商务部十二五规划教材

全国外经贸院校高职高专英语系列精品教材

国际商务函电

（全新版）

主　审　陈祥国

主　编　姚　元

副主编　丁礼章　　袁秋红　　张晓玲　　孟雅楠

参　编　刘启萍　　郝冠军　　梁燕丽　　杜颖新

中国商务出版社

图书在版编目（CIP）数据

国际商务函电：全新版 / 姚元主编 . —2 版 . —
北京：中国商务出版社，2015.7（2020.7 重印）
商务部十二五规划教材　全国外经贸院校高职高专英
语系列精品教材
ISBN 978-7-5103-1317-2

Ⅰ.①国…　Ⅱ.①姚…　Ⅲ.①国际商务-英语-电报
信函-写作-高等职业教育-教材　Ⅳ.①H315

中国版本图书馆 CIP 数据核字（2015）第 158890 号

商务部十二五规划教材
全国外经贸院校高职高专英语系列精品教材

国际商务函电（全新版）
International Business Correspondence

主　审　陈祥国
主　编　姚　元
副主编　丁礼章　袁秋红　张晓玲　孟雅楠

出　版：中国商务出版社
社　址：北京市东城区安定门外大街东后巷 28 号
邮　编：100710
电　话：010-64218072（职业教育事业部）
网　址：www.cctpress.com
网　店：www.cctpress.taobao.com
邮　箱：cctp@cctpress.com；bjys@cctpress.com
照　排：北京科事洁科技开发有限责任公司
印　刷：廊坊市长岭印务有限公司
开　本：787 毫米×980 毫米　1/16
印　张：22.75　字　数：390 千字
版　次：2015 年 8 月第 2 版　　2020 年 7 月第 4 次印刷
书　号：ISBN 978-7-5103-1317-2
定　价：38.00 元

再 版 说 明

　　随着我国职业教育事业的蓬勃发展，全国外经贸职业院校专业外语教学改革也日益深化。新专业不断拓展，课程设置不断更新，相应地对专业英语教材提出了新的要求。《教育部关于"十二五"职业教育教材建设的若干意见》特别指出，教材应"反映产业技术升级、符合职业教育和技能型人才成长规律"。

　　为了适应社会经济形势和职业教育发展的新变化，满足各高职院校对商务英语教材的需求，全国外经贸职业教育教学指导委员会组织以辽宁对外经贸学院为龙头的全国十多所职业院校的双师型骨干教师和部分行业企业专家，在对各地职业院校商务英语专业教学情况和毕业生用人单位的广泛调查和咨询的基础上，对原版"全国外经贸院校高职高专英语系列精品教材"进行了全面修订、调整、更新，进而推出了本套全新版教材。

　　本版教材做了以下更新和调整：

　　第一，优化作者资源，科学配置编者体系。

　　本版教材邀请了一批教育专家、课程专家和一线教师参与编写计划，他们教育成果丰硕，实践经验丰富，还增加了双师型骨干教师，壮大了编写队伍，保证了编写质量。依据商务英语专业培养目标，从课程设置、教学模式，到教学内容和手段，要求主编和参编人员加强责任意识，避免同质化和职业标准不对接、编写体例不一致等问题的产生。

　　第二，更新教材内容，优化教材类型结构。

　　本版教材注重吸收行业发展中的新知识、新技术，按照职业标准和岗位要求，丰富了实践环节的内容，增加了案例学习和项目学习等形式，有利于学生理解和掌握专业所需技能。此外，还引进和改编了体现国外先进职业教育理念、贴近商务英语专业教学实际的优秀教材和教学资源，并新增了实训类教材。

第三，改进教材呈现形式，充分利用现代教育手段。

本版教材的编写尽量做到简洁易懂。除了传统的纸质教材和教学课件，还开发了视频教学、互动教学等多媒体教学软件。通过引入现代教育手段，教学和实践将达到情境化、动态化、立体化效果，必将有效提高教学质量。

经过所有编者一年半的辛苦工作，这套教材终于陆续完成了。与旧版相比，本版教材课程覆盖面更广，内容全面更新，形式丰富多样，体现了以服务为宗旨、以就业为导向的总体编写思路，非常贴近社会和职业院校的需求，适合各职业院校以及其他开设商务英语专业的学校使用。

全国外经贸职业教育教学指导委员会
2013 年 5 月

编 者 的 话

　　随着中国对外开放的进一步扩大，从事国际商务活动的企业对人才的英语书面和口头表达能力要求不断提高。为适应岗位需求，按照国家对高职教育"能力本位"的培养要求，编者们在深入企业调研的基础上，结合课程改革探索和实践，编写了这本《国际商务函电》(全新版)，旨在为学习者从事经贸工作而提高英文信函的理解和表达能力，满足各大专院校培养高素质国际商务人才及社会上各阶层国际经贸工作者的需要。

　　全书由七个部分组成，即：函电格式及写作原则、客户开发函、交易条件磋商函、执行合同函、纠纷处理函、综合写作任务和附录。其中，基于业务流程共设计了十一项任务，包括开发新客户、询报盘、还盘、装运条件磋商、包装方式磋商、支付方式磋商、保险条件磋商、达成交易、支付货款、交货和索赔。每一课的结构安排为：(1) 信文范文：展示该业务环节的典型信文；(2) 注释：解释重要表达方式的常用用法；(3) 补充范文：扩充同一业务环节下不同的信文写作风格和技巧；(4) 练习：巩固词汇、句子用法和篇章写作技巧；(5) 要点重述：总结该课的语言要点和知识要点。

　　全新版的特点有：

　　1. 新：内容摒除老旧，体现业务最新做法，贴合实际；

　　2. 精：语言精炼规范，便于学习者参考和灵活掌握；

　　3. 真：取材真实可信，尽量选取真实的产品、单据，甚至是真实的公司；

　　4. 细：细节处理到位，体现"读者友好"，如：电子邮件头的设计、产品多样性的选择、重点表达方式的黑体显示以及要点重述等。

全新版的亮点是"综合写作任务"。该部分以"山东天意工艺品进出口公司"的一笔完整的出口业务和一笔进口业务为背景，设计了具有连贯性和真实性的写作实训任务，让"学中做、做中学"的思路贯穿教材始终。

本教材由陈祥国担任主审，姚元担任主编，山东外贸职业学院的老师参与编写完成。具体编写分工如下：姚元（格式、任务 1）、杜颖新（格式、附录 1）、丁礼章（任务 2、综合写作任务）、郝冠军（任务 3）、孟雅楠（任务 4、任务 11）、张晓玲（任务 5、任务 8）、袁秋红（任务 6、任务 7）、刘启萍（任务 9）、梁燕丽（任务 10，附录 2～5）。

在教材调研和编写过程中，青岛贝来国际贸易有限公司、青岛益诚戴客贸易有限公司、青岛恒驰远贸易有限公司和青岛奥纳特贸易有限公司提供了大量真实素材并提出了诸多宝贵意见，特表示衷心感谢！

由于编者水平有限，书中难免有错误或不妥之处，欢迎专家和读者批评指正。

编　者
2015 年 6 月

CONTENTS

目　　录

FORMS AND WRITING PRINCIPLES OF BUSINESS EMAILS AND LETTERS

Learning Objectives

To be able to write emails in a complete and correct format

To get familiar with the parts，writing principles and techniques of business emails and letters

商务电子邮件和书信的格式及写作原则

电子邮件的组成部分

在国际商务活动中，随着时代的发展和通信技术的进步，信息传递、交流、联系的主要媒介也在不断变化发展着。早期使用的电报、电传现在已经淘汰，信函、电子邮件、电话、传真、全球即时聊天工具如 Skype、WhatsApp 等成为使用广泛的通信方式。特别是从 20 世纪 90 年代中期以来，互联网浏览器诞生，全球网民人数激增，电子邮件因其收发速度快、成本低廉且安全性较高而成为最流行的国际交流通信方式。

电子邮件的格式因网站的不同而不同，但其组成部分基本是一致的。例 1 和例 2 展示了商务电子邮件的邮件头和正文的基本要素。

例 1：外发的邮件

例 2：收到的邮件

From : jackywang <jackywang@ziplip.com>　①
Reply-To : jackywang <jackywang@ziplip.com>　②
To : moris_scarv@hotmail.com　8
CC : jason@hotmail.com　9
Subject : enquiry for articles　③
Date : Fri, 29 Nov 2002 00:01:45 -0800 (PST)　10
Attachment : EnquirySheet.xls (32k)
Reply　Reply All　Forward　Delete　Put in Folder...　▼　　**Printer Friendly Version**

Dear Moris,　④

Attached please find the Enquiry Sheet and let us have your best FOB prices.

If favorable, we intend to place large orders.　⑤

Your prompt reply will be highly appreciated.

Best regards,　⑥
Jacky　⑦

Purchase Manager — Globalking Co.
12/F, Jinhai Bldg., 85 Taiping Rd.
Qingdao 266001, P.R.China
Mobile: +86 13853290001
Tel: +86 532-82746501　⑦
Fax: +86 532-82746009
www.globalking.com

　商务电子邮件包括 7 个基本组成部分和 3 个附加组成部分：

基本组成部分	① 发件人电子邮件地址	附加组成部分	8 抄送
	② 收件人电子邮件地址		9 事由
	③ 日期		10 附件
	④ 称呼		
	⑤ 正文内容		
	⑥ 结尾敬语		
	⑦ 签名		

1. "From"：发件人电子邮件地址

发件人的电子邮件地址是由电子邮件服务器在收件人收到邮件时自动显示的，无须发件人手动键入。"Reply-To"后面就是发件人电子邮件地址，意思是直接回复给发件人。电子邮件的地址有统一的标准格式：用户名@服务器域名。@符号是电子邮件的定位符，通常读成"at"，也就是"在"的意思。在商务电子邮件中，用户名往往可以反映出发件人或收件人的姓名，而域名通常能反映出所使用的邮件服务商名称或者发件人/收件人的公司名称。

例3：电子邮件地址

(1) maoyibu@vip.163.com

(2) amy_Zhang@outlook.com

(3) horris.hill@sgs.com

(4) 121386942@qq.com

2. "To"：收件人电子邮件地址

此栏填写收件人的电子邮件地址。当收件人多于一人时，应该使用";"号分隔电子邮箱地址，并按职务从高到低的顺序排列。

例4：群发电子邮件

To: David.Li@walmart.au; Belinda@hotmail.com; Joy.Wu@yahoo.com

3. "Date"：日期

此栏由网站的服务器自动生成，不需要发件人手动键入，显示的是发件时间。英式日期格式是"日/月/年"的次序，而美式日期按"月/日/年"的次序。月份通常用英文单词（或缩写）来表示，避免用数字。日期用基数或序数表示。月份和日期之间不用逗号，月份和年份之间用不用逗号皆可，而日期和年份之前必须用逗号点开。此外，服务器通常还会显示"星期"、"钟点"等信息。有的邮件服务器显示日期用的是"Sent"，而不是"Date"。

例5：日期

(1) Date：31th January, 20—13：20

(2) Date：31 January, 20—09：20

(3) Date：September 21st, 20—5：56 PM

（4）

> Date：Thursday，February 26，20—

（5）

> Sent：Fri.，March 19，20—8：40：27 GMT

4. 称呼

邮件的开头要称呼收件人。这既显得礼貌，也明确提醒某收件人，此邮件是面向他的，要求其给出必要的回应。使用何种称呼，要根据发件人的具体情况以及发件人与收件人之间的关系而定。此外，开头称呼应与结尾敬语相呼应。

称呼常用"Dear"开头，当不知道收件人姓名时，英式使用"Sir/Sirs"（男士）或"Madam/Mmes"（女士）来称呼，美式则使用"Gentlemen"或"Ladies/Gentlemen"，意思是"敬启者"；当知道收件人姓名时，正式场合一般使用 Mr.、Mrs.、Ms.、Miss 等尊称加收件人的家族姓；非正式场合或关系亲密时，可以直呼其名。但要注意：直呼对方的全名是非常不礼貌的。此外，称呼的首字母应使用英文大写。称呼后面一般使用"，"号，或不使用任何标点符号，"Gentlemen"后面使用"："号。

关系亲密的场合，有时还会用到"Hi"、"Hello"等非正式的用语。

例 6：称呼

（1）Dear Sir 或 Dear Madam 或 Dear Sir or Madam（Dear Sir/Madam）

（2）Dear Sirs 或 Dear Sirs or Mmes

（3）Gentlemen：或 Ladies/Gentlemen：

（4）To Whom It May Concern：

（5）Dear Mr. Duncan，

（6）Dear Michael，

（7）Hi，Jacky 或 Hello Jacky 或 Morning Jacky

5. 正文内容

正文内容是电子邮件最重要的部分，传递发件人的写信意图、详细信息和具体要求。正文格式一般采用齐头式（Blocked Style），即每行都是从最左侧开始写，不缩进，段落之间空一到两行。这种格式便于打字和节省时间，提高工作效率。邮件正文语言表达要简练，尽量使用短小的句子和段落，一般一段讲一件事情，切忌长篇大论，层次不清。

商务电子邮件的正文一般写有开头句和结尾句。开头句通常表达写信意图，或者确认收到某物并致以谢意。结尾句通常是表示友好和良好愿望的习惯用句，如：

Awaiting your good news.

Looking forward to your early reply.

We hope to receive your early reply.

6. 结尾敬语

结尾敬语是发件人在邮件结尾以礼貌的方式向收件人表达祝愿、勉慰之情的短语，意思是"××谨上"、"商祺"、"谨此致意"等。结尾敬语要根据发件人和收件人之间的关系选择用词，并与开头称呼相呼应。

在国际商务活动中，通常会与某一客户进行经常性邮件往来，因而 Best regards 和 Best wishes 成为了国际商务邮件中最常用的结尾敬语。

结尾敬语中，只需要第一个单词的首字母大写，其余的单词全部小写。结尾敬语后可以加标点符号，也可以不加，应与开头称呼的标点符号保持一致。

开头称呼	结尾敬语	使用场合
Dear Sir（s） Dear Sir（s）/Madam（Mmes）	Yours faithfully Faithfully yours	正式场合 标准用法
Gentlemen Ladies/Gentlemen	Yours（very）truly Very truly yours	正式场合 美式表达
Dear Mr. Malone Dear Jenny	Yours sincerely/ Sincerely Best wishes（英式） Best regards/ Regards（美式）	非正式场合 双方熟悉 场合

7. "Signature"：签名

电子邮件中的签名是邮件内容不可缺少的组成部分，既是对发件人信息（邮件显示信息）的补充，也是收件人进一步建立对发件人信任的必要信息。同时，电子邮件签名是一个公司品牌形象的组成部分，对企业网络品牌具有一定的影响。正规公司在邮件签名（尤其是对外部联系时的邮件）都有统一的格式设计，这样不仅看起来比较规范，而且也体现了公司品牌形象。

签名包括发件人姓名、公司名称、地址、联系方式和网址等。

（1）发件人姓名，可以是昵称、名或者全名。如："Jennie"、"Jenny YANG"、"YANG Limei"。现在，在国际商务信函中，中国商人更倾向于用汉语拼音大写来表示自己的姓，放在名前或名后，也方便了外国客户辨认。

（2）发件人如果有职务的话，要写明，首字母大写。如："Sales Manager"。

（3）公司名称，可以是全称或简称，还可以进一步写明部门。首字母应大写或全部字母大写。此外在签名栏显示公司标识和经营理念，也能起到很好的营销效果。

例 7：发件人公司名称

① Sinochem Jiangsu Import and Export Corporation

② AOL GL-Strategic Research & Innovation

③ OFFICE SYSTEMS PTY. LTD.

④ Bentonville Walmart Supercenter

（4）公司地址。在签名处标注发件人公司地址，有助于对方了解发件人公司的地理位置和通信方式。有些公司在设计签名格式时，则省略了公司地址信息。英语地址书写原则应遵循由小到大的顺序，先写门牌号码、街路名称，再写城市、省（州）和邮政区号，最后写国家名称。作为电子邮件结尾处的签名栏，公司地址应尽量设计在一行写完或分两行书写，不宜分多行，否则签名栏过长，不美观。特别值得注意的是，地址中的标点符号需正确使用。习惯做法是：行末一般不加标点符号，但行中间该加标点的地方，还是不应省略；门牌号码与街道名称之间不加标点，但是在城市与国家名称之间必须用逗号分开。

例 8：发件人公司地址

① 2076 West Main Street，Devon，EX14 0RA，U. K.

② Jiangsu International Business Mansion，50 Zhonghua Rd Nanjing 210001，P. R. China

中国的地名可以用汉语拼音直译；一个地名只大写第一个字母，如"山东青岛"，可写作"Qingdao, Shandong"。地址中的常用简写，如：F.（=Floor，楼层）、Sec.（=Section，段）、Rd.（=Road，路）、Ave.（Avenue，街）、Blvd.（= boulevard，大道）、St.（= Street，街道）、Bldg.（= Building，楼）、Rm.（=Room，房间）、Ste.（=Suite，套间）等。

（5）发件人联系方式通常包括手机（Mobile，或简写为 M）、固定电话（简写为 Tel 或 PH）、传真（Fax）的号码、电子邮件地址以及国际实时通信工具账号，如 Skype 账号等。其中，国际电话由国家电话区号＋当地城市电话区号＋当地电话号码组成。

例 9：发件人联系方式

Mobile：+86 138-0057-5116

Tel：+86-10-5969-3008

Fax：+86-10-5969-3002

Skype：jacky. wang@hotmail. com

（6）发件人公司网址能够方便客户通过浏览网站，了解更多发件人公司和产品的信息，起到宣传和营销的作用。

例 10：签名

Yours faithfully,

Morten Rolly
Program Director

AOL GL – Strategic Research & Innovation
Mobile: +47 91359247
Morten.Rolly@aolgl.com

Best regards,
Fran Fan
Sales Manager
JIELI PLASTIC
LEADING INJECTION PLASTICS MANUFACTURER

QINGDAO JIELI INDUSTRIAL CO.LTD
NO.398,EAST YUTAI STREET,QINGDAO CITY,CHINA,260012
PH: (86) 532-6278701 FAX: (86) 532-6278702
EMAIL: fran@jlplastics.com
M: 0086-15265353026
www.jlplastics.com

8. "Cc" 和 "Bcc"：明抄和暗抄

抄送分为明抄和暗抄。

"Cc"（Carbon copy）明抄：如果发件人想让收件人知道该邮件同时发给

了第三方，即被抄送人，可在 Cc 后填加被抄送人的电子邮件地址，这叫作明抄送。明抄送的目的是告知，被明抄送的人不需回应，当然如果被明抄送的人有建议，也可回复邮件。

例 11：明抄

收件人是销售部，同时邮件明抄送给采购部；销售部知道采购部也收到了这封邮件。

"Bcc"（Blind carbon copy）暗抄：如果发件人不想让收件人知道这封信抄送给了谁，则在 Bcc 处填写被抄送人的电子邮件地址即可，这叫作暗抄送，也叫密送。

例 12：暗抄

收件人是 Mr. Henry Hanks，同时邮件暗抄送给 Mr. Sam Brown；Mr. Henry Hanks 不知道 Mr. Sam Brown 也收到这封邮件。

9. "Subject"：主题

主题是邮件的事由或标题。主题应该明确，用少量的关键词说明邮件要阐明的问题，以引起收件人重视，尽快处理，并方便以后查找。主题中句首的单词和专有名词的首字母应该大写，或者也可将除了少于 5 个字母的介词、连接词或冠词之外的每一个单词的首字母大写。

当收件人回复（reply）或全部回复（reply to all）邮件时，主题栏会自动在原主题词句前显示 "Re:" 字样，表示 "关于" 该主题；当收件人转发（forward）邮件时，主题栏会自动在原主题词句前显示 "Fw:" 字样，表示 "转发" 该主题。当然，发件人也可以不使用这样自动产生的主题词句，而自行设定邮件主题。

例 13：主题

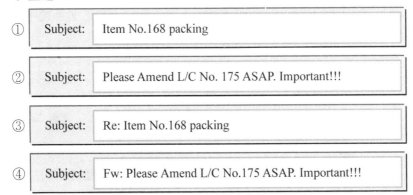

① Subject: Item No.168 packing

② Subject: Please Amend L/C No. 175 ASAP. Important!!!

③ Subject: Re: Item No.168 packing

④ Subject: Fw: Please Amend L/C No.175 ASAP. Important!!!

10. "Attachment"：附件

也可用"Attached"表示，即：在附件中添加文件、图片等。如果邮件带有附件，应在正文里面提示收件人查看附件。邮件的附件必须写上题目，能够概括附件的内容，方便收件人下载后管理。附件数目较多时应打包压缩成一个文件。此外，邮件服务器会清楚显示出所附文件或图片的格式及大小。带有附件的邮件，通常会被系统标注一个曲别针记号"📎"，提醒收件人此邮件有附件。

例 14：附件

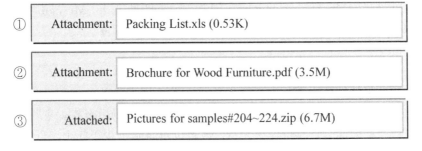

① Attachment: Packing List.xls (0.53K)

② Attachment: Brochure for Wood Furniture.pdf (3.5M)

③ Attached: Pictures for samples#204~224.zip (6.7M)

商务信函的格式及组成部分

通信技术的发展，让纸质商务信函的使用场合大幅缩小，仅在极为正式的场合使用，如银行公函、正式邀请函、推荐信等。在此，对商务信函的格式和结构做一简要介绍。

商务信函常见的格式有三种，其中最通用的是齐头式：

1. 齐头式（Block Style）

主要特征就是每行均从左边顶格写，信中各部分之间和各段落之间均空一行。

2. 缩进式（Indented Style）

主要特征是正文各段的第一行都从左边空白边缘往右缩进 3～5 个字母的位置；封内地址每逢换行时，下一行要比上一行往右缩进 2～3 个字母的位置，即层层缩进；日期在信纸的右上端；结尾敬语和签名在信文结尾处中间偏右下方；经办人栏和事由栏居中书写。

3. 混合式（Modified Block Style）

主要特征是日期、结尾敬语、签名等采用缩进式的格式，其余部分采用齐头式。

一般来说，商务信函的信头已印制于公司专用信纸的顶端中央。此外，也有采用信头左对齐或靠右对齐的个性设计。

商务信函一般包括 7 个基本组成部分和 6 个附加组成部分：

基本组成部分			附加组成部分		
	①	信头		8	经办人
	②	参考编号和日期		9	事由
	③	封内地址		10	经办人代号
	④	称呼		11	附件
	⑤	正文		12	抄送
	⑥	结尾敬语		13	附言
	⑦	签名			

例 15：商务信函结构（齐头式）

P.O. Box 4088 Frederick, MD 21705-0590, U.S.A.

Tel:+1(703)907-4352

E-mail: InternationalReg@ce.org

①

November 18, 2011　②

Smart Computer Information Co., Ltd.
2301 Yili Bldg., 39 Nanjing Road
Shanghai 200041, China　③

ATTN: Haitao Yang, Sales Dept.　8

Dear Haitao Yang,　④

RE: Registration Confirmed　9

Thank you for registering to attend the 2012 International CES®. Your confirmation number is 209864.

The International CES® 2012 trade show takes place on January 10-13, 2012 in Las Vegas, Nevada, USA. It is the world's largest annual trade show for the broad-band consumer electronics market. For additional information about International CES®, please see the enclosed Brochure 2012 and visit our website at www.CESweb.org.

Please apply for your visa early as it is our hope that you get the temporary admittance into the U.S. to attend the 2012 International CES®.

⑤

Legal Name: Haitao Yang
Title:　　　Sales Manager
Gender:　　Male

If I can be of further assistance, please do not hesitate to contact me.

Sincerely,　⑥

⑦

Christina M. Corrado
Sr. Manager, Registration
CESweg.org

RT/CMC　10
Enclosure: Brochure 2012　11
Cc: International CES® Shanghai Office　12　13
P.S.: The Consumer Electronics Associate (CEA) does not assume any financial, legal, or other type of responsibility for any person during their attendance at CES.

（1）信头（Letterhead）

很多公司都会印制带有信头的信纸，内容包括发件公司的名称、标志、通信地址、电话号码、传真号、电子邮箱等。书写信头的目的是为了方便收件人了解信函来自何处，并为回复提供联系方式。

（2）参考号码和日期（Reference No. and Date）

参考号码是为了方便信函存档备查，使用"Your reference No."和"Our reference No."加上各自存档编号。日期分为英式日期和美式日期两种格式。

（3）封内地址（Inside Name and Address）

封内地址包括收件公司的名称和通信地址。

（4）称呼（Salutation）

称呼在信函中是必不可少的部分，选词和书写要求与电子邮件的称呼一样。

（5）正文（Body of the Letter）

正文指信文内容，通常会有开头句和结尾句。信文内容要分层次、分段落书写。

（6）结尾敬语（Complimentary Close）

结尾敬语和电子邮件的结尾敬语要求一样，和称呼相呼应。

（7）签名（Signature）

签名包括写信人的打印签名，手写签名，职务（如果有），公司名称和地址。

（8）经办人（Attention）

经办人指的是承办本信件的具体部门或个人。通常使用"Attention："，"Attention of"，"To the attention of"，"ATTN："字样，后接部门或个人。一般使用下划线以突出强调。

（9）事由（Subject）

事由指的是该信函的主题。可以使用"RE："或者"Re："字样，后接主题词或主题句。一般使用下划线以突出强调。

（10）经办人代号（Reference Notation）

经办人代号是由秘书（打字员）和信件口授者的姓名首字母组成，用冒号或斜线号分开。

（11）附件（Enclosure）

商务信函的附件是指信封内除了信文，还装有其他文件等资料。通常用"Enclosure："、"Enc."、"Encl.："、"Enclosures："等字样来表示。

（12）抄送（Carbon Copy）

抄送和电子邮件抄送一样，分为明抄和暗抄。

（13）附言（Postscript）

附言是指如果信文遗漏了某事或者需要提醒对方某事，可在附言中补写。

英文信封格式

英文信封的书写格式采用缩进式或齐头式，要与信文格式统一起来。

英文信封由发信人名称和地址、收信人名称和地址以及邮票组成，有时还包括邮路和信件的机密等级。

英文信封的布局与中文信封不同：

（1）发信人的名字和地址：在信封左上角位置。

（2）收信人的名字和地址：在信封中间偏右下角位置。如果信件经由第三人"捎交"给收信人，应使用"Kindness of（Politeness of，Favored by，Through the Courtesy of，Per Kindness of，Forwarded by，With Favor of，Per Favor of)"加上捎交人的名字；如果信件经由第三人"转交"给收信人，应使用"care of（c/o）"加上转交人的名字。

例 16：捎交

```
Mr. Charles Wood
Kindness of Mr. J. W. Smith
```

例 17：转交

```
Mr. Part Davis
c/o Mr. Harold Bean
32 Bright Street
Rangoon，Burma
```

（3）邮路：在信封左下角的位置。

例 18：邮路

（1）Per S/S "Empress of Canada"

（2）Via Cape Town

（3）Via Air Mail（By Airmail，or Par Avion）

（4）Registered

（5）Parcel Post

（6）Express

（7）Samples Post

例 19：英文信封（齐头式）

2012 International CES
P.O. Box 4088 Frederick
MD 21705-0590 USA

Stamp

Mr. Haitao Yang
Smart Computer Information Co., Ltd.
2301 Yili Bldg., 39 Nanjing Road
Shanghai 200041, China

Confidential
Par Avion

商务电子邮件和信函的写作原则

商务电子邮件和信函的写作应遵循清楚（clarity）、简洁（conciseness）和礼貌（courtesy）的原则，即 3C 原则。

1. 清楚（Clarity）

清楚原则指层次清楚，用词准确。内容要适当分段并尽量使用短段落，必要时可标上段落号；用词要准确，切忌使用语义模糊、模棱两可的词或词组，以免产生歧义，造成误解，延误商务沟通和贸易。

2. 简洁（Conciseness）

简洁原则是商务英语写作最重要的原则，指在不影响完整性和礼貌性的前提下，尽量使用简单句子和简短词语（如缩略语），这样不仅能节约双方的时间，让人一目了然，而且还能给对方以干练和高效的良好印象。一封拖沓冗长、措辞复杂的电子邮件既浪费时间，也会给阅读者带来不必要的麻烦。

3. 礼貌（Courtesy）

礼貌原则指措辞婉转，语气自然诚恳，礼貌得体，使对方容易接受，同时遵守国际商务往来惯例，尊重对方风俗习惯。注意做到：（1）表示批评、建议、要求时，避免使用命令和生硬的口气，多用友好、肯定的语气和适当使用被动语态;(2) 适当使用虚拟语气、委婉语气等提出要求;(3) 对坏消息表示歉意,并说明问题的原因;(4) 回复邮件要及时。

除了以上原则外,商务电子邮件和信函的写作还应该遵循准确(correctness)、完整(completeness)、体谅(consideration)和具体(concreteness)的原则。

EXERCISES

1. Fill in each blank in proper form according to the following information.

收件人名字:Jill

收件人电子邮箱地址:hintingwro@outlook. com

抄送:qilida@kh. com. cn

邮件内容:

Your email of Mar. 15 has been noted with thanks. We agree to change the quantities considering our long term friendly relationship. Attached is the new P/I made out accordingly in PDF. Please sign back if everything is OK.

发件人名字:Mary Wang

发件人职务:Sales Manager

发件人公司名称:Kanghai International Trading Co. , Ltd.

发件人公司地址:10/F Fuda Bldg. , 132 Gutian Rd. ,

Fuzhou 350001, P. R. China

发件人联系方式:Tel:0591-28564625

Fax:0591-28564672

E-mail:mary. zhang@kh. com. cn

发件人公司网址:www. kanghai. com

To:	
Cc:	
Subject:	
Attachment:	

2. Write an email based on the situation below.

假设你是山东天意工艺品进出口公司出口部经理吴明（Aaron Wu），现需要你给美国客户 Bill 发一封邮件，内容如下：

"I will go to LA on business 10th-13th next month, hoping we can meet then. Are you available? Attached is a catalogue for our new products. Please check. If you are interested in some of them, please let me know so that I can take the samples to you. I am looking forward to your early reply."

山东天意工艺品进出口公司地址：

青岛市香港西路 65 号山东工艺品大厦 16—17 层，邮编 266071。

公司联系方式：电话：0086-532-82748906

传真：0086-532-82748909

公司网页：www. tyarts. com

其他信息请自拟。

PART ONE

PROMOTING BUSINESS

Task 1

Establishing Trade Relations

Learning Objectives

To be able to write emails asking for the establishment of business relations

To grasp the writing plans, useful sentences and phrases of developing new customers

Lesson 1

A Trading Company Introduction

Nidera

Nidera is a major international agribusiness and **trading company** with an annual **turnover** in excess of USD17 billion. The **firm**, which was **established** in 1920 with its **headquarter** in Rotterdam (The Netherlands), focused its early commercial activities on grain and foodstuffs. Nidera is an acronym formed by the first letter of the names of the countries and colonies in which its business centered: the **N**etherlands, the Dutch East **I**ndies (today Indonesia), **D**eutschland (Germany), **E**ngland, **R**ussia and **A**rgentina. On February 28, 2014, 51% stake in Nidera was acquired by China National Cereals, Oils and Foodstuffs Corporation (COFCO) .

Nidera is an expert in the trading, origination, processing, merchandising, handling, storage and logistics of grain, grain by-products, oilseeds and vegetable oils. In addition, Nidera is **engaged** in the **distribution** of crop technology and it is a **leading** seed research and production company in South America. Our plants in Argentina have been **certified** to ISO9001 : 2008, ISO 22000 : 2005, ISO 14001 : 2004, OHSAS 18001 : 2007, and HACCP Codex Alimentarius. In September 2010, Nidera became one of the first international Sustainability and Carbon Certification (ISCC) certified trading companies in the Netherlands.

Today, the company has **domestic** and international operations in more than 20 major **export** and **import** countries and distributes its products to more than 60 countries worldwide. This **privately held company employs** around 3,800 people globally and has 29 **wholly owned** operational facilities. The company serves as a **liaison** between **markets** in its **capacity** as a domestic and international trader of agricultural commodities and maintains an in-house freight **division** to accommodate **customers's** pecific shipping requirements. Our **brands** include Super series，Labrador series in the crop technology business and Legitimo in the edible oil business.

The Corporate **Vision** is to create **sustainable** economic，social and environmental value through our role as a leading **multi-commodity** originator and distributor in the global agriculture markets. We strive to be a reliable，innovative and dynamic business partner that provides the highest quality business **solutions** and forges strong and long-term relationships with our customers and **stakeholders** at large，fostering **partnerships** and open dialogue.

The Corporate **Values**：**Integrity**，**Commitment**，**Respect** and **Accountability**，guiding the company's operations and business worldwide in a responsible manner. These values help us to fulfill our purpose and to achieve our vision. They reflect who we are，what we do and what we expect from ourselves and others.

NOTES

1. Nidera：荷兰尼德拉公司，世界知名农产品和大宗产品交易集团
2. trading company：贸易公司

    trade *n.* 贸易；买卖

    Seventy per cent of the country's trade is with Europe.

    该国70％的贸易是和欧洲做的。

    trade *v.* 从事……贸易，进行……交易

    Nidera trades in leading hybrids and varieties of five of the world's main staples（wheat，corn，soybeans，sunflower seeds，and sorghum）.

    Nidera从事世界五种主要粮食作物（小麦、玉米、黄豆、葵花籽和高粱）的主要杂交品种和变种的贸易。

    trading partner 贸易伙伴

    trade agreement 贸易协定

    trader *n.* 商人，交易商

    a wool/sugar trade 毛料商/糖商

3. turnover：*n.* 营业额，成交量，在给定的时间成交的总额

    annual turnover 年营业额   export turnover 出口交易额

    foreign trade turnover 对外贸易额   sales turnover 营业额

4. firm：*n.* 公司，商号

a law firm 律师事务所

an accountancy firm 会计事务所

5. establish：*v.* 建立，可以用 found 或 set up 表示

6. headquarter：*n.* 总部 *v.* 总部设在，常用缩写 HQ 表示

GM is headquartered in Detroit，Michigan.

通用汽车总部设在美国密歇根州的底特律城。

表示公司总部地点还可以说：

The WTO is based in Geneva.

世贸组织设在日内瓦。

The company has its base in London and branches in all European countries.

公司总部设在伦敦，分公司遍布所有欧洲国家。

7. acquire：*v.* 收购，购得

mergers and acquisitions 企业兼并与收购，简称"并购"，缩写为 M&A

8. COFCO：中粮集团，中国最大的粮油食品进出口公司

9. storage and logistics：储存和物流

10. by-product：副产品，也可以写作 byproduct

grain byproducts 农副产品

native produce and animal byproducts 土畜产品

11. be engaged in：从事，从事……经营活动

表示公司"经营"，还可以用以下表达方式：

deal in：经营

This firm deals in furs.

这家公司经营皮货。

类似的表达方法有：

handle 经营

We have been handling chemicals for more than 20 years.

我们经营化工有 20 多年了。

specialize in 专营

We specialize in the import and export of textiles.

我们专营纺织品进出口业务。

in... line（business）经营

We are in Arts and Crafts line.

我们做手工艺品。

12. distribution：*n.* 分发；分配

    distribute *v.* 分发；分配

    The company aims eventually to distribute（= supply for sale）its products throughout the European Union.

    公司计划最终让产品行销欧盟国家。

13. leading：*a.* 主要的；领先的

14. certify：*v.*（以书面形式）证明；发证书给……

    The companies are required to obtain third-party audits to certify that they adhere to the standards.

    这些公司必须取得第三方审核，以证明他们坚持了上述标准。

    BV has certified our factory to ISO9001：2000.

    必维（即法国船级社）已按照 ISO9001：2000 标准给我们工厂颁证。

    certificate *n.* 证书

    SGS is the legal third party to issue such conformity certificate.

    通标公司是可以签发这种合格证书的合法第三方机构。

    certification *n.* 认证

    Obtaining ISO 9001 certification is extremely difficult，and many aftermarket parts manufacturers are hesitant to adopt this standard.

    通过 ISO 9001 质量体系认证十分困难，很多售后（汽车）配件厂商对是否采用这一标准犹豫不决。

    third-party independent certification body 第三方独立检验机构

15. ISO：国际标准化组织，全称是 International Organization for Standardization

    ISO 9001：2008 质量体系认证

    ISO 22000：2005 食品安全体系认证

    ISO 14001：2004 环境管理体系认证

    OHSAS 18001：2007 职业健康安全管理体系认证

    OHSAS 是 Occupational Health and Safety Assessment Series 的缩写

    HACCP Codex Alimentarius 危害分析及关键点控制体系食品规范

    HACCP 是 Hazard Analysis and Critical Control Point 的缩写

    International Sustainability and Carbon Certification（ISCC）

    国际可持续发展与碳认证

16. domestic：*a.* 本国的，国内的

    domestic market 国内市场　　　　domestic demand 国内需求

    domestic airlines 国内航空公司　　domestic flights 国内航班

Domestic opinion had turned against the war.

国内舆论已转而反对战争。

17. export：*n.* 出口；出口商品 *v.* 出口

    exporter *n.* 出口商

    import *n.* 进口；进口商品 *v.* 进口

    importer *n.* 进口商

    We have been handling import and export of textiles for many years.

    我们经营纺织品的进出口业务已有很多年了。

    Our exports now exceed our imports in value.

    目前我们出口值超过进口值。

    The company imports raw materials and exports the finished products.

    该公司进口原料而出口成品。

18. privately held company：私营企业，私人控股企业

19. employ：*v.* 雇用

    How many people does your company employ?

    你公司雇用多少人?

    More people are now employed in service industries than in manufacturing.

    现在服务业雇用的人员要比制造业多。

    employer *n.* 雇主

    employee *n.* 雇员

    表示公司雇员数量，还可以说：

    Our company employs 1,500 members of staff.

    我公司雇用 1500 员工。

    As of September 30，2013，Nidera had a total workforce of 3,174（headcount）.

    以 2013 年 9 月 30 日计，Nidera 拥有职员总数计 3174 名。

20. wholly owned operational facilities：全资的经营机构

21. liaison：*n.* 联络；联络人

    liaison office 联络处，联络办公室

    head office 总部

    branch office 分部，分公司

    subsidiaries 子公司

    parent company 母公司

22. market：*n.* 市场

the stock market 股票市场　　　　the job market 就业市场

the money market 金融市场　　　　the emerging market 新兴市场

23. capacity：*n.* 办事能力；生产能力（详解见 Lesson 3）

24. in-house freight division：公司内设的货运部门

    freight *n.* 货运；运费

    ocean freight 海运费　　　　　　air freight 空运费

    freight forwarder 货运代理商　　container freight station 集装箱货运站

    division *n.* 部门，处，室，科。如：

    the sales division 销售部门

25. customer：*n.* 顾客，主顾；客户

    相当于 client，外贸中 customer 一词更常用，如：

    regular/old customer 老客户　　new customer 新客户

    valued customer 重要的客户　　customer satisfaction 客户满意度

    customer preference 客户喜好　　customer reference 客户（提供的）资信证明

    potential customer 潜在顾客　　customer service department 客户服务部

26. brand：*n.* ＝brand name 品牌

    imitation brand 冒牌

    brand identification / recognition 品牌识别

    brand image 品牌形象

    branded goods 品牌货

    The company is launching a new brand of soap.

    那家公司正推出一种新牌子的香皂。

    The seller's brand is to be clearly stamped on the end of each piece.

    每件的末端应清楚地加印卖方的品牌。

27. Corporate Vision：公司愿景

28. sustainable：*a.* 可持续的

    sustainable development 可持续发展

29. multi-commodity：多商品的

    commodity *n.* 商品（详解见 Lesson 4）

30. originator：*n.* 原产国负责人

31. solution：*n.* 解决方案

32. stakeholder：*n.* 股东；利益相关者

33. partnership：*n.* 伙伴关系；合作关系

34. Corporate Values：企业价值观

35. Integrity，Commitment，Respect and Accountability：
    诚实、守信、尊重与责任

EXERCISES

Ⅰ. **Translate the following sentences into English.**

1. 我公司成立于 20 世纪 70 年代，从事医药保健品（medicines and health products）的进出口已有 40 多年了。公司总部设在北京。

2. 我公司拥有 6 家合作工厂（cooperative factory）和 1 家自属工厂。自属工厂占地（occupy an area of）约 1 万平方米，已通过 ISO9001：2000 质量体系认证。

3. 我们的注册资本（registered capital）是 3000 万元人民币。在伦敦、汉堡、马来西亚各有一家分公司。国内雇员达 2500 人。

4. 盛家工艺品厂是一家集研发、生产、经营于一体的工艺家具生产企业。

5. 我公司去年营业额达 2 亿美元，位于（rank）中国进出口额 500 强企业前列。

Ⅱ. **Translate the following excerpts of company introductions into Chinese.**

1. Founded in 1978，Versace（范思哲）is one of the world's leading international fashion houses. The Italian parent company of the Versace Group，Gianni Versace S. p. A. designs，markets and distributes luxury clothing，accessories，fragrances，makeups and home furnishings under the various brands of the Versace Group.

2. When we were founded in 1802，DuPont（杜邦）was primarily an explosives company. One hundred years ago，our focus turned to chemicals，materials and energy. Today，we deliver science-based solutions that make a real difference in people's lives around the world in areas such as food and nutrition，health care，apparel，safety and security，construction，electronics and transportation. Look closely at the things around your home and workplace，and chances are，you'll find dozens of items made with DuPont materials.

3. General Motors Corp.（通用汽车公司），the world's largest vehicle manufacturer，employs 349,000 people globally in its core automotive business and subsidiaries. Founded in 1908，GM has been the global automotive sales leader since 1931. GM today has manufacturing operations in 32 countries and its vehicles are sold in more than 190

countries. GM sold just over 9. 92 million cars and trucks in 2014，up 2 per cent from the previous year，setting a company record for global sales. GM's global headquarters is at the GM Renaissance Center in Detroit，USA. More information on GM and its products can be found on the company's consumer website at www. gm. com.

4. Ever since being established in 1881，SEIKO（精工）has contributed to society with one revolutionary product after another-initiating the production of wrist watches in Japan in 1913，and the world's first Quartz watch in 1969. While its focus is on watches and clocks，its operations cover many diverse fields，including camera components，other precision instruments，eyeglasses，jewelry as well as sports and toiletry products. Seiko is committed to offering attractive new products and services to our customers around the world.

Ⅲ. Writing task.

Please refer to Task A1-1 on Page 321.

RECAP

Language Focus	Knowledge Focus
establish，employ engage，certify leading，acquire	trading company，firm，turnover，headquarter，certificate，acquire，import，export，market，brand，customer，corporate vision，stakeholder，corporate value
Writing Tips	
➢ Introducing a trading company in various aspects： history，ownership，business scope，size，offices，product/service，employee，department，market，business figures（turnover，profit，registered capital，market value etc. ），partnership，business connections，brand，logo，corporate vision，corporate value，development，prospects，awards，etc.	

Lesson 2

Sellers Asking to Establish Trade Relations（1）

From：Tony. Zhang@shantex. com
To：m. woort@hers. com
Date：Mar. 20，20—
Subject：Shantex home textiles supplier
Attachments：Table Cloth Catalog. pdf（2. 3M）

Dear Sirs,

We **note** your information posted on Alibaba. com and are glad to learn that your **company** is **in the market for** table cloths. We hope we can work together with you in this field.

Our company **specializes** in home textiles for over 15 years. We can **offer** table cloths，chair covers，curtains，towels，bedspreads etc. with high quality and competitive prices. We are also **in a position** to accept orders **against** customers' design and **OEM** orders as well.

Attached is our latest **catalogue** in PDF file for some **best-selling** table cloths. If you **find** them **interesting，** we'll send quotations **upon receipt of specific inquiry** and **samples** via air for your evaluation.

We **look forward to** your **favorable** reply.

Sincerely yours,
Tony Zhang
Sales Manager for Shantex Imp. /Exp. Co. ，Ltd.
ADD：51 Taiping Rd. Qingdao，China
Mobile：0086 13853201101
Tel：0086-532-83531658
Fax：0086-532-83531660
Website：www. shantex. com

NOTES

1. establish：*v.* 建立，成立，设立
   to establish/enter into trade relations 建立贸易关系
   The company was established in Scotland in 1823.
   该公司于 1823 年在苏格兰成立。
   established *a.* 已建立的；信誉良好、地位牢固的；证实的，确认的
   the established order in the home market 国内市场已建立的秩序
   a well-established exporter 信誉良好的出口商
   established principle of international law 公认的国际法准则

2. home textiles：家用纺织品

3. supplier：*n.* 供应商
   Paperworks Ltd is a leading stationery supplier with over 100,000 customers.
   Paperworks 是一家大的文具供应商，有 100000 多个用户。
   supply *n.*/*v.* 供应（详解见 Lesson 4）

4. note：*v.* 留意，注意
   They noted the consumers' growing demand for quicker service.
   他们留意到消费者对便捷服务与日俱增的需求。
   Please note（that）we will be closed on Saturday.
   请注意我们周六不营业。

5. Alibaba.com：阿里巴巴网站（全球企业间电子商务平台）

6. company：*n.* 公司
   关于名称中"公司"的说法，常用的有 company（常缩写为 Co.）和 corporation（常缩写为 Corp.）两词，如：
   Ford Motor Company 福特汽车公司
   British Broadcasting Corporation 英国广播公司
   有限公司称作 limited liability company 或 limited company，用在名称中则用 Co. Ltd.（英式英语）或 Inc.（Incorporated 缩写，美式英语）。如：
   Sanyo Electric Co. Ltd. 三洋电气公司
   America Online Inc. 美国在线公司
   其他常用在公司名称当中、带有"公司"含义的词还有：
   PLC（Public Limited Company，英，股份公司），如：
   British Petroleum PLC 英国石油公司
   Pty Ltd（Proprietary，澳大利亚）：

JED Microprocessors Pty. Ltd

下面是其他语言中表示"公司"的常见词，供参考：

GmbH（德语，有限责任公司）

AG（德语，股份公司）：

SA（法语或葡萄牙语，公司）

S. p. A. 或 S. P. A.（意大利语，股份公司）

S. R. L.（意大利语/西班牙语/罗马尼亚语，有限公司）

7. in the market for：想要买

8. specialize：*v.* 专门从事，与 in 搭配，构成 specialize in sth. /doing sth. 专门从事

9. offer：*v.* 供应，还可以用 supply、provide 来表示

10. competitive：*a.* 有竞争力的

11. bein a position to do sth：能够做某事

这个词组表示的不仅仅是有没有能力做某事，更强调是否适合于、是否有权力、有资格、有资金或有经验做某事

As I say，I'm not in a position to reveal any of the details of the project at present.

依我说，我目前无权透露该项计划的任何细节。

I'm sure they'd like to help her out financially but they're not in a position to do so.

我肯定他们愿意资助她，但是他们没有资金。

She'd be in a much better position to get a job if she had more experience.

如果她经验再多一些，她找到工作的机会就会更大一些。

12. against：*prep.* 凭借，根据，按照

goods against the above mentioned order 根据上述订单（所约定的）货物，上述订货

Remittance has been made to cover the goods against the Commercial Invoice.

已汇款支付商业发票所开列的货物。

也可以用 under，表示"按照"，"凭"，"……项下的/所指的"。如：

The shipment under the Contract No. 639 has arrived here duly.

639 合同项下的船货已如期抵达。

Delivery can be made under/against Banker's guarantee.

可凭银行担保交货。

Under/Against instructions from our Head Office，we are quoting our prices as follows：

按照我们总公司指示，我们报价如下：

Shipment should be made this week under Article 12.

按照第 12 条规定，货物应于本周装运。

13. order：*n.* 订单（详解见 Lesson 25）

14. OEM：原始设备制造商，是 original equipment manufacturer 的缩写

    OEM 生产，也称为定点生产，俗称代工、贴牌生产。

    OEM customer：OEM 客户，即委托其他厂家生产的品牌方

    OEM manufacturer：OEM 厂商，即承接加工任务的制造商

15. attach：*v.* 附上

    I attach a copy of our latest report.

    兹附上我们的最新报告一份。

    Please attach the picture to your return email.

    请在回复邮件时附上图片。

    Attached is a copy of our price list for your reference.

    兹附上报价单一份供您参考。

    Attached please find a copy of our price list for your reference.

    兹附上报价单一份供您参考，请查收。

    attachment：*n.*（用电子邮件发送的）附件

    I'll email my report to you as an attachment.

    我把报告用电子邮件附件形式发给你。

16. catalogue：*n.* 商品目录

    关于商品的宣传材料（sales literature，销售说明书），通常有：

    illustrated catalogue 插图目录　　　　　manual 产品手册

    booklet/brochure/pamphlet 小册子　　　data sheet（产品）数据表

    leaflet（单张的）广告单　　　　　　　 bulletin（产品）简报

    sample 样品　　　　　　　　　　　　　broadside 广告宣传单；宣传单

    sample book 样品本　　　　　　　　　 circular letter 通函；通销函

    sample cutting 剪样

17. in PDF file：以 PDF 文件形式

    PDF：Portable Document Format 的简称，是一种便携式文件格式

18. best-selling：*a.* 畅销的

    bestseller 畅销品

19. find：*v.* 认为，感觉

We find Code X0146E a popular item to start with.

我们认为可以从 X0146E 号畅销品开始销售（推广）。

We find Model 201 suitable for European market.

我们认为 201 型号适合欧洲市场。

Our customers find it difficult to sell at your quoted price.

我们的客户认为很难按你们所报价格销售。

20. interesting：*a.* 令人感兴趣的

interest *n.* 兴趣

We have/feel/take special interest in your light industrial products.

我们对你方轻工产品特别感兴趣。

Canned goods are of special interest to us.

我们对罐头食品特感兴趣。

interest *v.* 使……感兴趣

The new packing will certainly interest you.

这种新的包装肯定会使你们感兴趣。

interested *a.* 感兴趣的，有兴趣的

We are very interested in importing medical equipment from your side.

我们对从你处进口医疗设备感兴趣。

We are very interested to know what you can offer in this line.

我们非常想知道你们可以供应什么。

21. quotation：*n.* 报价（详解见 Lesson 5）

22. receipt：*n.* 收到；收据；收到之物或款项

upon / on receipt of 一收到（就立即）

On receipt of your L/C, we shall effect shipment without delay.

一俟收到贵方信用证，我们将毫不拖延立即装船。

Mate's Receipt 收货单，大副收据

23. specific inquiry：具体的询盘

inquiry *n.* 询盘（详解见 Lesson 5）

24. sample：*n.* 样品

counter sample 回样   confirming sample 确认样品

auction sample 拍卖样品   sample survey 抽样调查

25. via air：通过航空（邮寄）

via：*prep.* 经过；通过，凭借；取道

Your order has been shipped via "Browick".

你方订货已由"Browick"号轮运出。

Did potential clients evercontact you via twitter?

曾有潜在客户通过推特联系过你吗?

As there is no direct steamer to your port, we have to ship via Rotterdam.

因没有直达你方港口的轮船,我们不得不在鹿特丹转船。

26. for your evaluation:供你评价

英语中类似格式的词组还有:

for your information 供你参考,告诉你方一下

for your reference 供你参考　　　for your consideration 供你研究/考虑

for your record 供你记录　　　for your file 供你存档

for your perusal 供你详阅

27. look forward to sth. / doing sth.:希望,盼望(to 是介词,后接名词或名词性短语)

We are looking forward to your letter.

盼望收到你方来信。

I look forward to hearing from you soon.

盼望尽快收到你的音讯。

28. favorable:*a.* 良好的;有利的;优惠的

We look forward to your favorable reply.

盼佳音。

A further understanding is favorable to business between our two sides.

进一步了解对我们双方业务有利。

The market situation looks favorable.

市场形势看来有利。

favorable balance of trade 贸易顺差

favorable price 优惠价格

29. fax:n. facsimile 的缩写,传真

30. website:*n.* 网站,网址

For more information about our company, please visit our website at www. shantex. com. cn.

欲知我公司详情,请访问我们的网站 www. shantex. com. cn。

A SUPPLEMENATRY SAMPLE EMAIL

Dear Sirs,

Your company has been kindly introduced to us by Messrs. Freeman &. Co. Ltd. , Lagos, Nigeria, as prospective buyers of Chinese cotton piece goods. As this item falls within our business scope, we shall be pleased to be your business partner in the future.

We attach a brochure and a price list for various kinds of cotton piece goods now available for export. Sample cuttings and quotations will be sent to you if you are interested.

We look forward to your early reply.

Yours faithfully,

EXERCISES

Ⅰ. Fill in the blanks with the proper forms of the following expressions.

attach, specific, look forward to, establish, note, interest, market, specialize, in a position to, receipt

1. We _____ meeting you at the Fair.
2. If you find _____ in any of the articles mentioned above, please let us have your _____ inquiry.
3. _____ please find a price list with full specifications.
4. Upon _____ of your letter, we contacted the factory at once.
5. We are writing you for the _____ of trade relations with you earlier.
6. Thanks for the offer, but I'm not in the _____ for auto parts right now.
7. Glad to _____ from your ad. in newspaper that you are _____ make to order according to customers' request.
8. Our company _____ in the import and export of outdoor sports products.

II. Translate the following sentences into Chinese.

1. The Bank of China has recommended your company as being interested in working with a Chinese company for importing electronic goods from China.

2. The Commercial Councilor's Office in this city has advised us of your business scope，which coincides with ours.

3. We have learned from the China Council for the Promotion of International Trade （CCPIT）that you are in the market for straw and willow products.

4. We learned of your name and contact information at the International Exhibition of Natural Health Products held in Beijing in October. As we handle these goods，we shall be glad to enter into direct business relations with you.

5. Your name and email address have been given to us by the Chamber of Commerce in your country as a well-established importer of arts and crafts.

III. Translate the following sentences into English.

1. 我们专营纺织品出口业务，愿与贵公司建立业务关系。

2. 我们可以根据客户要求来生产。

3. 如想了解产品的具体情况，请直接电邮我方。

4. 一俟收到你方具体询价，当即寄送产品报价和样品。

5. 附件是我公司部分畅销品的图片。

IV. Put the following words and phrases in right order to make up a sentence.

1. let，introduce，please，products，our，latest，to，me，you

2. one of，we，the largest，in China，importers，electrical appliances，are，of

3. quality，are interested in，we，you，learn from，printed shirting，that，the Internet

4. best regards，you，to，with，your manager，and

5. the sample books，send，you，by DHL，will，we

RECAP

Language Focus	Knowledge Focus
note your information on. . . and learn that. . . establish, specialize, in the market for offer(supply), attach, look forward to interesting, in a position to	company, textiles Alibaba, OEM orders catalogue, samples

Writing Tips

➢   Stating sources of information
➢   Introducing your company briefly
➢   Attaching sales literature
➢   Welcoming specific inquires
➢   Offering samples if necessary

Lesson 3

Sellers Asking to Establish Trade Relations（2）

From：Amy. Lin@Globalking. com. cn
To：Horris@dqs. com
Date：July 8，20—
Subject：Office Depot **vendor**-pens/ Globalking Co.
Attachments：Pen Brochure. pdf （1. 5M）

Dear Sir/Madam，

I'm Amy，the sales manager of Suzhou Globalking-one of the biggest pen **manufacturers** in China.

Thank you for taking your time getting to know our company **as follows**：
—**Product category**：ball pen，marker，highlighter
—**Capacity**：30,000 m² workshops，40-60HQ/month
—**Key customers**：**Office Depot，Kmart，Askul and etc**
—**Factory Audit**：**BSCI**

We are **dedicated** to product development and providing reliable delivery，competitive prices，and professional services for customers all over the world.

Attached please find our brochure. Should any **item** draw your **attention**，please **feel free to** inquire specifically. We'd like to provide our best prices and send free samples for you to compare.

Looking forward to your early response，and have a nice day!

Best regards，
Amy Lin
Sales Manager, Globalking Stationery Imp. & Exp. Corp.
Mobile：+86 13851200000 Tel：+86-512-2971666，2971718
Fax：+86-512-2971698
MSN & Skype：Amy. Lin@hotmail. com
Website：www. globalking. com

NOTES

1. vendor：*n.* 卖主，即 seller

2. manufacturer：*n.* 制造商

   manufacture：*v.*（批量）生产，制造，还可以说 make，produce

   We are well connected with over 20 factories that manufacture car parts.

   我们与二十余家汽车零件厂商有良好的业务关系。

   国际贸易中卖方统称 sellers，suppliers 或 vendors，具体角色有：

   exporter 出口商、factory 或 manufacturer 厂商；

   国际贸易中买方统称为 buyers，具体角色有：

   importer 进口商、distributor/dealer 分销商、wholesaler 批发商、retailer
   零售商等

3. as follows：如下，还可以说 as below

   Our solutions to this issue are as follows：…

   我们对此问题的解决方案如下：……。

4. product category：产品类别

5. capacity：*n.* 生产能力

   The factory has a capacity of 80000 tons yearly.

   工厂年生产能力 8 万吨。

   All our factories are working at（full）capacity.

   我们所有的工厂都在满负荷运行。

   We are running below capacity because of cancelled orders.

   因为订单取消，我们的工厂开工不足。

6. 40-60HQ/month：每月出货 40～60 个高柜

   HQ 也可以写作 HC，是 High Cubic 的简称，即 40 尺集装箱高柜。国际上
   常见的集装箱规格还有：20GP（General Purpose）20 尺普柜，40GP 40 尺
   普柜等。

7. key customer：重要客户，关键客户

8. Office Depot：欧迪办公（美），世界 500 强企业，提供办公产品与办公
   服务

9. Kmart：澳大利亚百货公司

10. Askul：日本办公产品邮购公司

11. audit：*n.* 审核，查验

    factory audit：验厂

12. BSCI：商业社会标准认证，全称是 Business Social Compliance Initiative，

是倡议商界遵守社会责任组织

13. dedicated：*a.* 尽心尽力的；专门的

J&J is dedicated to health and well-being.

强生公司深耕于健康与福利事业。

Our company is dedicated to delivering solutions tailored to customers' needs.

我公司致力于根据顾客需求提供定制的解决方案。

We are dedicated suppliers of security equipment.

我们专门从事安全设备的供应。

14. item：*n.* 货物，商品。尤指表格中列出的一系列产品。

some of the items 部分产品

an export item 一个出口项目（或一项出口商品）

an item of business 一个营业项目（或经营的一个产品）

Attached is an order for the following items from your catalogue.

附件是一份订单，订购你方目录中的下列商品。

15. draw your attention：引起你方注意

attention *n.* 注意（详解见 Lesson 6）

16. feel free to：尽管做，可以随便（做……）

17. response：*n.* 回答；回应

Responses to our advertisement have been disappointing.

人们对我们的广告反应平淡，令人失望。

18. MSN：即 MSN Messenger，是微软推出的即时通信软件

Skype 是微软推出的另一款即时通信软件，基本取代了 MSN，可以实现视频聊天、多人语音会议、多人聊天、传送文件、文字聊天等功能。

现在国际贸易中的通信手段常用的有 mail/post 信函、email 电子邮件、voice mail 声音邮件、telephone 电话、videophone 可视电话以及 Skype、MSN、QQ、WeChat 等网络实时通信软件。

A SUPPLEMENATRY SAMPLE EMAIL

Hi Sir/Madam,

Glad to hear that you're looking for Chinese suppliers of furnitures. Hope we can be a partner of your company.

Ningbo Natureyard Co. is a factory with 10 years' experience in making and exporting quality wooden and leather furnitures to US, Europe and Japan. We have been certified ISO9001 : 2000 by SGS. Besides, we have our own professional designers to meet any of your requirements.

An e-catalog with full specifications is attached for your information.

Email me or just call me directly for more details.

Thanks and best regards,
Leon

EXERCISES

Ⅰ. **Fill in the blanks with the proper forms of the following expressions.**

> as follows, attention, feel free to, capacity, attachment, vendor, dedicated, response, item, audit

1. We'd like to draw your _____ to the superior quality of this new product.
2. The _____ of the house wants to exchange contracts this week.
3. We have passed the factory _____ from Disney.
4. The terms and conditions of the technical offer are _____ :
5. We have a _____ team of production and service professionals who are specialists in their individual fields in the high-tech industry.
6. If you have any questions, please _____ to contact me.
7. Our factory is equipped with 12 sewing lines with a yearly _____ of nearly 1. 4 million pieces of Jeans Jackets and Skirts.
8. Waiting for your immediate _____ and thanks for your kind

cooperation.

9. We've an inquiry for glitter Christmas balls. Please see _____ for your reference.

10. Should any _____ interest you，please let us know.

Ⅱ. **Translate the following sentences into Chinese.**

　　1. LED SPIRIT Co.，Ltd.（HK）is engaged in the design and production of a wide range of professional LED lighting products.

　　2. Our own lab can carry out the chemical test according to the ITS standards.

　　3. We have long-term cooperation with many international companies，including Toshima，IKEA，DENDRO，COM40 with products of CONVERSE，AIRWALK，DISNEY，the IKEA sleeper and other famous brands.

　　4. To new buyers we offer：(1) price 10% off；(2) free samples；(3) OEM&ODM；(4) factory audit & goods inspection welcomed.

　　5. Thanks for your response. I need to see your product category. Can you give me the website of your company? Do you have Skype ID?

Ⅲ. **Translate the following sentences into English.**

　　1. 以下是我公司简介和我的联系方式。真诚希望与您合作。

　　2. 我们主营家纺、针织服装和床上用品的生产和进出口。

　　3. 工厂占地23万平方米，年产500万件。

　　4. 工厂通过了沃尔玛验厂，并获得了通标公司（SGS）的BSCI认证证书。

　　5. 关于该产品规格的所有细节都写在所附小册子里了。

Ⅳ. **Put the following in order to make up an email. Then translate it into Chinese.**

　　1. We wish you can list us as the supplier for the LED Screen from China.

　　2. Good day. This is Henry from Normarous LED Screen in China.

　　3. Knowing you are in the LED Screen business，

　　4. Your earliest response is highly appreciated.

　　5. Dear Purchasing Manager of Ergo LED Screen Limited，

　　6. We have been a professional LED Screen Factory since 2010

　　7. and famous for our competitive price，high quality，and swift loading time.

8. Best regards,

9. （1）Normarous LED Screen；

（2）Outdoor LED Screen；

（3）Indoor LED Screen；

（4）Conference LED Screen... （pictures attached below）

10. Recently, there are abundant styles of LED Screen in our catalogue as below：

11. Henry

V. Writing task.

Please refer to Task A1-2 on Page 322.

RECAP

Language Focus	Knowledge Focus
I'm... （name）, ... （job title） of... （company） as follows, be dedicated to, feel free to	manufacturers, product category capacity, key customers factory audit, item
Writing Tips	

> Introducing who you are and your job title
> Highlighting the advantages of your company, products and services
> Showing business figures and certificates

Lesson 4

Buyers Asking to Establish Trade Relations

From：Rick. Yang@walmart. com. cn
To：Jennie@finev. com
Date：Sep. 6，20—
Subject：Wal-Mart looking for cup suppliers

Dear Sirs，

You were **recommended** to us by the **Chamber** of **Commerce** of Copenhagen.

We wish to buy **quality** tea and coffee cups and saucers **of different shapes**, fully decorated with flowers or other designs.

If you can **supply** this type of **merchandise**，**kindly** send us sample cups via **courier**. Also，please let us have your **price** list and all suitable **illustrations**.

Please note that we are able to buy large quantities if your prices are favorable.

We **await** your early reply.

Yours faithfully，
Rick Yang
Purchasing Manager
Wal-Mart Supercenter
Add：254 Zhongshan Road，Harbin，China
Tel：86-431-82750798

NOTES

1. recommend：*v.* 推荐；建议

   You have been recommended by the CCPIT as a potential buyer of Chinese chinaware.

   中国国际贸易促进委员会向我们推荐说你们是中国瓷器的潜在买主。

   We recommend that you try the Scandinavian markets.

   我们建议你们试一试斯堪的那维亚市场。

   We recommend you to buy a small quantity for trial.

   我们建议你们试购少量的货物。

   We strongly recommend acceptance as our stocks are running low.

   由于我方存货减少，我们力荐接受（报价）。

   recommendation *n.* 推荐；建议

   We are contacting you on the recommendation of Johnson & Company.

   经约翰逊公司的推荐，特与你司联系。

   recommended：*a.* 推荐的；介绍的

   recommended retail price：建议零售价

2. Chamber of Commerce：商会

   International Chamber of Commerce（ICC）国际商会

   Chamber of Shipping 航运协会

   Chamber of Trade（英）零售商公会

3. quality：*n.* 质量

   Our products are famous for their superior quality.

   我们的产品以其优良的品质闻名。

   These shoes are of good/high/poor/low quality.

   这些鞋的质量很好/很高/很差/很低。

   a. 高质量的，上等的

   The market for quality cars remains strong.

   高档车市场持续强劲。

4. tea and coffee cups and saucers：tea cups and saucers，coffee cups and saucers

   带杯托的茶杯和带杯托的咖啡杯

5. ...of different shapes：各种形状的······

   of：表事物的材料、属性、特征等，可根据实际情况

翻译成"用……制造的"、"拥有……的"等，如：

plates of gold and silver 用金银做的盘子

a rod of iron 铁制的竿子

genuine leather of high quality 高质量的真皮

cotton piece goods of Chinese origin 中国产的棉布

shirts of various sizes and materials 各种尺寸、料子的衬衣

a matter of great importance 一件重要的事情

Our goods are of high quality and favorable price.

我们的货物质优价廉。

6. supply：*n.* 供应；供货，货源 *v.* 提供，供给

   n. 供应；供货

   be in short / scarce /light supply 供应短缺

   be in large / abundant / ample supply 供应充足

   Information indicates that supply exceeds demand.

   有消息表明供大于求。

   Our supply of tea is running low.

   我方茶叶货源已不多。

   There are no supplies on hand.

   手头无货可供。

   v. 提供，供给

   to supply a factory with spare parts 给工厂提供备件

   We believe we can supply all kinds of leather shoes to you.

   我们相信能够提供给你们各式各样的皮鞋。

   We believe we can supply you with all kinds of leather shoes.

   我们相信能够提供给你们各式各样的皮鞋。

7. merchandise：*n.* 商品，货物（总称，无复数形式）如：

   general merchandise 杂货

   The merchandise is shipped through two ports.

   商品通过两个港口装运。

   注意以下几个词的区别：

   GOODS（pl.）商品，货物。既用于统称，又可以特指。还用于表示货物的名称。一般用复数形式。

   Twenty pieces of goods were stolen at the port of discharge.

20 件货物在卸货港被盗。

consumer goods 消费品

captioned goods 标题商品

piece goods 布匹

cotton piece goods 棉布

canned goods 罐头食品

electric goods 电器

COMMODITY 商品，日用品。一般用来指类别。还特指一个国家的主要商品。

Labour is bought and sold like any other commodity.

和别的商品一样，劳动力也可以买和卖。

Wine is one of the many commodities that France sells abroad.

葡萄酒是法国众多的出口商品之一。

CARGO 货物（常指运输中的货物）；一批船货

The steamer sailed with full cargo.

该轮满载航行。

It's a cargo steamer.

这是条货轮。

A cargo（several cargoes）of sugar is（are）arriving on this steamer.

一（几）批食糖将由该轮运到。

ARTICLE，ITEM 表示编号的商品、列表中的商品。

Article / Item No. 5 五号商品

This list comprises the main articles/items the exporter deals in.

此清单包括该出口商经营的主要商品。

LINE（一系列同类）货色，商品的一种

This is a new line of ready-made suits.

这是一种新款式的成衣套装。

We don't have any beachwear in stock at the moment-we're still waiting for our summer line to come in.

我们目前没有沙滩服的库存，我们仍在等待这种夏季商品的到货。

PRODUCT（工厂生产的）产品

Nowadays there's such a range of skin-care products to choose from.

现今有很多护肤产品可供选择。

I'm trying to cut down on dairy products.

我正尽力减少食用奶制品。

primary product 初级产品

end/final/finished product 最终产品

semi-finished product 半成品

8. kindly：*ad.*（用作请求时的礼貌用语）请

Please kindly help to confirm with the client.

请帮忙跟客户确认。

You are kindly requested to provide your lowest quotation for cotton shirting.

请告知棉质细布的最低价格。

kind：*a.* 不吝啬的，慷慨的（礼貌用语，一般不翻译）

Thanks for your kind reply.

感谢您的回复。

9. courier：*n./v.* 快递；递送员；发快递

DHL Express offers shipping, tracking and courier delivery services.

敦豪快递提供运输、跟踪和快递服务。

If it is so urgent, I would suggest you arrange courier to collect it on tomorrow morning.

如果非常紧急，我建议您安排快递员明早上门来取件。

10. price list：价目表，价格单

11. illustration：*n.* 说明；图解

illustrate：*v.* 举例说明；图解

illustrated catalogue 有插图的目录

illustrated price list 有说明的价格单

The specifications are not fully illustrated in the contract.

合同中没有清楚地说明规格。

The book was illustrated by a very famous cartoonist.

本书由一位著名的漫画家插图。

The book has a lot of beautiful illustrations.

这本书有大量精美的插图。

This delay is a perfect illustration of why we need a new computer system.

这次延误充分说明了为什么我们需要一个新的电脑系统。

12. await：*v.* ＝wait for 等待

They are awaiting the decision of the board.

他们正等待董事会的决定。

A SUPPLEMENATRY SAMPLE EMAIL

Gentlemen:

I visited your stall at the International Hardware Fair in Cologne, 2014 and noticed that you manufacture garden trimming machines.

There is a good demand for garden trimming machines of high quality. We are interested in your products and would be grateful if you would send us your catalogue with full specifications and the latest price list.

Please let us know what discount you can give us for substantial orders as well as some other favorable terms.

We look forward to receiving an early reply.
Sincerely
George

EXERCISES

Ⅰ. Fill in the blanks with the proper forms of the following expressions.

recommend, quality, supply, kindly, airmail
note, large quantities, favorable, await, of

1. We can _____ him as a good agent (代理) here for the sale of your products.
2. The market has so changed as to be _____ to the big importers.
3. There is an ample _____ of this article.
4. Please note that we usually import this product in _____ .
5. Mail charges, including _____ rates, have risen by 10%.
6. We _____ from your letter that you are in the market for chemicals.
7. We are _____ your early response.
8. You will stand much chance to gain orders as long as you offer _____ products at reasonable prices.
9. We strive to deliver customer service _____ the highest standard.

10. _____ let us know your detailed requirements.

II. Translate the following letter into Chinese.

Dear Susan，

Hoping that all is going well and that your business is flourishing daily.

I'm planning to attend the PREMIERE（法兰克福国际博览会）on/about Jan. 18.

Please tell us your stand number and let us know if you have carpet stocks in your warehouse and what types.

I am also interested in importing office furniture to China and saw a lot of exporters at the Fair before. Do you have any friends or contacts in this field?

Awaiting your kind reply.

With best regards to you and your manager，

Jerry

III. Translate the following sentences into English.

1. 我公司有意从贵国进口银制品，请寄样品、价格单及带插图的目录。
2. 很遗憾，目前我方不能供应这种特殊规格。
3. 装潢材料在我处供大于求。
4. 我方从伦敦商会了解到，你公司生产高级服饰用品用于出口。
5. 我们是本地最大的棉织品进口商，目前收到许多有关你方印花细布的询盘。

IV. Writing task.

Please refer to Task B1 on Page 334.

RECAP

Language Focus	Knowledge Focus
You are recommended to us by...	Chamber of Commerce
supply	merchandise, commodity, cargo,
kindly	line, article, item, product
await	courier, price list, illustrations

Writing Tips

➢ Identifying what you want to buy
➢ Requesting for sales literature
➢ Expressing or implying you are a large buyer

PART TWO

NEGOTIATING A CONTRACT

Task 2

Making Inquiries and Offers

Learning Objectives

To be able to write emails making general inquiries, specific inquiries, quotations and offers

To get familiar with the writing plans, useful sentences and phrases of inquiries and offers

Lesson 5

A General Inquiry

From: jzzmd@aol. com
To: maoyibu@vip. 163. com
Date: Aug. 7, 20—
Subject: An Inquiry for Oolong Tea

Dear Sir/Madam,

Thank you very much for your email of Aug. 6 from which we know that you are exporting various kinds of Chinese teas.

We have an **inquiry** here for your **Oolong Tea.** Kindly let us have your **MOQ**, packing, terms of payment, **quotation** sheet and etc. in detail as soon as possible for our **reference.** We would like to have your **latest** samples. Also please **let us know** the quantities **available** for export at present and whether you can supply them from stock.

We shall really **appreciate** it if you will **quote** us your most favorable prices.

Best regards,
Mike Daniel

NOTES

1. inquiry：*n.*（美语）询盘，询价，询购，英语常用 enquiry

   inquire：*v.*（美语）询盘，询价，询购，英语常用 enquire

   inquiry note 询购单

   general inquiry 一般询盘

   specific inquiry 具体询盘

   Thank you for your email of May 8 inquiring about Mountain Bicycles.

   贵方五月八日询盘山地自行车的电子邮件收悉，谢谢。

   The goods you inquire for are out of stock at present.

   你们所询购的货物现已售完。

   We are inquiring for Sunflower Seeds.

   我们正在询盘葵花籽。

   to make（send，give，email）sb. an inquiry for sth. 向某人询购某货

   to make（send，give，email）an inquiry to sb. for sth. 向某人询购某货

   We are making you an inquiry for Sunflower Seeds.

   现向你方询盘葵花籽。

2. Oolong tea：乌龙茶

3. MOQ：Minimum Order Quantity 最小订量，起订量

   Our monthly MOQ is 3000KGS of every kind.

   我们每月的最小订量是每种 3000 千克。

   类似表达还有：MOV Minimum Order Value 最小订单值

4. packing：*n.* 包装（详解见 Lesson 17）

5. terms of payment：付款条件，支付条件

6. quotation sheet：报价单

7. in detail：详细地

8. for our reference：供我方参考

   for your information 告诉你们一下，供你方参考

For your information，Indian dealers are offering the same item at a price about 5 per cent lower than yours.

现告知你方，印度交易商正以比你方低5%的价格对同一产品报价。

9. let us know：让我们知道，告诉我们

相当于 tell，但是语气更礼貌。这种用法在商务信函中很常见，再如：

let us have 给我们，相当于 give

Please let us know the name of the vessel.

请告知船名。

Please let us have your best quotation.

请报我最低价。

10. available：*a.* 可利用的，可用的，可得到的

The swimming pool is available only in summer.

这个游泳池只在夏天开放。

The Prime Minister was not available for comments.

首相无暇做出评论。

Do you have a room available?

你们有空房间吗?

11. stock：*n.* 存货，库存

supply sth from stock 现货供应……

have sth in stock 有……现货

be out of stock 无货，缺货

a stock of... 一批……现货

We can supply walnut meat from stock.

我们能够供应核桃仁现货。

If you have pine kernels in stock，please send us some samples.

如你们有松籽仁现货，请寄来一些样品。

Fresh shrimps are now out of stock.

鲜虾现在缺货。

We have a large stock of canned fruits.

我们有一大批水果罐头。

12. latest：*a.* 最新的

Attached is our latest price list for your information.

随附我们最新的价目单，供你参考。

13. appreciate：*v.* 感谢，感激

（1）appreciate sth.

We highly appreciate your close cooperation.

我们十分感激你们的密切合作。

Your prompt reply would be appreciated.

如能立即答复，不胜感激。

（2）appreciate（one's）doing sth.

We shall appreciate hearing from you again.

我们将乐于再次收到你方来信。

（3）appreciate it if/when...

We should appreciate it if you could send us your samples immediately by airmail.

如能立即航寄样品，不胜感激。

（4）It will/would be appreciated if...

It will be appreciated if you can quote us the lowest prices.

如能报最低价，不胜感激。

14. quote：*v.* 报价

（1）quote（sb.）a price

Please quote your lowest price CIF Singapore.

请报成本加运费加保费新加坡最低价。

Please quote us your lowest price CIF Liverpool.

请向我方报成本加运费加保费利物浦最低价。

（2）quote sb.（a price）for sth.

Please quote us for Snow White Neutron Gel Pens.

请向我报"白雪"中性笔价。

Please quote us the price for 34" color TV sets.

请向我报 34 英寸彩电价。

（3）quotation：*n.* 报价

常与动词 make，give，send 等连用，后接介词 for 或 of：

Please make/give us your lowest quotation for Nike basketball shoes.

请报耐克篮球鞋最低价。

Your quotation of iron nails is too high to be acceptable.

你方铁钉报价太高，无法接受。

A SUPPLIMENTARY SAMPLE EMAIL

Dear Sirs,

We are in the market for Melon Seeds of the first and second grade and should appreciate it if you could let us have your offers with some representative samples by airmail. When offering the goods, please state the earliest possible time of shipment and quantities available.

Best regards,
Lanny

EXERCISES

I. Fill in the blanks with the proper forms of the following expressions.

appreciate, kindly, inquire, quote,
for your reference, from which, export, in detail

1. We thank you for your email _____ we know that you are interested in your dehydrated vegetable.
2. Please _____ us your best price for the foods attached in your email.
3. If you can _____ the goods we asked for, please let us know soon.
4. We thank you for your email of Aug. 18 _____ about our products.
5. We would _____ it if you could send us your samples by airmail.
6. We examine the wording _____ before deciding on the final text.
7. We have attached you our quotation sheet _____ .
8. Will you _____ obey the instructions I am about to give?

II. Multiple choice.

1. We'll appreciate it very much if you can quote us your best prices _____ Sony Brand Color TV Sets of 24 and 29 inches.

   A. in   B. to   C. for   D. with

2. Kindly _____ us your most favorable price FOB China.

   A. giving   B. gave   C. to give   D. give

3. We thank you for your email of March 18 _____ our silk blouses.

   A. inquiring for   B. inquiry for

   C. inquires for   D. inquired for

4. We are pleased _____ your inquiry of July 15 for our Chinese Cotton Piece Goods.

   A. to receiving   B. as received   C. receiving   D. to have

5. We are looking forward to _____ from you soon.

   A. hearing   B. hear   C. heard   D. be heard

6. The Italian Commercial Bank informed us that you are in the market _____ table-cloths.

   A. for   B. with   C. with   D. for

7. It may interest you to know that there is a good demand here for Chinese Black Tea _____ prices.

   A. at moderate   B. in cheap   C. for low   D. on dear

8. We are a specialized corporation, _____ the export of animal by-products.

   A. dealing   B. handling   C. dealing with   D. dealt in

Ⅲ. Put the following words and expressions in right order to make up a sentence.

1. your email, we, inquiring for, have received, of May 15th, the packing machines.

2. waiting for, are, we, your, reply, early.

3. we, you, our, your, sample, at, have sent, request.

4. appreciate, we, you, us, it, would, should, quote, if, the best price.

5. your, reply, early, be, appreciated, would, highly.

Ⅳ. Translate the following email into English.

敬启者：

目前我们对中国棉布感兴趣，并从阿里巴巴网上得知你们从事这个行业。请报每码的价格及付款条件。如报价优惠，拟向你们购进我们目前的全部所需。

盼早日答复。

谨上
托尼

Ⅴ. Writing task.

Please refer to Task A2 on Page 329.

RECAP

Language Focus	Knowledge Focus
inquire for make an inquiry to sb. for sth. supply... from stock, be out of stock appreciate, available, let us know for your reference/for your information	inquiry MOQ, MOV quotation sheet

Writing Tips

➢ Acknowledging receipt of the seller's email of establishing trade relations
➢ Making an inquiry with general requirements in terms of prices, MOQ, packing, payment terms, etc.
➢ Asking for quotation sheet, price list, samples, etc.
➢ Describing your expectation for favorable prices

Lesson 6

A Specific Inquiry

From：giwsdc@spspa. au
To：sunfine@vip. 163. com
Date：Aug. 10，20—
Subject：An inquiry for peanuts

Dear Sirs，

We thank you for your email of Aug. 9 from which we learn that you are an exporter of peanut products.

We are a **grocery importer and wholesaler based** in Sydney，Australia. I am **interested** in most of your products. So can you kindly provide the following information **ASAP** since we are about to **place an order** very soon?

    1. The actual photos of products

    2. Products packing and **description**

    3. Prices **in terms of** FOB China

The products I am interested in are as follows：

    1. Blanched Peanuts

    2. Peanut Kernels

    3. Roasted peanut in shell

    4. Chocolate products

Your immediate **attention** and early reply will be appreciated.

Best regards，
Andley

NOTES

1. peanut products：花生制品

   chocolate products：巧克力制品

   常见的花生制品和巧克力制品有：

blanched peanuts 脱皮花生	peanut kernels 花生米，花生仁
roasted peanut in shell 烤花生果	peanut chocolates 花生巧克力
sunflower seed chocolates 葵花籽仁巧克力	stone chocolates 石春巧克力

2. a grocery importer and wholesaler：食品杂货进口商和批发商

   零售商 retailer

3. based in Sydney：位于悉尼

   Both groups are based in Athens and listed in New York.

   这两家企业都位于雅典，并在纽约上市。

4. interested：*a.* 感兴趣的，有兴趣的

We are/feel very interested in importing medical equipment from your side.

我们对从你处进口医疗设备感兴趣。

We are very interested to know what you can offer in this line.

我们非常想知道你们可以供应什么。

interest：*n.* 兴趣

We have/feel/take special interest in your light industrial products.

我们对你方轻工产品特别感兴趣。

Canned goods are of special interest to us.

我们对罐头食品特感兴趣。

interest：*v.* 使……感兴趣

The new packing will certainly interest you.

这种新的包装肯定会使你们感兴趣。

5. ASAP：尽快，是 as soon as possible 的缩写

6. place an order：下订单（详解见 Lesson 25）

7. description：*n.* 描述

This description didn't seem to tally with what we saw.

这一描述似乎与我们目睹的情况不符。

Description of Goods：货描

Name of Commodity：品名

Commodity：商品

8. in terms of：根据；用……的话；就……而言

In terms of quantity, production grew faster than ever before.

从数量上看，产量增长的速度比以往任何时期都要快。

He thought of everything in terms of money.

他是从钱的角度来看每一件事。

9. attention：*n.* 处理；办理；关注，注意，注意力

Your immediate attention to our proposal will be appreciated.

如对我方建议立即处理，将不胜感激。

The letter is marked "for the attention of Mr. Kramer".

信上注着"由克莱莫先生处理"。

All your future inquiries will receive our prompt attention.

你方今后的一切询盘都会得到我方迅速办理。

They attract attention regardless of their quality.

不管品质，只需吸引注意力。

Facebook might get all of the attention as the world's largest social network.

Facebook（脸谱）作为全球最大的社交网站可能吸引了所有的注意力。

Facebook 是创办于美国的一个社交网络服务网站，用户可以通过它和朋友、同事、同学以及周围的人保持互动交流，分享无限上传的图片，发布链接和视频。类似的知名网站还有 Twitter（推特）、Youtube 等。

A SUPPLIMENTARY SAMPLE EMAIL

Dear Sirs，

It was a pleasure meeting you in Anuga（德国科隆国际食品展览会）.

Please visit our website in order to get familiar with our company. We are importing goods from China for many years already，always looking for qualitative suppliers.

Could you please send me your best offer CIF Rijeka and FOB Chinese Port for：
　　Peanuts 29/33，28/32 and 11/13
　　Shine Skin Pumpkin Seeds size 11
　　Dark Green GWS AA and AAA grade?

Please also name packaging sizes and terms of payment.

Best regards，
Olja

EXERCISES

Ⅰ. Fill in the blanks with the correct word.

interest *n.* ，interest *v.* ，interested，interesting

1. Thank you for your introduction but we are not _____ in this line at present.
2. The new movie is not _____ to most of us.
3. The extraordinary function of the new model _____ us a great deal.

4. We have no _____ in the goods shown at the fair.

5. Among the goods on display，this one is of special _____ to us.

II. Put in the missing words.

Dear Sirs

Thank you for your email _____ Jun. 12. We note _____ pleasure that you intend to develop business with us in the subject goods.

We have gone _____ your catalogue and find that Cotton Table Cloths Art No. 345 and No. 348 are _____ interest to us. We shall be pleased _____ your quotation also indicates the quantities of the various sizes _____ you can supply for prompt delivery. If your prices are reasonable and quantity satisfactory，we shall consider placing substantial orders.

We have _____ handling Table Cloths for more _____ 20 years and have goods connections all over this country. We have also some associated firms in the neighboring countries where we can find a ready market for your products as well.

We trust you will _____ this inquiry your immediate attention and let us have your reply _____ an early date.

Best regards

Funny

III. Translate the following sentences into Chinese.

1. The sample that we asked for has not reached us yet.

2. We have done substantial business with that company，which has some good connections in Paris.

3. We would like to know whether you can quote price for Head & Shoulders Shampoo.

4. Your immediate attention to early reply will be appreciated.

5. You may rest assured that we shall certainly give your inquiry our serious consideration.

6. I wonder whether this article comes under your export programme.

7. Do you think there is any opportunity to work up a good deal in this time?

8. Please send us your catalogue along with your quotation.

9. We'd like to know what discount you offer on bulk purchase.

10. There is a promising market in our area for moderately priced goods.

Ⅳ. Translate the following sentences into English.

1. 如果你们对这几项商品感兴趣，请寄来你们具体的询盘。

2. 请告知你们何时才能给我们提供样本。

3. 随附价格单一纸，请查收。

4. 如果能航寄来你们最新的样品，我们将不胜感激。

5. 对你们这样的老客户，我们给的毫无疑问都是最优惠价。

6. 我们有自己的工厂，因此货源是稳定可靠的。

7. 你们所有的询盘都会得到我方迅速办理。

8. 你方 8 月 8 日询盘我们的出口产品的电邮收到了，谢谢。

9. 请报 1000 辆 "Trend" 牌自行车成本加运保费至新加坡价。

10. 报价时，请说明付款条件及装运日期。

Ⅴ. Writing task.

Please refer to Task B2 on Page 334.

RECAP

Language Focus	Knowledge Focus
be interested in...，be of interest...	grocery，importer，wholesaler
in terms of	actual photo
place an order	product description
attention	nut products
ASAP	FOB Qingdao
Writing Tips	

➢ Appreciating the seller's intention to establish trade relations

➢ Introducing your company

➢ Making an inquiry，specifying your detailed requirements in terms of particular articles，trade terms，etc.

➢ Describing your expectation for immediate attention

Lesson 7

An Offer (A Reply to Lesson 5)

From：maoyibu@vip. 163. com
To：jzzmd@aol. com
Date：Aug. 8, 20—
Subject：Oolong Tea
Attachment：Quotation Sheet. pdf (1. 2M)

Dear Daniel,

We have received your email of Aug. 7 with many thanks.

As **requested**, we are sending you **herewith** our quotation sheet for Oolong Tea Art. Nos. 206 and 208. The **respective quantities** available for **prompt shipment** are **indicated** therein, and the prices are quoted **on the basis of CIFC2%** New York. This **offer** is **subject to** our final confirmation. **As to** the relative samples, we have sent them to you by **FedEx**. Its **tracking number** is 6800 3569 2256 3908.

It is known to all that Chinese teas are of best quality and moderate price.

You will certainly **agree** to that when you have examined our samples and quotation sheet. As the **season** is **approaching**, it is hoped that you will send us your orders as early as possible. If you have any other requirements, please **let us know without any delay**.

Your prompt reply will be appreciated.

Best regards,
Sunny

NOTES

1. as requested：根据要求

2. as requested by you 按照你的要求

   as requested in your email of May 5 按照你方 5 月 5 日电邮的要求

   As requested，we have changed the color of the sample and are now sending you a new piece for your study.

   根据要求，我们修改了样品的颜色，现寄去新样品一份，供你研究。

   （1）request：*n.* 要求，需求

   Chambermaids will bring an iron or hair dryer on request.

   只要提出要求，清理房间的女服务员就会送来熨斗或电吹风。

   The price quotes on selected product categories will be sent upon request.

   所选产品类别的报价承索即寄。

   （2）at your request：按照你的要求

   We have sent you our samples at your request by DHL.

   按照你的要求，我们用 DHL 快递给你寄去了我们的样品。

   （3）request：*v.* 要求，

   She had requested that the door to her room be left open.

   她要求不要关闭通向她房间的门。

   They requested him to leave.

   他们要求他离开。

   Mr Dennis said he had requested access to a telephone.

   丹尼斯先生说他已经请求使用电话。

3. herewith：*ad.* 在此，随同此信，＝with this

   此类词在商业信函、公文等正式文件中很常见。类似词语还有：

   （t）herein，（t）herewith，（t）hereof，（t）hereafter，（t）herefrom，

   （t）hereinafter，（t）hereon，（t）hereto，（t）hereunder 等。如：

   We hereby recommend to you our newly developed model as a substitute for the one you requested.

   我们在此向你方推荐我们新开发的一个型号，作为你方需求型号的替代。

   Under CIF terms，the sellers are responsible for the shipment of the goods to the port of destination and pay the freight thereto.

   在 CIF 条件下，卖方负责将货物运至目的港，并支付到目的港的运费。

4. Art. Nos. 206 and 208：编号为 206 和 208 的商品

   Art. 是 Article 的缩写。article number 表示货号，公司还常用 code

number 或 item number。

5. respective：*a.* 各个的，各自的

一般情况下 respective 后用名词的复数，如：

Types 22 and 32 have their respective merits.

22 型和 32 型各有优点。

6. quantity：*n.* 数量

The minimum order quantity we require is 80 M/T.

我们所要的起订量是 80 公吨。

Our customers prefer quality to quantity.

我方客户重质量过于数量。

a large quantity of＝large quantities of 大量的

We know that you are in need of a large quantity of coal.

我们知道你们需要大批量的煤。

in（large）quantities 大量地

Chain stores usually make purchases in large quantities.

连锁店通常大批量进货。

7. prompt shipment：即期装运

8. indicate：*v.* 表明，标示，指示

The last figures so far this year indicate a rise of 13.8%.

今年到目前为止的最新数据显示增长了 13.8%。

He told us when to indicate and when to change gear.

他告诉我们何时打转向灯、何时换挡。

9. on the basis of：＝on...basis 以……为基础，在……基础上；根据……，按照……

Please make us an offer on CFR basis.

请按成本加运费价格给我们报盘。

The business was booked on the basis of sight L/C.

这笔业务是按照即期信用证成交的。

We trade with people in all countries on the basis of equality and mutual benefit.

我们在平等互利的基础上和各国人民进行交易。

10. CIFC2%：成本运费加保费含 2% 佣金

也可以说 CIFC2，其中第二个 C 代表 commission（佣金）。

11. offer：*n.* 报盘

to make/give /send sb. an offer for/on sth 向某人报盘某物

Please make us an offer CIF London for/on 20 metric tons of Brown Cashmere.

请向我们报 20 公吨棕色开司米羊毛成本加运保费伦敦价。

"对……的报盘"还可以说 offer of sth

We are studying your offer of 2,000 kilos of Black Tea.

我们正在研究你方 2000 公斤红茶的报盘。

offer：v. 报盘

to offer sb. sth. 或 to offer sth. to sb. 向某人报盘某物

We can offer you wood pulp at attractive prices.

我们能以具有吸引力的价格向你方报木浆。

We hope that we can offer you firm some time next week.

我们希望能于下周某天向你方报实盘。

We can offer motorcycles of various brands.

我们能报各种品牌的摩托车。

Please offer as soon as possible.

请尽早报盘。

12. subject to：... 以……为准，以……为条件

to 是介词，后接名词或动名词。

This offer is subject to our final confirmation.

此报盘以我方最后确认为准。

This offer is firm，subject to your reply reaching us before March 20.

此报盘为实盘，以你方 3 月 20 日前复到有效。

an offer subject to our final confirmation 就是报盘人想留有余地，不想一锤定音，即过去所说的"虚盘（non-firm offer）"。类似说法还有：

We are offering without engagement the following goods.

我们向你报下列产品，该报盘无约束力。

Our offer is subject to alterations without prior notice.

我们的报盘在不通知你方的情况下可以修改。

Our offer is subject to prior sales.

我方对该报盘保留先卖权。

13. as to：至于；关于；按照；根据

I have no doubts as to your ability.

关于你的能力我毫不怀疑。

We sorted the eggs as to size and color.

我们按照大小和颜色挑选鸡蛋。

We have found some drivers clueless as to the law.

我们发现有些司机对这一法规一无所知。

14. FedEx 联邦快递公司（美）

国际知名的快递公司有：

FedEx 联邦快递公司（美）	DHL 敦豪快递公司（比）
UPS 联合包裹服务（美）	EMS 邮政特快专递服务（中）
TNT 天地快运（荷）	SAGAWA 佐川急便（日）
AAE 美亚快递（美）	DPEX（澳）

15. tracking number：查询号，追踪号

快递公司运送的每一笔货物都会有一个查询号码，方便客户在网上追踪邮件，随时获知有关货物在递送途中的信息。

16. agree to：同意

（1）agree to sth（to 是介词）

We agree to a friendly settlement of the dispute.

我方同意友好解决这一争端。

（2）agree to do sth（to 是动词不定式符号）

We agree to share the expenses.

我们同意分担费用。

as agreed upon 按照约定

17. season：*n.* 季节，这里指 selling season 销售季节

shopping season 购物季节

peak/hot/busy season 旺季

off/dead/slack season 淡季

18. approach：*v.* 靠近，接近＝draw near

We could just see the train approaching in the distance.

我们可以看到火车从远处开来。

The total amount raised so far is approaching ＄1,000.

筹集的资金接近 1000 美元。

19. without（any）delay：＝with the least possible delay 立即，马上

Should the position improve in the future，we will contact you without delay.

若将来情况好转，我们将立即与你联系。

We hope that you will ship our order with the least possible delay.

望立即装运我方订货。

A SUPPLEMENTARY SAMPLE EMAIL

Dear Mr. Crane

We are pleased to inform you that we have enlarged our business machine department and are considering the addition of new lines to our stock.

Your various typewriters and calculators would fit in well. Please send us a full range of catalogues and samples that are in production. We expect you to quote your lowest prices and would like to know whether you can supply from stock.

If we decide to put your goods on the market，we want your assurance that you will not sell them to other firms in our district.

Weare looking forward to your early reply.

B/RGDS
CAUSIO

EXERCISES

Ⅰ. Fill in the blanks with the proper forms of the following expressions.

> subject to，as to，let us have，look forward to，be known to，
> on the basis of，as agreed upon，prompt shipment，approach，without delay

1. We are _____ hearing from you soon.

2. It _____ to our buyers that our products are of good quality and reasonable price.

3. Please quote us the prices for our needed goods _____ FOB China.

4. Would you please offer us the goods _____ .

5. As the selling season _____ , you are requested to ship our order ASAP.

6. This offer is firm _____ your reply received by us before the end of this month.

7. Please _____ your detailed information about your export goods.

8. _____ payment terms，we'd like to make all the payments by sight L/C.

9. _____ , we have sent you the contract made out by our sales- manager.

10. If your needed goods are available，we'll send them to you by air _____ .

Ⅱ. Translate the following terms into English.

报价单	即期装运
起订量	虚盘
根据商定	销售季节
毫不延误	最终确认

Ⅲ. Rewrite the following sentences with the hints given in parentheses.

1. It is known to the buyers that our canned goods are moderately priced. (as known)

2. Do not hesitate to write us if you are in need of any other articles. (need)

3. Please send your specific inquiry as early as possible if you find our goods marketable. (let us have)

4. Your quotation sheet has been noted but the quantity available for September shipment is not indicated in your quotation sheet.

(therein)

5. We assure you that we shall certainly give your inquiry our serious consideration.

(assure you of)

6. The item required by you is unavailable at the moment.

(that-clause)

Ⅳ. Translate the following sentences into English.

1. 请尽快告知你们的具体询盘。

2. 如果你们已快递所要样品，请告知追踪号。

3. 你们给的是 CIF 报价，但我们希望你们能在 CFR 基础上报价。

4. 如果你们同意我们的报价，请告知，以便我们备货。

5. 市场调查表明这种商品供不应求。

Ⅴ. Writing task.

Please refer to Task A3 on Page 330.

RECAP

Language Focus	Knowledge Focus
offer sb. sth.	offer
make/give sb. an offer for/on sth.	Art. No.
as requested, to send…herewith…	CIFC2%
as to, on the basis of, subject to…	prompt shipment
approach, agree to	FedEx, Tracking number
without any delay	moderate prices, season

Writing Tips

> Acknowledging having received the buyer's inquiry
> Making a general offer by attaching a quotation sheet
> Advising the buyer of courier's name and tracking number if samples are sent
> Explaining the popularity of the product
> Describing your expectation for orders

Lesson 8

An Offer（A Reply to Lesson 6）

| From：sunfine@vip. 163. com |
| To：giwsdc@spspa. au |
| Date：July 9，20— |
| Subject：Offers for peanut & chocolate products |

Dear Andley，

Your inquiry of July 8 has been noted with pleasure and thanks.

As one of the leading suppliers of dried fruits and nuts for many years，we can assure you that our goods are **superior** in quality and **moderate** in price. We are now making you the offers for your **selections** as follows：

1. 25/29 blanched peanuts，packed in 2 × 12. 5kgs bags/carton at USD1200/**MT** FOB Qingdao
2. 24/28 peanuts，packed in25 kgs vacuum bag at USD1250/MT FOB Qingdao
3. 11/13 roasted peanut in shell，packed in 10kgs vacuum bag at USD800/MT FOB Qingdao
4. Chocolate peanuts，packed in 10kgs cartons at USD1600/MT FOB Qingdao
5. Chocolate sunflower seeds，packed in 10kgs cartons at USD1650/ MT FOB Qingdao
6. Stone chocolate，packed in 10kgs cartons at USD1550/MT FOB Qingdao

Attached are the actual photos of our products. This offer is **firm** subject to your reply reaching us by the end of this month. We hope that the above offers will be **acceptable** to you and are looking forward to your early orders.

Best regards，
Mike Liu

NOTES

1. dried fruits and nuts：果脯和干果

2. assure：*v.* 使确信，使放心；向······保证

   （1）assure sb. of sth.

   We assure you of our readiness to cooperate with you.

   我们保证愿与你合作。

   I can assure you of the reliability of the information.

   我可以向你保证这个消息是可靠的。

   （2）assure sb. that 从句

   We assure you that we shall do our best to expedite the shipment.

   我们保证将尽速装运。

   （3）商业书信中还常用下面句型：

   Please be assured of... （或 that 从句）请放心······

   Please rest assured of... （或 that 从句）请放心······

   You can be assured of... （或 that 从句）请放心······

   You can rest assured of... （或 that 从句）请放心······

   Please be assured of our continued cooperation.

   请相信我方将继续与你合作。

   You can rest assured that we shall revert to your inquiry as soon as possible.

   请放心，我方以后将尽速重新处理你的询盘。

   （4）assurance：*n.* 保证，担保

   They had given an absolute assurance that it would be kept secret.

   他们信誓旦旦地保证将对此绝对保密。

   Progress is the activity of today and the assurance of tomorrow.

   进步是今天的活动和明天的保证。

3. superior：*a.* 比······好的，高的，优的

   We chose her for the job because she was the superior candidate.

   我们选择她做这一工作，因为她是更优秀的候选者。

   We can assure you that the quality of our goods is superior to that of other similar products.

   我们可以保证我们货物的质量比同类其他产品的质量都好。

   反义词 inferior：*a.* 比······劣的，次的

   Please always bear in mind that goods of inferior quality will find no market here.

请永远记住，劣质货在这儿是没有销路的。

4. moderate：*a.* 适当的，中等的，稳健的

Futures prices recovered from sharp early declines to end with moderate losses.

期货价格在早盘深幅下跌后反弹，收盘时未见严重损失。

It is known to all that our canned fruits are moderately priced. and selling very well.

众所周知，我们的水果罐头定价适中并十分畅销。

5. selection：*n.* 被选中的东西，相当于 the selected items

6. 25/29，24/28，11/13 花生的规格，指一盎司（ounce）25～29，24～28，11～13 粒。

7. MT：＝Metric Ton 公吨

The best price we can accept is USD 138/MT.

我们能够接受的最好价格为每公吨 138 美元。

8. 25/29 blanched peanuts, packed in 2×12.5kgs bags/carton at USD1200/MT FOB Qingdao：25/29 脱皮花生，用纸箱包装、每箱 2 袋、每袋 12.5 千克，每吨 1200 美元 FOB 青岛。

We are glad to offer you 500 sets of HP ink-jet printers at USD120 per set FOB China for shipment during March 20—.

我们很高兴向你报 500 台惠普喷墨打印机，每台 120 美元，FOB 中国，20—年 3 月份装运。

9. vacuum bag：真空袋

10. This offer is firm subject to your reply reaching us by the end of this month.

此报盘以本月月底前复到为有效。

同样的意思，还可以说：

This offer is subject to your reply arriving here by the end of this month.

This offer is firm subject to your reply being received by us by the end of this month.

有确切有效期的报盘，常被称为"实盘（firm offer）"。表示报盘有效期的说法通常有：

The offer is firm/good/open/valid/effective for three days.

此报盘以有效期三天。

The offer is firm/good/open/valid/effective until. . . .

本报盘有效至……

Our offer remains open for three days only. Please act quickly.

本报盘有效期只有三天，请赶快行动。

How long do you usually keep your offer open?

你们的报盘通常有效期多长？

11. acceptable：*a.* 可接受的，合意的

A 10 to 15 percent deviation is considered acceptable.

10％至15％的离差是可以接受的。

We have made an acceptable start，but it could have been better.

我们起了一个好头，但本可以更好一些的。

A SUPPLEMENTARY SAMPLE EMAIL

Hi Connie，

As per your requirements and photos，the pricing for the baseball caps with the 50 applique（贴花）is as follows：

(1) Materials：washed polo

(2) Color：light blue

(3) Logo：50 applique

(4) Q'ty/ Unit price：

      (a) 100,000 pcs：USD5. 6/pc FOB Ningbo

      (b) 300,000 pcs：USD5. 2/pc FOB Ningbo

(5) Lead time：

      (a) 100,000 pcs：30～45 days

      (b) 300,000 pcs：60 days

(6) Sample time：5～7 days

(7) Sample fee：USD15 including shipping

Please advise your comments.

Best regards,
Leon

EXERCISES

Ⅰ.**Complete the following sentences.**

  1. We are interested in _____ .
    （1）从你方进口纺织品
    （2）你方的报价
    （3）惠州产"TCL"牌彩色电视机
    （4）你们的新产品

  2. We are interested to _____ .
    （1）从你方购买化工产品
    （2）与你方建立直接的贸易关系
    （3）得到你方最新价格表
    （4）在你地设立一个办事处

  3. As requested，_____ .
    （1）我们给你寄去我方最新目录一份
    （2）我们航寄给你所要样品
    （3）我们报花生价如下
    （4）我们已和厂商取得了联系

  4. We look forward to _____ .
    （1）在交易会上再次与你见面
    （2）早日收到你方样品
    （3）尽快收到你的音讯
    （4）一个愉快的假期

Ⅱ.**Multiple choice.**

  1. We should _____ if you would inform us of their financial standing.
    A. appreciate   B. be appreciated
    C. oblige   D. be obliged

  2. We have _____ the shipping company for booking the space.
    A. contacted   B. contacted with
    C. got contacted   D. got contacted with

  3. Your products would not have been sold so well but for a lot of ads _____ TV and _____ newspapers.
    A. in，in   B. on，on   C. in，on   D. on，in

  4. Please reply to our inquiry _____ your earliest convenience.
    A. by   B. upon   C. at   D. to

5. Replying _____ your inquiry of 26th January，we are glad to quote as follows：

    A. for   B. with   C. on   D. to

6. Would you please supply _____ a complete set of catalogues for textiles accessories so that we may make choice and work on them?

    A. us   B. us with   C. us by   D. us for

7. As _____ , we make you the offer on the basis of CIFC2％ Rotterdam.

    A. request   B. requested   C. requesting   D. requests

8. We are pleased to inform you that the item you requested can be supplied _____ stock.

    A. upon   B. out   C. in   D. from

9. We would like to suggest that you _____ orders for goods required for winter sales earlier.

    A. will place   B. place   C. have to place D. shall place

10. This offer is firm subject to your reply _____ by the end of this month.

    A. arriving   B. receiving   C. reaching   D. received

Ⅲ. Translate the following sentences into English.

1. 如对我方报盘有兴趣，请即来电。

2. 好久没有收到你方音信，请告知是否对我方报盘感兴趣。

3. 你方报价太高，我们认为很难接受你方报盘。

4. 我们正在仔细研究你方报盘，希望将此报盘保留到月底有效。

5. 因为商品数量有限，我们建议你方立即接受这个报盘。

6. 我的一个客户要求通过我们与你联系建立贸易关系。

7. 我们非常高兴地通知你方，本地有顾客对你方产品很感兴趣。

8. 我们向你们报 100 件中国玉雕 (jade carvings)，每件 600 美元，成本价运费到利物浦价，6 月装运。

9. 我们向你们报 20 辆农用拖拉机 (farm tractors)，每辆 4000 美元，深圳港船上交货价，5 月装运。

10. 我方产品品质上乘，价格公道，在国内外市场上很畅销。

Ⅳ. Translate the following email into Chinese.

Dear Sophie,

Thank you for your email and are very pleased to learn you are interested in our rompers.

As known to you, our Baby's wear is good in quality, moderate in price and attractive in style. Each romper is packed in a poly-bag, two dozen in a carton, and 24 cartons on a pallet with equal assortments of pink, green and yellow. The price is USD6 per set CIF Los Angeles. Please note that this offer is subject to your acceptance within one week.

Our usual practice is that we make shipment within 30 days after receipt of 30% deposit by T/T and the balance needs to be wired to us after we complete the loading.

We are awaiting your order soon.

Best regard,

Lang Rong

Ⅴ. Writing task.

Please refer to Task A1-3 on Page 322.

RECAP

Language Focus	Knowledge Focus
offer sb.… （quantity） of… （goods） at… （unite price） for shipment in… （shipment date） packed in… （packing） assure sb. of sth., to assure sb. that… be superior in quality and moderate in price acceptable	leading suppliers MT （M/T, mt, m/t） KGS 2×12. 5kgs bags/ctn non-firm offer

续　表

Writing Tips

➢ Showing appreciation of the buyer's specific inquiry
➢ Introducing your experience and capability
➢   Making a specific offer, stating products description, unit price, packing, etc. in detail
➢ Indicating the validity of the offer
➢ Explaining the popularity of the product and the soundness of your price
➢ Describing your expectation for orders

Lesson 9

A Voluntary Offer

From：cherry106@163. com
To：carvlin@yahoo. com
Date：July 9，20—
Subject：Best Offers for Crystallized Gingers
Attachment：Quotation Sheet. xls（120K）

Dear Carvlin，

We found your name and company on the **Internet.** We are pleased to know that you are **looking for** a supplier of the **Crystallized Gingers** in China.

We have been **in** this **line** for many years and we are one of the leading dealers of Crystallized Ginger Products in China. Every year， we export various **kinds of** the **above** products in large quantities to Japan， Southeast Asia， Europe and South Africa.

As your requirements **fall within our business scope**，we would like to **take this opportunity to** approach you. In order to let you have more **detailed** information about our company and our products，we are attaching you our quotation sheet.

Shipment can be made within 30 days after receipt of your order.

Payment is to be made by an irrevocable L/C payable by draft at sight.

Your prompt attention and early reply would be highly appreciated.

Best regards，
Cherry Han

Attachment:

QUOTATION SHEET OF CRYSTALLIZED GINGER SERIES

Commodity Name	Specifications	FOB QINGDAO		Quantity/20FCL & Delivery Time	Sample Photo	Packing
		Size	USD			
Crystallized Ginger Sticks	Green food without any additives and preservatives SO_2: 30ppm max H_2O: 16%~18% max Sugar: 65~70%	Sticks: (irregular) $8 \times 8 \times 20 \sim 50mm$	$ 4300/mt	14mts/20fcl About: 700ctns		5×4bags/20kgs/ctn
Crystallized Ginger Cubes Regular	Ditto	Cubes: $8 \times 8 \times 8mm$ $10 \times 10 \times 10mm$	$ 4750/mt	14mts/20fcl About: 700ctns		5×4bags/20kgs/ctn
Crystallized Ginger Cubes Irregular	Ditto	Cubes: $8 \sim 10mm$	$ 4150/mt	14mts/20fcl About: 700ctns		5×4bags/20kgs/ctn

续　表

Commodity Name	Specifications	FOB QINGDAO Size	FOB QINGDAO USD	Quantity/20FCL & Delivery Time	Sample Photo	Packing
Crystallized Ginger Dices	Green food without any additives and preservatives SO_2: 30ppm max H_2O: $16\%\sim18\%$ max Sugar: $65\sim70\%$	Dices: $12\sim20$mm	$3750/mt	14mts/20fcl About: 700ctns		5×4bags/20kgs/ctn
Special Crystallized Ginger Slices	Ditto	Slices thickness: 3mm Round flat type	Now we can't produce because the cost is too high	14mts/20fcl About: 700ctns		5×4bags/20kgs/ctn
Crystallized Ginger Slices Irregular	Ditto	Slices thickness: 3mm	$3750/mt	14mts/20fcl About: 700ctns		5×4bags/20kgs/ctn

NOTES

1. Internet：*n.* 互联网，又称因特网

   Surfing the Internet is fun，but it's also a time waster.

   上网很有意思，但也很浪费时间。

   Postings on the Internet can be accessed from anywhere in the world.

   互联网上的帖子在世界任何一个地方都能读到。

2. look for：寻找，寻购

   We are looking for a new supplier of building materials.

   我们在寻找新的建材供货商。

   One of our clients is looking for high quality umbrellas.

   我们的一个客户正在求购高质量雨伞。

3. crystallized ginger：糖姜，蜜饯生姜

4. be in...line，to be in the line of：从事……业务（行业）

   We have been in this line for many years.

   我们从事这种业务好多年了。

   We are not in the chemical line.

   我们不从事化工业。

5. various kinds of：各种各样的

   In the showcases were displayed various kinds of goods.

   橱窗里陈列着各种商品。

   They also engage in various kinds of sideline production.

   他们也从事各种副业生产。

6. the above products：以上产品，上述产品

   The above products have been manufactured as per IEC standard.

   以上产品的生产均按照 IEC 标准。

7. fall（lie）within our business scope：属于我们的贸易范围

   We are glad to tell you that the goods you require fall within our business scope.

   很高兴告知，你方需求的货物正在我经营范围之内。

8. take this opportunity to do sth.：借此机会做某事

   We'd like to take this opportunity to express our thanks for your close cooperation.

   我们愿借此机会感谢你们的密切合作。

9. detailed：*a.* 详细的

Attached please find a detailed catalogue of our new products.

现随函寄去我方新产品的详细目录一份，请查收。

10. Payment is to be made by an irrevocable L/C payable by draft at sight.

用不可撤销的凭即期汇票付款的信用证支付。

A SUPPLEMENTARY SAMPLE EMAIL

Dear Galley，

We learn your name and company from www. alibaba. com and are pleased to know that you are in the market for color packing bags.

We have been handling the above products for many years and have many experience and good connections in this line. Our packing bags are enjoying good sales in European and American markets. As known to all，our products are famous for its high quality，fashion design and moderate price.

Attached please find our quotation sheet and the product photos. Should any of the items listed in the sheet be of interest to you，please let us have your specific inquiry ASAP.

Your prompt attention and early reply would be appreciated.

Best regards，
Chally Den

EXERCISES

Ⅰ. Put in the missing words with the first letter or letters given.

Dear Sirs，

We are pleased to l _____ from the I _____ that you are l _____ importers of textiles.

We have the p _____ of informing you that we have been e _____ such commodities for many years. If you are in _____ in en _____ into business relations with us in this l _____ ，we shall be glad to pr

_____ samples and ca _____ as well as d _____ information upon r _____ .

We assure you o _____ our best attention to any en _____ from you and anticipate your prompt response in this re _____ .

Best regards,
Daniel

Ⅱ. Put the following words and expressions in right order to make up a sentence.

1. we, our, your, have received, August 18, of, for, inquiry, woolen blanket.

2. we, you, an offer, are making, for, as follows, 50 metric tons Dried Apple Rings.

3. our customers, of, is, one, looking for, foodstuffs, high quality, in China.

4. we, you, want, pay, to, by, letter of credit, an irrevocable, sight.

5. you, us, the above offer, find, please, acceptable, know, let, by email, if.

Ⅲ. Translate the following sentences into English.

1. 我们从事此项业务已 20 年了。

2. 目前我们正在寻找新的贸易伙伴。

3. 如果你们能大量供货，我们将给予优惠的付款条件。

4. 我们是东南亚主要的轻工业产品贸易商。

5. 你们所要货物属于我们的贸易范围。

6. 我们借此机会与你们联系建立贸易关系。

7. 我们新产品的详细目录已航寄给你们了。

8. 兹给你们我方最有竞争力的报盘如下，请给予及时关注。

9. 对上述建议，希望听取贵方的意见。

10. 我们相信，研究了我们的目录和价格单之后，你们会发现我们的价格是有竞争力的。

Ⅳ. Translate the following email into Chinese.

Dear Sirs,

We would like to have your best quotation for Model L2219-20 LED

Ceiling Lighting on the terms and conditions mentioned below:
Quantity Required: About 20,000 pieces. (1×20'FCL)

Packing: in cartons
Price: FOB Chinese Port
Terms of payment: By irrevocable sight letter of credit.
Time of Shipment: June/July, 20—.

We trust that you will send us your reply as soon as possible.

Best regards,

Daniel

Ⅴ. Writing task.

Please refer to Task A4 on Page 330.

RECAP

Language Focus	Knowledge Focus
be in the line of... fall within the scope of... take this opportunity to... various kinds of, detailed Shipment is to be made... Payment will be made by....	voluntary offer internet dealer business scope in large quantities

Writing Tips

➢ Stating sources of information
➢ Introducing your company and products
➢ Making a voluntary offer, stating prices, shipment terms, payment terms, etc.
➢ Describing your expectation for the buyer's interest and favorable response

Lesson 10

Offering Substitute

From: sunfine@vip.163.com
To: jones@bissma.com
Date: Oct.19, 20—
Subject: Upgraded model as substitute
Attachment: Auto Packing Machinery.flv (5.1M), Quotation Sheet.pdf (1.2M)

Dear Ms Jones,

We thank you for your email of Oct.18 enquiring for our Auto Packing Machine Art. No. PM203. We appreciate your interest but we can no longer supply it as the **production** line has been upgraded and the processing technology improved. We are **confident** that our new machine Art. No. NPM 303 is a good **replacement**.

We use the stainless steel instead of the cast iron. The quality and **specifications** are much improved at very little **extra cost** and its appearance is very excellent. It must be **enjoying fast sales** in your country. We have sent you the working video presentation **as per** the attachment together with the quotation sheet.

We are 100% sure that you will find it easy to use and will find a good market on your side. It will give you complete **satisfaction**.

Kind regards,
Petty Boss

NOTES

1. Auto PackingMachine：自动包装机

2. production：*n.* 生产，制造

   The company's new model will be going into production early next year.

   该公司的新型产品将于明年初投入生产。

   The goods you want are out of production at present，so we regret our inability to quote on them.

   你所要的货物目前已停止生产，抱歉我方无法报价。

   produce：*v.* 生产，制造

   We are producing for export hand-made gloves in a variety of natural leathers.

   我们制作各种各样手工真皮手套供出口。

   product：*n.* 产品，制品

   We are very interested to place large orders with you for chemical products.

   我们十分想从你处大量购买化工产品。

   producer：*n.* 生产者；制造商；厂商

3. confident：*a.* 有信心的；确信的

   Management is confident about the way business is progressing.

   管理层对业务发展的态势充满信心。

   We feel/are confident of the superior quality of our products.

   我们对产品优越的品质有信心。

   I am confident that everything will come out right in time.

   我坚信一切终究都会好起来。

   confidence：*n.* 信心，把握，信任

   Consumers' confidence in the economy is strong.

   消费者们对经济形势信心十足。

   have/place/put confidence in ... 对……给以信任，对……有信心

   If your price is competitive，we have confidence in securing the order for you.

   如果你方价格有竞争力，我们相信能为你方获得订单。

4. replacement：*n.* 调换；替代品

   The damaged computers need replacement.

   损坏的电脑需要调换。

   We offer a slightly different material in replacement for what you enquire for.

我们提供一种稍有区别的料子，以代替你们所询购的品种。

replace：*v.* 替代

Tourism has replaced agriculture as the nation's main industry.

旅游业已经替代农业，成为该国的主要产业。

replace A with/by B：用 B 替代 A

The factory replaced most of its workers with robots.

这家工厂用机器人代替了大部分的工人。

substitute：*v.* 用……代替，代之以；取代，代替

substitute A for B：用 A 替代 B

The company illegally substituted cheap bolts and screws for more expensive materials.

这家公司非法地用劣质螺母和螺帽替代了更昂贵的材料。

Gas-fired power stations will substitute for less efficient coal-fired equipment.

以煤气为燃料的发电站将会代替效率较低的燃煤装置。

substitute ：*n.* ＝replacement 替代品，代替物

Model 501 is an ideal substitute for Model 401.

5. cast iron：铸铁

6. specification：*n.* 规格，常用复数

   We make curtains to customers' specifications.

   我们按照客户的规格定做窗帘。

7. extra：*a.* 额外的；附加的

   The extra charges are to be for our account.

   额外的费用将由我方负担。

   We agreed on a price but afterwards they wanted £10 extra.

   我们谈好了价格，但后来他们又想多要 10 英镑。

8. cost：*n.* 成本，费用

   The total cost of the project would be more than $ 240 million.

   该项目的总成本会超过 2.4 亿美元

   Copies of the CD can be sold at cost.

   这种光盘可按成本价销售。

   The new shopping centre was constructed at a cost of 1. 1 million U. S. dollars.

   新建成的购物中心耗资 110 万美元。

9. enjoy fast sales：畅销

表示"畅销"通常还有下列表达方法：

Our goods enjoy excellent sales.

我们的产品很畅销。

Cashmere coats always sell well.

羊绒大衣总是很畅销。

Home fitness equipments are very popular nowadays.

目前家用健身器材很受欢迎。

Wearable technology products will find a good/ready sale in a few years.

可穿戴的科技产品几年后将有很好的销路。

Digital products are enjoying fast sales these days.

数码产品近来非常畅销。

Our garments have a ready market in your region.

我们的服装在你地区销路很好。

This is a widely salable product.

这种产品销路很广。

Our goods have won a high appreciation among our customers.

我们的货物得到客户的好评。

Our goods are well received.

我们的货物很受欢迎。

Our ceramics have met with great favor in the US market.

我们的陶瓷在美国市场上很受欢迎。

This product is very marketable.

这个产品很畅销。

Our products have been well established in the world.

我们的产品已在世界上建立了良好声誉。

10. working video presentation：视频演示

11. as per：按照

    The report was sent to the general manager as per your instructions.

    按照您的指示，报告送给总经理了。

12. on your side：在你处（市场）

    表示"在你处（市场）"的表达还有：at your end, in your market/district/place

13. satisfaction：n. 满意

    If the first shipment turns out to the satisfaction of our customers, we will place repeat orders with you.

如果首批船货令我方客户满意，我们将向你方续订。

satisfy：*v.* 使满意

The patterns of your carpets satisfy us. We will order 1,000 pieces.

你方地毯的图案使我们很满意。我们将订购 1000 件。

be satisfied with：对……感到满意

We are not satisfied with your quotation. It is apparently out of line with the market.

我们对你方报价不满意，它显然和市价不符。

satisfactory：*a.* 令人满意的

If the price of your products is satisfactory, we shall be able to place substantial orders with you.

如果你方产品的价格令人满意，我们将能够向你方大量订购。

A SUPPLEMENTARY SAMPLE EMAIL

Hi Mike，

Thanks for your email of May 15，inquiring for our truck tires.

Pattern 668 is our most popular item，which is your wise choice to start with. We can offer at USD70/pc FOB Shanghai for delivery within 3 weeks after the order and MOQ has to be 300pcs.

Pattern 718 is a hi-tech tire with the price at USD100/pc. Based on our marketing experience，our recommendation for you is Pattern 698 with the lower price at USD80/pc. MOQ is 200pcs. Tires are packed according to customers' requirements. Payment is to be made by an irrevocable letter of credit payable by draft at sight.

Please check our photo quotations in the attached file. If any further information is needed，please contact me without hesitation.

Your prompt response will be highly appreciated.

Best regards，
Amro Yan

EXERCISES

Ⅰ. Translate the following sentences into Chinese.

1. Since the required articles are not available at present，we would like to recommend herebelow a few popular items for forward shipment.

2. Thank you for your inquiry for Art. 269 but we regret this item is out of stock for the time being. But we may accept your order for shipment in April.

3. As the selling season is drawing near，we would propose in all sincerity that you buy a certain quantity of Art. 9903 which can be delivered promptly.

4. We would like to recommend as follows a few popular items available for immediate shipment.

5. We have pleasure in introducing to you the following goods for prompt shipment similar to the samples given by you.

Ⅱ. Fill in the blanks with the correct words.

satisfactory，satisfy，satisfied，satisfaction

1. We hope the goods will give you every _____ .

2. We are confident that this shipment will be _____ to you.

3. Unfortunately your packing failed to _____ our end-users.

4. We are sure that this shipment will prove _____ .

5. We are not quite _____ with the quality of your goods.

Ⅲ. Complete the following sentences.

1. We have received your email in which 你们询问我们新产品 .

2. If our offer 让你们感兴趣，please let us know immediately.

3. If it is possible，you are recommended to order Art. No. AB02 以替代 你们所要的 Art. No. AB01.

4. Our latest generation of DVD players 在你们邻近国家销路很好 .

5. If the first order 执行得令我方客户满意，we will order with you in large quantities.

Ⅳ. Writing task.

Please refer to Task A5 on Page 330.

RECAP

Language Focus	Knowledge Focus
substitute A for B	cost
replace A with/by B	specifications
substitute, replacement	production line
be/feel confident of/that clause...	processing technology
enjoy fast sales	working video presentation
find it... (a. /prep. phrase) to do... / that...	
be satisfied with... , satisfactory	

Writing Tips

➤ Appreciating the buyer's interest in your products
➤ Showing regret over the inability to offer the needed articles due to products update, no stock, or other reasons
➤ Offering substitutes
➤ Explaining reasons for recommendation
➤ Justifying the higher prices
➤ Persuading the buyer to accept

Task 3

Making Counter-offers

Learning Objectives

To be able to write emails expressing reasons for non-acceptance of the sellers' or buyers' price ideas

To get familiar with the writing plans, useful sentences and phrases of counter-offers

Lesson 11

A Counter-offer （1）

From: giwsdc@spspa. au
To: sunfine@vip. 163. com
Date: July 10, 20—
Subject: Your offer for blanched peanuts

Dear Mike,

Thank you for your offer of July 9 for the blanched peanuts at USD1200/ MT FOB Qingdao.

After careful study, we find your price **on the high side** and **out of line with** the **prevailing** market. For your information, **competition** here is very fierce. Most of the competing goods are **selling** at a level about **10% lower than** yours.

We are fully **aware** that their products are not as good in quality as yours, but 10% is really too big a difference. **Should you** be prepared to **lower your price** by about 8%, i. e. at USD1,100/MT, we might be able to **come to terms**.

As **the market is weak**, we hope you will consider our counter-offer acceptable and send us your confirmation as soon as possible.

Best regards,
Andley

NOTES

1. counter-offer：*v.*/*n.* 还盘

   counter-表示方向相反、相对的意思，再如：

   counter-sample 对等样品　　　　counter-signature 会签

   counter-trade 对等贸易　　　　counter-purchase 互购

   to counter-offer sth at...：对……还盘价格为……

   We'd like to counter-offer 1,000 suitcases at US $95 each FOB Los Angeles.

   我们愿还盘 1000 个手提箱，每个 95 美元洛杉矶船上交货价。

   We'd like to counter-offer 50 euros.

   我们还价 50 欧元。

   to make a counter-offer for sth. at...：对……还盘，价格是……

   Now we'd like to make you a counter-offer for 1000 bottles of Vitamin C at USD16 per bottle CIF Shanghai.

   现在我们向你还盘 1000 瓶维生素 C，每瓶 16 美元成本加运保费到上海价。

2. on the high side：高，高于平均水平的任何价格都是 on the high side。

   on the low side：低，低于平均水平的任何价格都是 on the low side。

   While appreciating your offer，we find your price rather on the high side.

   感谢你方报盘，但我方发现你方价格偏高。

   To tell you frankly，our prices have always been on the low side compared with the international prevailing prices.

   坦白说，与国际市场价格相比，我方价格一向偏低。

3. out of line with：与……不符，脱离……

   in line with：与……一致，符合……

   Though we would like to conclude a deal with you，we find your price out of line with the ruling market.

   虽然我们想跟你达成交易，但我们认为你方价格脱离现行市价。

   We can assure you that our prices are always in line with the market.

   我们可以向你保证我们的价格总是符合市场价格的。

4. the prevailing market：现行市场

   the prevailing price：现行价格，时价。其他说法还有：

   the ruling price, the going price, the present price, the current price 等。

5. competition：*n.* 竞争

   Competition in the market is fierce/intense/keen.

市场竞争激烈。

Foreign competition had reduced their sales.

国外竞争使他们的销量减少。

competitive：*a.* 竞争激烈的；有竞争力的；竞争性的

Small firms are trying to find their way to survive in the competitive world of business.

小公司试图寻找出路，以在当今充满竞争的世界里生存。

The prices we offer are very competitive. You can't find any other company offering prices lower than ours.

我们报的价格非常有竞争力，你不可能找到别的公司报价比我们低。

As a sole agent，you are not allowed to deal in competitive goods.

作为独家代理，你们不允许经营竞争性的货物。

competitive goods 竞争性货物。也可以说 competing goods。

compete：*v.* 竞争

The two companies are competing against/with each other to get people to buy their goods.

这两家公司相互竞争客源。

competitor：*n.* 竞争者，竞争对手

We are trying to keep our new product a secret from our competitors.

对于我们的新产品，我们试图对竞争者保密。

6. sell：*v.* 销售

注意很多情况下 sell 用主动语态表示被动意思，如：

These baskets sell well/fast in the American market.

这些篮子在美国市场上卖得非常快。

Cashmere coats always sell.

羊毛大衣总是很畅销的。

由此派生的一个词是 seller，表示畅销品。如：

This car model is our biggest seller at the moment.

这款汽车是我们目前最畅销的。

Of the ten top sellers，six are women's magazines.

销量居前十位的当中，有六位是妇女杂志。

7. 10% lower than：比……低 10%

10% higher than：比……高 10%

We can't cut our prices as they are already 5% lower than quotations from our competitors.

我们不能降价，因为它们比竞争者的报价已经低出 5%。

We're surprised to find your quotation for computer floppy disks are 7% higher than last month.

我们吃惊地发现你们电脑软盘的报价比上月高出 7%。

8. be aware：知道，明白，清楚，了解，意识到

We are well/fully/acutely aware of the sticky situation in the present market.

我们完全明白目前市场的困难处境。

Are you aware that your service needs to be improved?

你们意识到你们的服务需要改善了吗?

Maybe you are not aware what quality means to a product.

或许你没有意识到质量对一个商品来说意味着什么。

9. lower one's price by（to）...：将某人的价格降低（至）……

类似的说法还有：

cut one's price by（to）...

reduce one's price by（to）...

bring down one's price by（to）... 等等

There is not much possibility of business unless you can reduce your price by 5%.

除非你能降价 5%，否则没有太大成交希望。

Provided you cut your price to £95，we think we can increase our order by 500 sets.

如果你们把价格降至 95 英镑，我们就能多订 500 台。

10. Should you be prepared to lower your price ...：如你方愿意降价

Should 放在句首表示假设，是一种虚拟语气，等于 If you should ...。再如：

Should any of the items on the list be of interest to you, please let us know.

如果你们对单子上哪些商品感兴趣，请告知。

Should you ever need anything, please don't hesitate to contact me.

如果你需要什么东西，请尽管找我。

If anyone should ask for me, I'll be in the manager's office.

如果有人找我，我在经理办公室。

11. come to terms：＝to come to agreement 达成协议

    The two sides have come to terms on the unit price of the goods.

    双方就货物的单价达成一致。

12. The market is weak. 市场疲软

    表示市场状况的说法还有：

    The market is quiet/ easy /dull / gloomy / sluggish.

    市场清淡/疲软/黯淡/黯淡/呆滞。

    The market is steady/ firm/ active/ strong.

    市场稳定/趋升/活跃/坚挺。

A SUPPLEMENTARY SAMPLE EMAIL

Thank you Leon.

The below cost find to be high for my client... Their budget is USD6. 2 CNF Hamburg... Let me know if this is possible.

Navy blue color cap—100, 000/300, 000 units with single color logo embroidery/ printing. Let me know your best cost and mention the air freight charges separately please.

Awaiting your response.

Connie

EXERCISES

I . Fill in the blanks with proper forms of the following words.

compete，competition，competitive，competitor

1. To _____ on a market with the established brands，your products must be very _____ both in quality and in price.

2. Speaking of quality，our products are among the best ones，and can stand the keenest _____ anywhere at any time.

3. We must upgrade our product line; otherwise，we will lose in the international _____ ，for our _____ are already streets ahead.

4. As our sole agent，you are not allowed to handle any _____ products in your region within the duration of the agreement.

5. Without _____，an economy lacks the incentive to grow.

Ⅱ. **Choose the best answer for each of the following sentences.**

1. A recent market survey reveals that such articles are no longer _____ .

   A. in demand　　B. to demand　　C. on demand　　D. for demand

2. If you can accept payment by L/C，we will make you a very competitive _____ .

   A. order　　　　B. offer　　　　C. enclosure　　D. offer firm

3. By joint efforts we can _____ both friendship and business.

   A. increase　　B. expect　　　C. promote　　D. push

4. Materials of the same quality can be easily obtained at _____ much lower than yours.

   A. price　　　　B. a price　　　C. the price　　D. same price

5. If your prices are found _____，we intend to place large orders with you.

   A. accept　　　B. accepted　　C. accepting　　D. acceptable

6. Such growing demand has doubtlessly resulted _____ increased prices.

   A. in　　　　　B. from　　　　C. at　　　　　D. for

7. We would like to quote a price for our basketball shoes _____ :

   A. as follow　　B. as follows　　C. as following　　D. as followed

8. We suggest that you _____ our offer immediately.

   A. must accept　　　　　　B. will accept

   C. accept　　　　　　　　D. be acceptable to

9. We admit that the quality of your products is superior _____ the goods of Indian origin.

   A. to　　　　　B. than　　　　C. with　　　　D. over

10. If any of the items are _____ you，please let us know.

   A. interested in　　　　　B. of interest to

   C. interest　　　　　　　D. of interest

Ⅲ. **Translate the following letter into Chinese.**

Dear Liu，

We've been very pleased with your products，as you know.

However， we find that we can obtain a price of ＄4.00 per piece with a local firm. This is fifty cents lower than your price.

If you can see your way clear to meeting these figures, we would be pleased to place with you an order that will carry us for the rest of this year. That order is likely to be one of the largest that we have ever placed with you.

Best regards，

Alan De Yogurt

Ⅳ. **Translate the following sentences into English.**

1. 过去我们对你方的报价一直偏低。

2. 你方还盘与现行市价不符，我们歉难接受。

3. 我们的工艺品在国外市场上一直很畅销。

4. 你我双方都不愿做出让步，这样的话，我看只好取消这笔交易了。

5. 为鼓励交易，我方愿降价 3 美元，希望你们能接受。

6. 由于供大于求，目前市场疲软。

7. 你方产品在价格上没有多大竞争力，或许你们已经意识到这一点。

8. 如果你方能降价 10％，我们将向你方订货。否则，将转向其他供应商订货。

9. 我们现还盘 1000 打男士衬衣，每打 360 美元 CFR 洛杉矶价。

10. 我方产品采用的是上等材料，因此价格比同类产品高出 2％是可以理解的。

Ⅴ. **Writing task.**

Please refer to Task B3 on Page 335.

RECAP

Language Focus	Knowledge Focus
on the high side out of line with. . . , in line with. . . prevailing market，10% lower than lower one's price，come to terms This market is weak. Should. . . , we will . . .	counter-offer prevailing market competition competing goods

Writing Tips

➢ Appreciating the offer
➢ Explaining reasons why the prices cannot be accepted
➢ Stating necessary data tactfully
➢ Showing your consideration for the seller's benefits，e. g. weak market，fierce competition，etc.

Lesson 12

A Counter-offer（2）

From： sunfine@vip. 163. com
To： giwsdc@spspa. au
Date： July 11, 20—
Subject： Re： Your offer for blanched peanuts

Hi Andley,

Your email of July 10 has been received with many thanks.

While appreciating your counter-offer, we find that you have driven the price too close to our **cost** of **production.** We agree with you when you say that our prices are higher, but please note that our **materials** are carefully selected, which **adds to** our cost. This just **accounts for** the **superior** quality of our peanuts, and explains why our **clients** in Europe and America keep buying from us at our price level. So we do hope that you can **draw** your **end-users' attention to** the quality, rather than prices only.

However, **in view** of the **longstanding business relations** between us, we are willing to correspond to your counter-offer by reducing our price by 3%. As the stock of this item is running low, we hope that we can **strike a deal** at USD1160/MT FOB Qingdao.

Your early reply will be appreciated.

Best regards,
Mike Liu

NOTES

1. While ... ：尽管……，虽然……，

   While we would like to help you to push your sales，we don't think your price is competitive enough.

   虽然我们愿意帮你促销，但你方价格不具竞争力。

   While I fully understand your point of view，I do also have some sympathy with Michael's.

   虽然我理解你的观点，我对迈克尔的看法也有一定同感。

2. material：*n.* 材料

   raw material 原料

   finished product 成品

   semi-finished product 半成品

3. add to：＝increase 使……增加

   Your refusal to cooperate has added to the difficulties in solving the dispute.

   你方拒绝合作，增加了解决争议的困难。

   Her colleagues' laughter only added to her embarrassment.

   同事们的笑声只能使她更加窘迫。

4. account for：解释

   Can you account for your absence last Friday?

   你能解释上星期五为什么缺勤吗？

5. superior：*a.* 比……好的，高的，优的

   We chose her for the job because she was the superior candidate.

   我们选择她做这一工作，因为她是更优秀的候选者。

   We can assure you that the quality of our goods is superior to any other similar products available on the present market.

   我们可以保证我们货物的质量比现今市场上可以买得到的同类产品都要好。

   inferior：*a.* 比……劣的，次的，低的，差的

   Please always bear in mind that goods of inferior quality will find no market here.

   请永远记住，劣质货在这儿是没有销路的。

   They felt inferior to others until their success gave some pride.

   他们感到低人一等，直到取得成功才感到一些自豪。

6. draw sb's attention to：请某人注意

还可以说成 direct/invite/call sb's attention to

We wish to draw your attention to the wording of the contract.

我们想提请你们注意合同的措辞。

We would like to draw your attention to the fact that the delivery date is approaching，but we haven't received your relevant L/C so far.

我们想请你们注意，交期临近，但目前为止我们尚未收到你们的有关信用证。

7. end-user：最终用户

8. in view of：鉴于，由于

In view of the rising tendency in the market，we'd recommend you accept our offer.

鉴于目前市场的上涨趋势，我们建议你方接受我们的报价。

In view of what you said，I think we should reconsider our proposed course of action.

鉴于你所说的，我认为我们应该重新考虑我们提出的行动措施。

9. longstanding business relations：长期的业务关系

10. strike a deal：达成交易；达成协议

达成交易还可表达为：

conclude/ close/ complete/ finalize a deal

I think another cut of 5 dollars is necessary for us to strike a deal.

我认为，为达成交易，再降 5 美元是有必要的。

A SUPPLEMENTARY SAMPLE EMAIL

Hi Connie，

It seems that your price is a bit low. In order to close the deal，we can do the price at USD 5. 8/pc CFR Hamburg for navy blue cap with the logo embroidered/ printed. But this price will not include door to door service.

Please confirm it is acceptable and advise how to proceed.

Thank you.

Leon

EXERCISES

Ⅰ. Fill in the blanks with the proper forms of the following expressions.

drive, cost, note, add to, account for, superior
draw, rather than, in view of, appreciate

1. We _____ your sending us the latest catalogue.

2. Superior quality _____ the reason why the price of our goods is a little higher.

3. As we see it, the market is rising _____ falling as from your point of view.

4. Japan's increase in imports has been _____ by the government's spending plan to stimulate its economy.

5. Please _____ that competition is very strong in the local market, and your goods are likely to be priced out of the market should you stick to your previous quotation.

6. Please be assured that our goods are _____ to any other product in the same line.

7. One of the reasons that we have to raise our prices is that labor _____ have gone up recently.

8. We would like to _____ your attention to the new function of our products.

9. _____ the increasing demand, the rising tendency of prices are likely to continue for a while.

10. We regret to inform you that a general strike has just taken place, which _____ our difficulties in fulfilling your order.

Ⅱ. Translate the following sentences into Chinese.

1. We appreciate your counter offer but find it too low.

2. The market has been greatly affected by the world economic recession.

3. There is more crude oil available than is actually needed.

4. The best we can do is to reduce our price by another $2.

5. Information indicates that some parcels of Turkish origin have been sold here at a level about 10% lower than yours.

6. We don't deny that the quality of your goods is slightly better, but the difference in price should, in no case, be as big as 10%.

7. We have to point out that your bid is obviously out of line with the

ruling price in the present market.

8. Other buyers in your neighboring countries are buying freely at our quoted price.

9. We think that a 3% commission may also facilitate the conclusion of business.

10. As you are aware, there has been active demand for Steel Tubes in the market. Therefore it is impossible for us to keep this offer open for long.

III. Translate the following sentences into English.

1. 随附根据你方第 15 号询价单所开的报价单，期待你方确认。

2. 由于上述商品目前市场坚挺看涨，为你方利益着想，建议你接受我方报价。

3. 虽然我们对于你方所说的情况并不怀疑，我们的意见是西班牙货的质量远远比不上我们的产品。

4. 我们相信如果你方考虑到商品的质量，就可以理解我们的报价是很优惠的。

5. 由于目前存货不多，请尽快做出决定。

IV. Writing task.

Please refer to Task A1-4 on Page 323.

RECAP

Language Focus	Knowledge Focus
while...	cost of production
add to	materials
account for	client
superior, inferior	stock
draw one's attention to	
in view of, strike a deal	

Writing Tips
➤ Being aware that every customer will ask for cut in price
➤ Appreciating the counter-offer
➤ Justifying your higher prices
➤ Making a cost analysis
➤ Sticking to the original offer if a reduction is impossible
➤ Agreeing to make a concession in price if a reduction is possible
➤ Showing the buyer's benefits
➤ Urging the buyer to accept it

Lesson 13

A Counter-offer（3）

From：giwsdc@spspa. au
To：sunfine@vip. 163. com
Date：July 12, 20—
Subject：Your offer for blanched peanuts

Dear Mike，

Thank you for your prompt reply and your efforts toward closing a deal.

But **honestly**，a reduction of 3％ is **only too modest**，as we had expected something better than that. As we said before，your quality is good，but your price is absolutely **beyond** what we can accept. Yet in view of your above reduction，we think it's only fair that we make a corresponding move，so we'd be willing to **go up** to USD1,120/MT. This is the **best price** we can give you. We will not be able to **sign the contract at** any price higher than this.

Given the **declining market** and competition from low price goods，your price must be very competitive if you want to **push the sales** of your products here. We hope this **concession** of ours is acceptable to you and a contract can be signed at this level.

Best regards，
Andley

NOTES

1. honestly：*ad.* 说实话，坦白地说。一般放在句首。再如：

   Honestly speaking，To be honest，Frankly，Frankly speaking，To be frank 等。

   To be frank with you，only yesterday we received a quotation from a Chinese supplier at 5% lower than yours.

   坦白跟你说，昨天我们刚刚从中国的一个供货商那儿收到一份报价，比你低 5%。

2. only too：＝all too＝very 非常

   If you have any problems，please tell us and we will be only too pleased to help you.

   如果你有什么问题，请告诉我们，我们将非常乐于帮助你们。

   The holidays flew by all too quickly.

   假期过得真是太快了。

3. modest：*a.* 谦虚的；此处指幅度低的

   There has been a modest improvement in housing conditions for the poor.

   穷人的住房条件有小幅度的改善。

   While the Dow Jones industrial average pulled back，some stocks made modest gains.

   尽管道琼斯工业平均指数出现回落，有些股票价格却有些许上涨。

4. beyond：prep. 在……之外的；超过……的

   beyond what we can accept：是我们所不能接受的

   We are sorry to say that such terms of payment is beyond our financial strength.

   很遗憾，这种支付条件超出了我们的财力。

   Such accidents are beyond our control.

   这种事故是我们所不能控制的。

5. … we'd be willing to go up to USD1,120/MT.：我们愿意把价格提高到每吨 1120 美元。

   "提价"还可以表达为：raise/increase the price

   We have raised the price by 10 dollars，and we don't think we can go up any further.

   我们已经把价格提高了 10 美元，我们不能再提了。

6. the best price：最好的价格

注意该词随说话人的角度不同而有不同的意思，可以是"最高的价格"，也可以是"最低的价格"。

7. sign the contract：签合同

8. Given the declining market：考虑到下跌的市场

   given：考虑到

   Given the domestic weakness, Japan might further stimulate exports in order to sustain its economic growth.

   考虑到国内的疲软，日本可能会进一步刺激出口，以维持经济增长。

   the declining market：下跌的市场

   市场下跌还可表达为：

   The market is dropping/ falling/ going down/ weakening.

   Owing to worldwide economic recession, the international market has fallen sharply.

   由于世界范围的经济衰退，国际市场急剧下跌。

   相反，市场上涨可表达为：

   The market is rising/ going up/ strengthening/ advancing.

   Ever since we signed the last contract, prices for computer CPUs have gone up by 5%.

   自从我们签订了上笔合同后，电脑处理器的价格就上涨了5%。

9. push the sales of：推销

   也经常说 promote the sales of

   Thank you for your efforts in pushing the sales of our products.

   感谢你方在推销我方产品方面所做的努力。

   In order to get your products into the American market, you need a local distributor to push your sales.

   要使你方产品打入美国市场，你需要一家当地分销商进行推销。

10. concession：n. 让步

    Now that you have increased your order by 1,000 dozen, we'd like to reduce our price by 3 euros as a concession.

    既然你们把订货量提高了1000打，作为让步，我们愿意降价3欧元。

    Both sides involved in the deal made some concessions in yesterday's talks.

    交易双方在昨天的谈判中都做了一些让步。

A SUPPLEMENTARY SAMPLE EMAIL

Dear Tom,

I'm sorry but your quotations are still not within the range of other suppliers that we've found. To accept your price would leave us only a little profit.

Our target price is USD6. 8 per piece FOB Qingdao. Can you see your way clear to reduce your price to this figure?

Best regards,
Alan De Yogurt

EXERCISES

I . Fill in the blanks with the proper forms of the following expressions.

favorable, close, modest, beyond, in view of
level, best, sign, decline, push the sales of

1. Cars such as Ferraris and Porsches are priced _____ the reach of most people.

2. Thank you for your intention to _____ our products, but we think the time to talk about a sole agency agreement is premature.

3. If your prices are more _____ than those of other suppliers, we shall send you an order.

4. The _____ we can do is to give you a 2% discount.

5. Products of Chinese origin are selling at a _____ about 5% lower than yours.

6. A $2 cut in the price is too _____ . We'd suggest you cut the price by $8.

7. In our view, the European market for cars has been _____ owing to excessive supply.

8. I'm afraid we won't be able to _____ the transaction unless both of us make some concessions.

9. Once you have _____ the contract, you should abide by it.

10. _____ what I've said, I think you should reconsider the terms of payment.

II. Translate the following sentences into English.

1. 如你对我们的产品感兴趣，我们将十分乐意回答你们关于产品的任何问题。

2. 正如我们以前所说的，中国市场对进口食品的需求呈上涨趋势。

3. 鉴于供大于求，请你们调整价格，以便更好地促销。

4. 恐怕只有你们减价10%，才有希望成交。

5. 为表示我们合作的意愿，我们愿意再次提价，到99澳大利亚元，这是我们最高的价格了。

6. 考虑到这是我们之间的第一笔交易，能否在价格上做些让步?

7. 你方报价与欧洲市场不一致。

8. 类似质量的货物很容易在本地市场以较低的价格买到。

9. 对你方报价上涨，我们非常吃惊，并认为这是缺乏理由的，因为原料价格本季度一直疲软。

10. 虽说我方愿意继续从你处购买，但鉴于报价过高，我方客户决定从别处购买。

III. Writing task.

Please refer to Task B4 on Page 335.

RECAP

Language Focus	Knowledge Focus
go up to，increase given...，beyond，concession declining market，push the sale of	the best price modest reduction declining market

Writing Tips

➢ Appreciating the re-offer by the seller

➢ Stating the target price

➢ Presenting pertinent favorable, then unfavorable facts, e. g. (better quality, large quantities, future cooperation, declining market, fierce competition, etc.)

➢ Showing the seller's benefits

➢ Avoiding tug-of-war

➢ Making a final counter-offer

Lesson 14

A Counter-offer（4）

From: sunfine@vip. 163. com
To: giwsdc@spspa. au
Date: July 13, 20—
Subject: Re: Your offer for blanched peanuts

Hi Andley,

Having received your email of July 12, we are glad to see that the **gap** between your price and ours is **narrowing.** We think it would be unwise for either of us to **stick** to his own price. Why don't we **meet each other halfway,** i. e. at the price of USD1,140/MT? This is already our **rock bottom price,** and we really cannot **afford** any further concessions. If you agree, please send us your order. If not, then there will be nothing we can do.

Do consider our proposal and don't lose this chance to conclude a good deal.

Best regards,
Mike Liu

NOTES

1. gap：差距。在本文是指 the gap in price 价格上的差距

   还可说 the difference in price

   Both sides need to make further concessions to bridge the gap between our prices.

   为弥补价格之间的差距，双方都需做更多的让步。

   "弥补差距" 还可说：to cover/close/bridge the gap

2. narrow：v. 变窄；缩小

   In order to narrow the price gap, both parties are willing to make concessions.

   为了缩小价格差距，双方愿意做出让步。

3. stick to：＝insist on 坚持

   We are sorry we must stick to our usual practices and accept nothing but L/C.

   很抱歉，我们必须坚持惯例，只接受信用证付款方式。

4. meet sb halfway：互相折中，各让一半

   The best we can do is to meet you halfway.

   我们最多只能与你各让一半。

   Let's meet each other halfway and split the price gap 50-50.

   让我们各让一半，将价格差距对半平摊。

5. in one's opinion：在某人看来，照某人的意见

   In our opinion, the prices of paper will increase considerably in the near future.

   我们认为最近纸张的价格会大涨。

   It is our opinion that/Our opinion is that you should place a small order for trial.

   我们认为你们应该小量试订。

6. rock bottom price：最低价

   最低价还可表达为：

   lowest price, minimum price, floor price 等

7. afford：v. 负担得起

   We can not afford to accept such a big price increase.

   价格提高这么多，我们无法接受。

   This price has left us with only a moderate profit, and we really cannot afford any further reduction.

   按这个价格我们的利润已经很少，我们实在无法再让步。

A SUPPLEMENTARY SAMPLE EMAIL

Dear Chris,

Thank you for your email of May 1.

To be frank, our production cost has gone up by 10% because of the rise in the labor cost and the appreciation of Renminbi Yuan. Therefore, we regret to say that we are unable to accept your price at USD7. 80/pc.

However, if you can increase your quantity to 5, 000 pieces, we may consider allowing you a special discount of 5%.

Waiting for your early confirmation.

Best regards,
Joy

EXERCISES

I . Fill in the blanks with the proper forms of the following expressions.

> gap, stick to, meet each other halfway, counter-offer, narrow,
> contract, rock bottom price, afford, concessions, conclude

1. The prime minister has made it clear that no _____ will be made to the strikers.
2. In our trade with all countries, we always _____ the principle of equality and mutual benefits.
3. A _____ is an agreement, enforceable by law, by which two parties mutually promise to buy or sell some particular thing, or to do a certain work.
4. We can't _____ to buy your goods at such a high price.
5. —In order to step up the deal, we suggest _____ .
   —Do you mean splitting the difference in our prices 50-50?
6. We hope we can _____ a deal at USD10 per piece.
7. What would you suggest to bridge the price _____?

8. Since this is already our _____, we can't make any further concession on the price.

9. To step up the transaction, we have to _____ the gap between our prices.

10. We _____ you 1000 pieces of men's shirts at USD22 per piece CIF New York.

Ⅱ. **Translate the following sentences into English.**

1. 你们的订单数量太小,我们很难考虑降价。

2. 我方非常欣赏你方产品的质量,但价格太高不能接受。

3. 希望贵方能接受我方报价并尽早向我方下订单。

4. 接受你们的报价意味着我们将有亏损,更不用说利润了。

5. 由于该种商品供不应求,我们建议你方尽快接受报盘。

Ⅲ. **Put the following words and phrases in right order to make up a sentence.**

1. must, that, we, concession in price, we, any further, cannot, make, make it clear

2. a copy of, we are, price list, pictures of the products, together with some, attaching

3. counter-offer, as follows, you, men's shirts, 1000 pieces of, we

4. that, it is, enjoy fast sales, in the world market, our T-shirts, not surprising

5. we, rock bottom price, as, are, deserve, a, regular customer, your, we

Ⅳ. **Writing task.**

Please refer to Task A1-5 on Page 323.

RECAP

Language Focus	Knowledge Focus
narrow/bridge/cover the price gap meet sb. half way stick to	price gap rock bottom price

Writing Tips

➢ Appreciating the counter-offer by the buyer
➢ Analyzing factors that influence your prices, e. g. currency exchange rate, size of order, labor cost, raw materials cost, long-term cooperation, etc.
➢ Making a decision whether you accept the counter-offer
➢ Offering quantity discount, if possible
➢ Avoiding tug-of-war
➢ Wishing to reach an agreement

Task 4

Discussing Mode of Shipment

Learning Objectives

To be able to write emails negotiating time of shipment, transshipment and partial shipment

To get familiar with the writing plans, useful sentences and phrases of negotiating shipment terms

Lesson 15

Inquiring About Time of Shipment

Inquiring About Time of Shipment

From: Emil@hotmail.com
To: Amy@sina.com
Date: July 7, 20—
Subject: Time of shipment

Hi Amy,

We would like to **inform** you that we have persuaded our customers to accept your prices although they seem still high for this market.

However, they **expect** shipment **no later than** mid-July in order to catch the coming selling season. Failure to do so will cause them to acquire the goods from other sources. We think it would be **in your interest** to consider this **unharsh** condition.

We should be **obliged** if you would **take** our customers' request **into account** and arrange immediate delivery.

Your prompt response will be highly appreciated.

Best regards,
Emil

A Reply to the Above

From：Amy@sina. com	
To：Emil@hotmail. com	
Date：July 8，20—	
Subject：RE：Time of shipment	

Hi Emil，

We have received your email in **connection** with the shipment date.

Regretfully，our factory is finding it impossible to **meet** current **demand** for the required goods because the stock is **exhausted** but consecutive new orders are **pouring in.** By speeding up the production and putting off our supply to another customer，we can only guarantee shipment **on or before** 31 July. We **trust** this slight **alteration to** your proposal will meet with your **approval**.

Once the shipment date is **confirmed**，we shall manufacture the goods and handle all the shipping formalities and insurance.

Looking forward to your initial order and a happy cooperation between our two firms.

Best wishes，
Amy

NOTES

1. inform：*v.* 通知

    （1）inform sb. of sth.

    We shall inform you of the date of shipment soon.

    我们将马上通知你们装船日期。

    （2）inform sb. that（what，when，why，where，how，whether 等）从句

    We regret to inform you that your tender was not accepted.

    我们遗憾地通知，你们的投标未被接受。

    Please inform us what quantity you can sell per year.

    请告知你方每年可销售的数量。

    Please inform us when the L/C will be opened.

    请告诉我们信用证何时能开出。

    （3）Please be informed of sth. 或 that 从句

    Please be informed that we have already airmailed the samples.

    兹通知你方，我们已经将样品空邮寄出。

    （4）keep sb. informed/posted of sth. 随时告知

    Please keep us informed of any fluctuations of the prices.

    请随时通知我方价格的波动情况。

    information：*n.* 信息；情报

    This is a very important piece of information.

    这是一条重要的信息。

    For detailed information，please contact our local agents.

    欲知详情，请联系当地代理。

    We have reliable information that a terrorist attack is being planned for next month.

    我们有确切情报表明有人计划下月进行恐怖袭击。

2. expect：*v.* 预期；期待

    This is what we expect to happen.

    这就是我们所预期将会发生的。

    We are expected to get the goods ready by the end of this month.

    客户希望我们本月底前备货。

3. no later than：不迟于，相当于 on or before

4. We should be obliged if you would...：如蒙……，我们将不胜感激。

    be obliged：*v.* 感激，感谢。经常用来表示请求

We shall be obliged if you could make timely shipment.

如果你能及时装运，我们将不胜感激。

常用表示谢意的词，除了 appreciate 之外，还有 grateful（a.）和 thankful（a.）：

We should be grateful if you could let us know whether you consider it workable.

如能告知此事是否可行，则不胜感激。

We should be thankful if you could arrange for immediate shipment.

如能立即安排装船，则不胜感激。（请安排立即装船）

5. in your interest：为了你方的利益

也可以说 to your advantage，for your benefit

We suggest in your interest that you take advantage of the rising market and accept our offer without delay.

为你方利益着想，我们建议你们利用行市上升趋势，尽快接受我们的报盘。

6. unharsh：*a.* 不苛刻的

harsh terms 苛刻的条件

harsh words 刺耳的话

7. take sth. into account：＝to take sth. into consideration 考虑，考虑到

I think you have to take the rising cost into account.

我认为你得把上升的成本考虑在内。

8. in connection with：关于……，与……有关

In connection with the investment，we should like to know the local policy and market situation before we can reach a decision.

关于投资问题，我们想先了解一下当地政策和市场行情再作决定。

in this（that）connection 在这（那）一方面

Since we are both concerned about the delivery date，I'd like to make a proposal in this connection.

既然我们都很关心交货期的问题，我想在这方面提一条建议。

9. regret：*v.* 为……而遗憾；因……而抱歉

We very much regret our inability to comply with your requirements.

很抱歉，你们的要求我们无法满足。

We regret being unable to advance the shipment to early June.

很遗憾，我们无法将装运期提前到 6 月初。

We regret to say that we cannot accept your proposal.

抱歉，我们很难接受你方的建议。

We regret that you failed to open the L/C in time.

很遗憾，你方未能及时开出信用证。

It is to be regretted that you have lost the opportunity.

真可惜，你们没抓住机会。

n. 遗憾；抱歉

We wish to express our deepest regret over this unfortunate incident.

对此不幸事件，我们深表遗憾。

Much to our regret，the goods you inquired about are out of stock at present.

很抱歉，目前没有你们要的货物。

We note with regret that you are not interested in this offer.

得知你方对该报盘不感兴趣，甚感遗憾。

regretful：*a.* 遗憾的

We feel/are regretful for inability to accept your offer.

很遗憾，我们无法接受你方报价。

We feel regretful that we cannot meet your request for shipment in May.

很遗憾，我们无法满足你方五月装运的请求。

regretfully：*ad.* 遗憾地

Regretfully，we are not able to accept your payment terms，since this is the first deal between us.

很抱歉我们不能接受你方的支付方式，因为这是我们之间的第一次交易。

regrettable：*a.* 令人遗憾的

It is regrettable that your sample quality is not up to our customers' required standard.

很遗憾，你方样品质量未达到我们客户所要求的标准。

10. meet current demand：满足现在的需求

    meet 做"满足，符合"讲，比如：

    meet your expectations 符合你的要求（期望）

    meet your satisfaction 使你们满意

    Food must be produced to meet certain standards.

    食品必须按一定标准生产。

    The workers' demands for higher pay were not met by the management.

    管理层没有满足工人提高工资的要求。

    We haven't yet been able to find a supplier that meets our needs/

requirements.

我们还没有找到能满足我方需求的供货商。

They will only agree to sign the contract if certain conditions are met.

只有某些条件得到满足，他们才同意签订合同。

11. demand：*n.* 需求

Cheap goods are available，but not in sufficient quantities to satisfy demand.

有一些廉价的商品，但是数量不足以满足需求。

Moderately priced goods with high quality are in great demand.

品质高而定价适中的货物需求量很大。

We are in large demand for Peanuts.

我们对花生的需求量很大。

brisk demand 旺盛的需求

12. exhaust：*v.* 用完，耗尽

Our stock is completely exhausted.

本公司已无存货。

I felt exhausted after the long journey.

长途旅行之后，我感觉筋疲力尽。

13. consecutive：*a.* 连续的，相继的

For five consecutive years we ranked top in terms of the annual turnover.

我们连续五年年销售额排名第一。

This is the fifth consecutive weekend that I've spent working，and I'm a bit fed up with it.

这是我连续第五个周末加班，我真有点厌烦了。

14. pour in：蜂拥而至，源源而来

pour：*v.* 倒；倾泻；注入；流（出）

The government has been pouring money into inefficient state-owned industries.

政府一直向效率低下的国有企业注入大量资金。

The sweat was pouring down her face by the end of the race.

比赛接近尾声时，她已汗流满面了。

15. speed up the production：加速生产

Our factory is speeding up the production in order to avoid any delay in shipment.

我们工厂正在加速生产避免船期延迟。

16. guarantee：*v.* /*n.* 保证；担保

    Unless you guarantee delivery within two weeks，we'll have to cancel the order.

    除非你们保证在两周内交货，否则我们将取消订单。

    You must be aware that an irrevocable L/C gives the exporter the additional protection of the banker's guarantee.

    你们必须意识到不可撤销的信用证为出口商增加了银行担保。

    A famous old name on a firm is not necessarily a guarantee of quality.

    公司悠久的品牌并不能确保商品的质量。

    a Letter of Guarantee 银行保函

17. on or before：在······或之前

    on or about：在······或左右

18. trust：*v.* 相信并希望

    We trust that the superior quality of our products will appeal to the most selective buyers.

    我们相信我们产品的优良品质将会吸引最挑剔的买主。

19. alteration：*n.* 更改，变动

    Any alteration to the contract terms should be mutually approved by both parties in advance.

    合同条款的任何变动均需事先征得双方的同意。

    A non-firm offer is subject to alteration without notice.

    虚盘不经通知可以改变。

    alter：*v.* 改动

    We'd like to alter the destination port from London to Liverpool.

    我们想将目的港由伦敦改为利物浦。

20. approval：*n.* 批准；认可，赞同

    We should submit our plan to the council for approval.

    我们应该向理事会提交计划以求批准。

    The testing and approval of new drugs will be speeded up.

    新药品的检测和审批速度将会加快。

    approve：*v.* 批准；赞成

    The city council has approved the plan.

    市议会批准了这项计划。

    I presume you will approve of this plan.

    我相信你会赞成这个计划。

21. confirm：*v.* 确认；证实

该词后接名词或名词性短语，不接动词不定式。

We confirm your email of Dec. 2 regarding curly wigs.

兹确认已收到你方 12 月 2 日关于卷发型假发的电子邮件。

We are glad to write you to confirm Sept. /Oct. Shipment.

很高兴去函确认 9/10 月装船。

We confirm having telephoned you today in reply.

兹确认今天已电话回复你方。

confirmation：*n.* 确认；确认书

sales confirmation 销售确认书

purchasing confirmation 购货确认书

We await your confirmation.

等候你的确认。

If you accept our offer, please email us for our confirmation.

如接受我方报盘，请来传真索取确认。

22. initial order：首笔订单，也可以说 first order

A SUPPLEMENTARY SAMPLE EMAIL

Hi Sam，

We refer to our purchase contract No. 885.

We wish to remind you that we have had no news from you about shipment of the goods. As we mentioned in our last letter，we are in urgent need of the goods and we may be compelled to seek an alternative source of supply.

Under the circumstances, it is not possible for us to extend further our letter of credit No. 562 which will expire on 21 May. Please understand how serious and urgent it is for us to resolve this matter.

We look forward to receiving your shipping advice soon.

Best regards，
Wood

EXERCISES

Ⅰ. **Fill in the blanks with the proper forms of the following expressions.**

> in connection with, meet, exhaust, speed up, put off, on or before
>
> confirm, persuade, in your interest, arrange

1. We have to point out that we make this suggestion entirely _____ .

2. We are here to talk to you _____ an agency proposal.

3. Any tender （投标） should be submitted to the following address _____ October 20, 20—local time.

4. His bad behavior nearly _____ her patience.

5. The government is trying to _____ foreign businesses to invest in the project.

6. The introduction of the new equipment _____ our production rates by one-fold.

7. I'd like to _____ a reservation for a double room on the first of July.

8. They will only agree to sign the contract if certain conditions are _____ .

9. Extreme weather compelled us to _____ the shipment until a month later.

10. Please _____ for a technician to assist us in the installation of the new machines.

Ⅱ. **Translate the following sentences into Chinese.**

1. We can effect shipment within one month after your order has been confirmed.

2. Shipment will be made within one month after receipt of your deposit.

3. We have shipped, in partial fulfillment of your order No. 685, five sets of Art. No. NY565 Milling Machines per S. S. Five Star which sailed today.

4. We are sorry for the delay in the shipment under the above L/C, as there is no vessel available this week.

5. We are pleased to inform you that the Teddy Bear you ordered on May 25th will be shipped ex S. S. Maria, which is scheduled to leave for Guangzhou on July 30.

III. Translate the following sentences into English.

1. 最近几个月来，市场对我们新产品的需求不断增长，订单源源不断。

2. 尽管未造成严重损失，我们还是建议你方不要把此次装运延误仅仅看作是疏忽大意。

3. 让我们为贵方办理所有装运及海关手续，既省时又节约。

4. 我们期望你方能赶在销售旺季前两个月将货物运到我处。

5. 尽管我们的工人正加速生产以满足客户需求，有些买主仍需等到下月月底。

6. 我们只能保证在 25 号左右交货，很难再提前了。

7. 余下的货物采取等量、连续、每季度发货一次的分期装运方式。

IV. Rewrite the sentences to make them more effective.

1. We have to stress that you must effect shipment within the prescribed time limit，as a further extension will not be considered.

2. Having studied the recent change in the market，they made some alterations of the terms of the contract.

3. As your order has been ready for shipment，please inform your forwarding agent to make shipping arrangements.

4. We have your letter dated 16th this month in acknowledgement covering the above-mentioned subject.

5. Upon receipt of the same，please arrange shipment of the goods book by us without the least possible delay.

V. Writing task.

Please refer to Task A1-6 on Page 323.

RECAP

Language Focus	Knowledge Focus
inform sb. of sth. / that . . . , keep sb. informed of regret，to one's regret，regretful，regrettable expect，no later than，in one's interest We shall be obliged if you will. . . meet one's demand，on or before take sth. into account，trust	time of shipment shipping formality initial order

续　表

Writing Tips

➢ Stating buyers' requirement on shipment time
➢ Accepting shipment time if it is OK
➢ Rejecting shipment time if it cannot be met
➢ Explaining the product schedule of manufacturers
➢ Asking for buyers' understanding
➢ Guaranteeing timely shipment

Lesson 16

About Mode of Shipment

Inquiring About Mode of Shipment

From：Peterson@google. com

To：Cindywang@sina. com

Date：July 10，20—

Subject：Modification of shipment arrangement for Order No. 13/125A

Hi Cindy，

We would like to advance **shipment** for Order No. 13/125A，i. e. ，80% of the goods in November and the **balance** in December instead of **two equal shipments** in January and February.

Please confirm whether you could catch the shipment time and whether the shipping space is available for us.

Thank you in advance for your understanding.
We look forward to your early reply.

Best regards，
Peterson

A Reply to the Above

From: Cindywang@sina. com
To: Peterson@google. com
Date: July 11, 20—
Subject: RE: Modification of shipment arrangement for Order No. 13/125A

Hi Peterson,

Warm greetings!

We agree to advance shipment for 80% of the goods to November.

But after checking with the shipping company, we were informed that all the direct **vessels**, either **liner** or **tramp, sailing for your port** have been fully booked up till the end of November.

In this case, I think November shipment is only possible if **transhipment** is allowed at Hong Kong. In spite of it, it is still uncertain whether the goods will reach you earlier than your expected time.

Please take the above into consideration and kindly let me know your decision soon.

Best regards,
Cindy

NOTES

1. shipment：*n.* 装运，运输

   mode of shipment 运输方式

   time of shipment 装运时间

   shipment time/date 装运时间

   port of shipment 装运港

   partial shipments 分批装运

   shipment in installments 分批装运

   to effect / make shipment 装运

   to advance shipment 提前装运

   to expedite shipment 加速装运

   ship：*n.* 船；*v.* 装运，运输

   Goods will be shipped in 5 equal monthly lots of 10 tons each, starting from May.

   货分 5 批按月等量装运，从 5 月开始。

   shipping：*a.* 装运的，运输的

   shipping mark 运输标志，唛头

   shipping advice 装运通知

   shipping instruction 装运要求

   shipping space 舱位

   shipping order 下货纸

   shipping container 船运集装箱

   shipping agent/forwarding agent/forwarder 运输代理，货代

   shipping company 运输公司

   shipping documents 运输单据

   shipper：*n.* ＝consignor 托运人

   carrier：*n.* ＝ship owner/shipping company 承运人，船主，运输公司

2. balance：*n.* 余额，余数；差额

   The balance of 20％ will be remitted after a successful test run.

   20％的余额将在试运行成功后汇付。

   We have supplied most of your order; the balance will follow after the holidays.

   我们已供应你方所订的大部分货物；剩余部分将在假日后交货。

   trade balance：进出口贸易差额

favorable / unfavorable trade balance：顺差/逆差

We expect to ship the balance of 15 tons by the next available steamer.

我们打算剩余的 15 吨由下条船装运。

3. two equal shipments：分两批等量装运

分批装运（part shipment，partial shipment）的表示方法还有：

in one lot 一次性交货

in ... lots（parcels，shipments，installments）分……批交货

in ... equal monthly installments of ... each，beginning from ....分……
批按月等量

交货，每月……（数量），从……（时间）开始

12,000 sets of Fridges are to be shipped in three equal monthly installments
of 3,000 sets each，beginning from March.

12000 台冰箱分三批按月等量装运，每月 3000 台，从 3 月开始。

4. vessel：*n.* 船，船舶

steamer 汽船

steamship 汽轮，缩写为 S. S. 或 s. s.

motor vessel 轮船/内燃机船，缩写为 M. V. 或 m. v.

5. liner：*n.* 班轮

6. tramp：*n.* 不定期船

7. sail for your port：开往你方港口

sail：*v.* 航行；启航（for/to）

There is no direct steamer sailing to/for your port.

没有驶往你方港口的直达轮。

sail from ... to ... 从……开往……

The goods have been loaded on board S. S. "Red Star"，which is due to
sail from Qingdao to Copenhagen on or about April 7.

货物已装到红星轮上，该轮定于 4 月 7 号左右由青岛开往哥本哈根。

8. in this/that case：在这（那）种情况下

I wouldn't normally agree but I'll make an exception in this case.

通常我不会赞成，但在现在情况下我破例同意。

case：*n.* 情况

in some cases 在某些情况下

Over a hundred people were injured，in some cases seriously.

一百多人受伤，有些还很严重。

in most cases 在多数情况下

In most cases international transactions are paid by letters of credit.

多数情况下，国际贸易是用信用证支付的。

in any case 况且

I don't want to go and in any case, I haven't been invited.

我不想去，况且我也没接到邀请。

in no case 在任何情况下都不，决不

We should in no case sacrifice principles for profits.

在任何情况下我们都不应该放弃原则，一味追求利润。

in case of sth, in case (that) 如果，万一

Bring an umbrella in case of rain.

带把雨伞，万一下雨。

In case you need help, please call me.

如果你需要帮助，请给我打电话。

in the case of 在……的情况下

The law will apply equally to men and women except in the case of maternity leave.

除产假情况外，本法律对男女同等适用。

If that's/that's not the case 如果是（不是）那样

If that's the case then I will be very disappointed.

如果是那样，我将很失望。

9. book：v. 预订

Owing to congestion, we failed to book the necessary freight space on the pointed steamer.

由于舱位拥挤，我们未能在指定的船上订到舱位。

10. transhipment：n. 转船，也可以写作 transshipment

"在……转船"可以说 make transhipment at...，或 ship the goods via...

tranship：v. 转船

Do you wish to tranship the goods at Hong Kong or at Macao?

你希望在香港还是在澳门转船?

A SUPPLEMENTARY SAMPLE EMAIL

Hello Mr. Esses,

Thank you very much for your reply. We have discussed the delivery date with our manufacturer and are informed that we are not able to finish production before Apr. 1.

I suggest we ship the goods in 2 lots. The first half of the goods will be aired before March 15 with an increase of 50% in freight. The second half will be shipped by sea before Apr. 10. We have tried our best to expedite production of your order, but this is the best we can do as we are fully committed at this moment.

Your understanding will be highly appreciated and hope the above will be acceptable to you.

Best regards,
Wang

EXERCISES

Ⅰ. **Fill in the blanks with variations of "ship".**

1. Goods will be _____ in 3 equal monthly lots of 50 tons each, beginning from May.

2. We will have our goods _____ by the first available steamer next month.

3. _____ is to be effected during Oct. / Nov..

4. All the _____ space has been booked up till the end of November.

5. The _____ will be liable for any damage resulting from inadequacy or delay in delivery of such documents.

Ⅱ. **Fill in the blanks with the proper forms of the following expressions.**

M. V. Sunshine, balance, available, book up,
bear, transshipment, sail for, modify, for one's account, charge

1. It's your decision-you must _____ the responsibility if things go wrong.

2. For your information，we have sent you a catalogue covering the goods now _____ for export.

3. Direct vessels，which _____ your port are few and far between.

4. Your goods will be _____ at Boston，please make sure that you refer to the attached detailed notice and submit related documents before mentioned deadline.

5. The extra expenses caused by delay will be _____ .

6. The theater is fully _____ .

7. The company's success is reflected in its healthy bank _____ .

8. Please refer to our _____ to the previous arrangement for shipment and let us know your final decision.

9. Your goods have been shipped via _____，with ETA on or about May 8th.

10. The barber _____ me USD 5 for my haircut.

Ⅲ. **Translate the following sentences.**

A. from English into Chinese

1. Shipment is to be made before the end of this month and，if possible，we should appreciate your arranging to ship the goods at an earlier date.

2. The goods will be shipped in 2 equal installments of 20，000 m/t each, starting from June.

3. We are sorry to inform you that due to vessel operation constraints，your bookings have been forced to change from the old vessel CMA CGM VERDI/347W to new vessel HS OCEANO/1503 with ETD 3/3/2015.

4. The goods have long been ready for shipment，but owing to the late arrival of your L/C，shipment can hardly be effected as anticipated.

5. We inform you with pleasure that we have booked space for our Order No. MX23/A on S. S. Sunshine with ETD March 3. Please ensure that goods are delivered in time. For delivery instructions，please contact Maersk Line representative at ＋86-532-89765899.

B. from Chinese into English

1. 如果你方想早点交货，我们只能分批装运，9 月份 10 台，10 月份装余下的 10 台。

2. 很抱歉，我们无法满足你方一次性交货的要求。

3. 因装运延误所造成的任何损失由你方承担。

4. 我们会考虑你方在香港转船的建议。

5. 按照约定，货物分三批等量装运，每月 5 万辆，从 4 月份开始。

6. 维多利亚号定于 11 月 10 日由上海启航开往伦敦。

7. 我们再次和船运公司联系过，遗憾的是，我们被告知目前所有的舱位都已被预订。我们只能尽力将货物装下月第一艘便轮。

Ⅳ. **Writing task.**

Please refer to Task A1-7 on Page 324.

RECAP

Language Focus	Knowledge Focus
shipment in… （ equal ） lots/ installments of … each, beginning from … sail for/to book up	mode of shipment partial shipment，transhipment shipping space，liner，tramp balance

Writing Tips

➢ Noting the buyer's request for earlier delivery

➢ Specifying the arrangement of shipment in installments

➢ Describing the availability of shipping space

➢ Suggesting transhipment

➢ Reminding the buyer's of the uncertainty of shipment time in case of transhipment

➢ Describing your consideration in the buyer's interest and expectation for decision

Task 5

Discussing Mode of Packing

Learning Objectives

To be able to write emails negotiating way of inner packing, outer packing and shipping marks

To get familiar with the writing plans, useful sentences and phrases of negotiating packing terms

Lesson 17

Packing Requirements

From: Adam@Pacific. com
To: Cindy@Fashion. com
Date: Jun. 16, 20—
Subject: Beer Glass under Order No. SD1661

Dear Cindy,

We refer to our Order No. SD1661 for 100 card**board cartons** of beer glasses to be shipped to us during May. As the goods are highly **fragile**, we feel it **advisable** to **make it clear** that the goods must be **packed** according to our **instruction** lest they are damaged **in transit.**

We would like to have them packed half dozen in a box, 10 boxes to a carton. The boxes are to be **padded** with **foamed plastics. Apart from** this, we hope the inner packing will be attractive and helpful to the sales while the outer packing strong enough to **withstand rough handling** and the sea transportation.

We hope our goods will arrive in **perfect condition.**

Best regards,
Adam

NOTES

1. requirement：*n.* 要求，需要；需要之物

   We have noted your requirement of samples and catalogues.

   我们已注意到你们需要样品和商品目录。

   We can meet your requirements for（or：of）grape wine.

   我们可满足你方对葡萄酒的需求。

2. beer glass：啤酒杯

3. refer：*v.* 谈到，涉及（to）；参照；提交

   We refer to our letter of Oct. 12，20—.

   兹谈及我方 20—年 10 月 12 日的去函。

   Referring to your request in your letter，we attach a copy of our latest catalogue.

   应你方来信要求，现随函附寄我方最新目录一份。

   As regards the claiming procedures，please refer to Appendix Two.

   关于索赔程序，请参照附件二。

   Should friendly negotiations fail，we shall refer the case to arbitration.

   如果友好协商不能成功，就将该案提交仲裁。

   We are glad to refer you to a local dealer of high quality bamboo shoots.

   我们很高兴将你推荐给当地一个优质竹笋经销商。

   reference：*n.*

   with/in reference to 关于，谈及，相当于 referring to

   With reference to the complaints in your letter of May 14，we assure you that we will give the matter our serious attention.

   关于你方 5 月 14 日来信之投诉，我们保证将严肃对待。

   We have made all possible inquires with/in reference to the integrity of the firm you mentioned.

   关于你提到的公司的信誉，我们已做了最大程度的调查。

   Reference is made to ... 兹谈及……，是 make reference to 的被动语态，用于句首。

   We make reference to your delay in shipment.

   我们谈一谈你方延误装运的问题。

   Reference is made to your proposal of cash payment.

   兹谈及你方现金付款的建议。

4. cardboard carton：纸板箱

国际贸易中，常用 master carton，export carton 或 outer carton 来表示标准箱、外箱。

5. fragile：*a.* 易碎的

As porcelains are fragile，we insure them with a franchise of 3%.

因为瓷器是易碎物品，我们按 3% 的免赔率投保。

6. advisable：*a.* 适当的，明智的

As the market is advancing，we deem it advisable for you to accept our offer without further delay.

因为市价上涨，我们认为你方立即接受我方报盘是明智的。

7. make it clear：说明……，明确……

We have made it clear that the goods under S/C No. 123 should be shipped by direct steamer.

我们已明确说明销售合同 123 号项下的货物应用直达船装运。

We think it necessary to make it clear that the outer packing is strong and seaworthy.

我们认为有必要明确外包装应坚固并且适合海运。

8. pack：*v.* 包装，打包

Our usual way is to pack these goods in cartons.

我们通常用纸箱包装这些货物。

We require walnuts to be packed in double gunny bags.

我们要求核桃用双层麻袋包装。

packing：*n.* 包装

The packing must be seaworthy.

包装必须适合海运。

inner packing 内包装	outer packing 外包装
neutral packing 中性包装	seaworthy packing 适合海运的包装
export packing 出口包装	packing list 装箱单

包装方式常用以下几种句型表达：

(1) "in ..." 用某容器包装，用某种形式包装

Cement should be packed in double kraft paper bags.

水泥要用双层牛皮纸袋包装。

(2) "in ... of ... each" 或 "in ..., each containing ..."

用某容器包装，每个容器装多少

Men's shirts are packed in cardboard cartons of 10 dozen each.

男式衬衫用纸板箱装，每箱 10 打。

The goods will be packed in iron drums of 25 kg net（each）.

货物用铁桶装，每桶净重 25 公斤。

(3) "in ... of ... each, ... to/in ..."

用某容器包装，每个容器装多少，若干小容器装于一大容器中

Pens are packed in boxes of a dozen each，100 boxes to a wooden case.

钢笔要用盒装，每盒装一打，100 盒装一木箱。

(4) "... to/in a ..., ... to/in a ..."

多层次包装时可用此句型

Candles are packed 20 pieces to a paper box，40 boxes to a carton.

蜡烛每 20 支装一纸盒，40 纸盒装一纸板箱。

Cotton socks are packed each pair in a plastic bag，100 bags to a carton.

棉袜每双装一个塑料袋，100 袋装入一个纸板箱。

package：*n.* 包装物，包件（packing 指的是包装的方式，package 指的是包装之后的物品）

Upon examination，it was found that 10％ of the packages were broken.

经检验发现，10％的包装破损。

packaging *n.* 包装材料；打包

Unwanted items should be returned in their original packaging.

不想要的物品应连同原包装一同退回。

recycling plastic packaging 可回收的塑料包装（材料）

The price includes packaging and transport.

价格包装打包和装运。

9. instruction：*n.* 指示，要求

Please inform us of your shipping instructions so that we may make arrangements accordingly.

请告知装船要求，以便我方照此进行安排。

We've received instructions from our Head Office to postpone execution of the order.

我们收到总公司的指示，推迟执行订单。

instruct：*v.* 指示，通知

Please instruct your bank to make necessary amendment to L/C No. 123.

请指示银行对信用证 123 号进行必要修改。

We will instruct our warehouse to release the goods upon receipt of your remittance.

一俟收到你方汇款，我们将通知仓库放货。

10. lest：*conj.* 免得，以免

The wooden cases must be bound with metal straps lest they are broken during loading and unloading.

木箱必须用铁箍捆扎，以免在装卸过程中破损。

11. in transit：在运输途中

Goods should be packed in cartons to avoid any possible damage in transit.

货物必须用纸板箱包装以避免运输途中任何可能的损坏。

There is no doubt that breakage occurred in transit.

毫无疑问破损发生在运输途中。

12. The boxes are to be padded with foamed plastics.

纸盒内要垫上泡沫塑料。

pad：*v.* 填塞；给……装衬垫

The backrests are padded with camel's wool.

靠垫用骆驼绒填充。

padding：*n.* 填充物，如：

Padding：50% down, 50% feather 填充物：50%绒，50%毛

foamed plastics 泡沫塑料，又称作 polystyrene（英），Styrofoam（美，注册商标）

13. apart from：＝except 除……之外

You have no reason to cancel the contract apart from this minor one.

除了这个微不足道的理由之外，你们没有理由取消这个合同。

14. withstand：*v.* 顶得住，经受住

Cases should be strong enough to withstand rough handling.

货物必须足够坚固，以经得起粗鲁搬运。

Please note that your packing must be able to withstand the long sea voyage.

请注意你方包装必须能经受长途海洋运输。

15. rough handling：粗鲁搬运，野蛮搬运

The damage is apparently due to rough handling in transit.

损坏显然系由运输途中的粗鲁搬运所致。

16. in perfect condition：状况完好

in good condition：状况良好

in poor/bad condition：状况不好

The goods were in perfect condition when they left here，and the damage evidently occurred on the voyage.

货物离开此地时完好无损，损坏显然发生在运输途中。

We trust that the goods will reach you in perfect condition.

我们相信货物将完好抵达你处。

A SUPPLEMENTARY SAMPLE EMAIL

Dear Mr. Field，

Please see the following and come back to us on Monday.

Packaging （again）：The customer shipped the sample units via UPS all over the country and two came back damaged，so now they are requesting the following additions：

（1）Wrap each resin elf（树脂小精灵）in bubble wrap to protect them better.

（2）Fill each compartment in the Styrofoam（泡沫塑料）with bubble wrap or something similar.

（3）Tape the two（top & bottom）Styrofoam boxes better. There was only a small piece of tape applied to the samples. The tape should be wrapped around the entire seam between the top & bottom portions.

Best regards，
Wood

EXERCISES

Ⅰ. Fill in the blanks with the proper forms of the following expressions.

> refer to, advisable, make it clear that, lest, in transit
> apart from, helpful, withstand, in perfect condition, damage

1. At the same time, we should _____ goods must be packed in seaworthy cardboard cartons.

2. We have to state that the shipping company be held responsible for the losses because the damage occurred _____ .

3. She spoke for an hour without once _____ her notes.

4. Goods should be packed in cartons lined with water-proof paper _____ they should be damaged during sea voyage.

5. Should there be any _____ upon arrival of the goods at the port of destination, please feel free to contact us.

6. Owing to shortage in supply, it is _____ for you to place your order quickly.

7. The manufacturers _____ provide an instruction manual.

8. Your packing must be strong enough to _____ transportation on bad road.

9. _____ packing, punctual shipment is of same importance in your performance of our order.

10. We hope our goods will reach you _____ and prove to the entire satisfaction of your end users.

Ⅱ. Translate the following sentences into Chinese.

1. Pens are packed 12 pieces to a box and 200 boxes to a carton.

2. All the cases are strongly packed in compliance with your request.

3. The outer packing should be strong enough for ocean transportation.

4. Please pack each piece of men's shirts in a polybag, half dozen to a box and 10 dozen to a wooden case.

5. The wooden case should be not only seaworthy but also strong enough to protect the goods from damage.

6. According to your requirements, we have changed the packing to small wooden cases.

7. Under normal condition, this double oilpaper packing is workable.

8. This is the most popular packing for product of this nature in the world market today.

9. The wheat is to be packed in new gunny bags and each bag weighs about 1.5kgs.

10. The chocolate mints will be packed in 12-ounce packs, 24 packs to a case.

Ⅲ. **Translate the following sentences into English.**

1. 月光牌纯棉床单用纸箱包装，每箱 10 打。

2. 折叠椅（folding chairs）两把装一个纸箱。

3. 柔柔牌纯棉枕套用纸箱包装，每箱装 20 打。

4. 每套婴儿睡衣（Infant Pajamas）装一塑料袋，12 套装一盒。

5. 可口可乐 345 克装一听，24 听装一盒。

6. 人们常把真丝围巾作为馈赠的礼物，因此要求包装要美观。

7. 合同规定包装必须坚固，足以承受粗鲁装运。

8. 顺告我们的餐具过去一向是用木箱包装的，但经过多次用纸板箱试装后，发现纸板箱同样适宜于海洋运输。

9. 纸板箱价格较低，搬运较为轻便，运费也较低廉，所以现在有更多客户宁愿要纸板箱包装而不要木箱包装。

10. 请用带花卉图案的硬纸盒包装，以便在超市销售。

Ⅳ. **Translate the following email into Chinese.**

Dear Andres，

We have received the deposit today and will arrange production accordingly.

Kindly send us the artwork of labels & shipping marks within 10 days and we will send our printing version for your final confirmation.

Let me know if you need the pre-product sample to confirm or will you arrange inspection before shipment?

Thank you.
Jennie

RECAP

Language Focus	Knowledge Focus
pack sth in... (containers) of ... (quantity) each, ... (small containers) to a ... (larger container) pack... (quantity) in a ... (container) pack sth with... (packing materials) refer to, make it clear that ... bepadded with ... , in perfect condition	inner packing, outer packing cardboard carton sea transportation rough handling packing instructions foamed plastics fragile

Writing Tips

➤ Stressing the importance of packing
➤ Describing the packing requirements in detail, e. g. packing materials, packing containers, ways of packing, etc. of the inner and outer packing
➤ Sending illustrations or artworks of packing, if necessary
➤ Hoping goods will reach in good condition

Lesson 18

Packing Arrangements

From：Audrey@flower. com
To：Gregory@Roman. com
Date：June 28，20—
Subject：Silk Blouses

Dear Gregory，

Your email **concerning** packing requirements reached us the day before yesterday. We are now making arrangements **accordingly**.

As requested，we will put the **hangtag** by **apparel tag gun**，then each silk blouse is packed in a **polybag**，one dozen to a box，blue，yellow，white **equally assorted**，S/3，M/6 and L/3 per dozen，10 boxes to a carton，10 cartons on a **pallet**. All the cartons are to be **lined with damp-proof** paper，**bound** with double straps outside. All the cartons are **up to** export standard and are strong enough for ocean transportation.

We trust you will find the packing satisfactory.

Best regards，
Audrey

NOTES

1. concerning：*prep.* （略正式）关于

   I've had a letter from an African customer concerning the demand for Chinese green tea.

   我收到了非洲一个客户的来信，关于求购中国绿茶一事。

   Attached please find our latest price list concerning the main exports we handle at present.

   兹随附最新的关于我方目前经营的主要出口商品的价格单，请查收。

2. accordingly：*ad.* （句首或句中）因此；（句末）照办，相应地

   Our stocks are running low on account of heavy sales. Accordingly, we cannot offer you more than 10 tons.

   由于大量销售，库存日减，因此我们只能报给你们 10 吨以下。

   We have received your letter and have altered the contract accordingly.

   贵方来函收到，我们已经对合同做了相应的修改。

   Please inform us of your packing requirements, so that we may make arrangements accordingly.

   请告知你方包装要求，以便我方照此进行安排。

3. hangtag：*n.* 吊牌

4. apparel tag gun：吊牌枪

   apparel：*n.* 衣服，服装

5. polybag：*n.* ＝plastic bag 塑料袋，塑胶袋

6. equally assorted：平均搭配

   We are pleased to order 1,000 dozens of silk skirts, pink, blue, and yellow equally assorted.

   我们高兴地订购一千打丝裙，粉蓝黄平均搭配。

   assortment：*n.* 搭配

   Please pack our men's gloves in cartons of 60 dozen each, with equal assortment of S, M and L sizes.

   男式手套请用纸箱包装，每箱 60 打，大，中，小号平均搭配。

7. S：small 小号

   M：medium 中号

   L：large 大号

   XL：extra large 特大号

8. pallet：*n.* 托盘

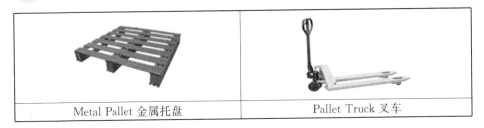	
Metal Pallet 金属托盘	Pallet Truck 叉车

9. be lined with：内衬

SuSu Brand Cotton Embroidered Table Cloth is packed in cartons lined with damp-proof paper.

苏苏牌纯棉绣花桌布用内衬防潮纸的纸箱包装。

lining：*n.* 内衬

The case has tin-plate lining.

这个箱子内衬锡箔。

10. damp-proof：*a.* 防潮的

类似的表达方式还有：

heat-proof 防热的　　　　　　waterproof 防水的

shockproof 防震的　　　　　　windproof 防风的

fireproof 防火的　　　　　　　mothproof 防蛀的

air-tight 密封的　　　　　　　rust-resistant 不生锈的

11. bound with double straps outside 外面用两根带子捆住

strap：*n.* 打包带

bound 是 bind（*v.* 捆，绑）的过去分词

加固包装的表达方式通常有：

We would suggest you strengthen the carton with double straps.

我们建议用两道打包带加固纸板箱。

The goods must be packed in strong wooden cases secured with iron hoops at both ends.

货物须以结实的木箱包装，两端用铁箍加固。

We do not object to packing in cartons, provided the flaps are glued down and cartons reinforced with metal bands.

如果盖子被粘牢而且箱子用金属带加固，我们不反对用纸板箱包装。

Packing in sturdy wooden cases is essential. Cases must be nailed, battened and secured with overall metal strapping.

用坚固木箱包装很重要。箱子须钉牢、加上压条并通体用金属带加固。

12. be up to: =measure up to 达到，及得上

You may rest assured that our export packing is up to international standards.

请放心，我们的出口包装达到国际标准。

According to the lab's records, one batch proved to be acceptable, but the other didn't measure up.

根据检验所的记录，一批货可以接受，但另一批不符合要求。

A SUPPLEMENTARY SAMPLE EMAIL

Hi, Grace!

Thanks for your email of June 29th. As requested, we make packing arrangements as follows:

Happiness brand Women's cotton T-shirts are packed one piece in a polybag, then in a paper box, 100 boxes to a carton lined with water-proof paper, bound with double straps outside. S/20, M/30, L/30, XL/20 per carton, with equal assortment of green, pink and white. You may rest assured that our cartons are strong enough and seaworthy.

We hope the above arrangements will turn out to your satisfaction and await your early confirmation, so that we may have the goods ready for shipment.

Best regards
Romy

EXERCISES

Ⅰ. Fill in the blanks with appropriate prepositions.

1. The outer packing is seaworthy cartons, 50 packs _____ one carton.

2. We guarantee that the boxes are safe _____ breakage.

3. Fortunately it did not cause any damage _____ the goods.

4. They are strong enough _____ sea transportation.

5. The cartons are made _____ cardboard.

6. The damage is caused _____ rough handling.

7. Men's Shirts are packed _____ cartons of 10 dozen each.

8. The pens are packed 12 pieces _____ a box and 200 boxes _____ a case.

9. We are satisfied that the packing is suitable _____ a long sea voyage.

10. To have the cases reinforced with double straps would call _____ extra labor and costs.

Ⅱ. Fill in each of the blanks with the most suitable word from the four choices given.

1. Rope or metal handles should be fixed to the cartons to _____ carrying.

    A. make   B. easy   C. convenient   D. facilitate

2. The goods are to be packed _____ strong wooden cases, suitable _____ ocean transportation.

    A. in, in   B. in, on   C. in, during   D. in, for

3. The goods will be _____ in 35 special waterproof lined cases and dispatched tomorrow by railway to Qingdao for shipment.

    A. pack   B. packed   C. packing   D. packs

4. Carpets wrapped _____ heavy oil waterproof paper and in a double thickness of jute canvas should have enough protection under normal condition.

    A. in   B. of   C. under   D. at

5. In the future, we will see to it that the end-packings are to be specially reinforced to _____ the hard long transit.

    A. make   B. match   C. take   D. stand

6. Each piece must be wrapped up _____ paper and packed in a zinc-lined case.

    A. on   B. below   C. in   D. after

7. Taking into consideration the transport conditions at your end, we have especially reinforced our packing so as to minimize the extent of _____ possible damage to the goods.

    A. many   B. some   C. the only   D. any

8. The goods are to be packed in cartons. If the cartons are not strong enough, most of them will be liable to _____ broken on arrival.

    A. do   B. be   C. take   D. see

9. We would suggest you _____ the carton with double straps.

    A. forward   B. strengthen   C. ship   D. enclose

10. The packing should be double bags _____ with kraft paper.

    A. line   B. lining   C. lined   D. lines

Ⅲ. Translate the following sentences into Chinese.

1. The goods must be packed in strong, seaworthy wooden cases, which are reinforced by straps.

2. We have transferred your proposal on packing to the manufacturers, who have agreed to adopt it in the next shipment.

3. Our cotton prints are packed in cases lined with kraft paper and waterproof paper, each consisting of 30 pieces in one design with 5 colourways equally assorted.

4. Traces of pilferage are easier to be found out for goods packed in cartons than those packed in wooden cases. This will help you to get compensation from the insurance company.

5. Please take necessary precautions that the packing can protect the goods from dampness and rain, since these shirts are liable to be spoiled by damp or water in transit.

Ⅳ. Translate the following sentences into English.

1. 纸板箱作为一种包装容器已在国际贸易中广泛使用。因此，对它们的适航性，你们不必担心。

2. 设计精美的包装能够促进销售。

3. 对你方的指定包装，我们要索取费用，因为这需要额外的费用和劳力。

4. 我们男衬衫的包装为每件装一塑料袋，五打装一纸箱，内衬防潮纸，外打铁箍两道。

5. 运到我们口岸的货物必须在汉堡转船，因此你们的包装必须具有适航性，并能经得起运输途中的粗鲁搬运。

6. 你们的人参酒质量很好，但包装太差，瓶子易碎，纸盒太薄，对我们今后的订货，请改进包装。

7. 我们希望你们的最终用户会对我们的包装安排感到满意。

8. 青岛啤酒一打装一纸盒，10 盒装一纸箱。

9. 女鞋每双装一纸盒，12 盒装一纸箱，大中小号平均搭配。
10. 我们出口的中国餐具每套先装一塑料盒，每盒再装一内衬塑料泡沫的纸盒内，10 盒装一纸板箱，外用铁箍加固。

RECAP

Language Focus	Knowledge Focus
equally assorted，be lined with be bound with，damp-proof accordingly，be up to	hangtag，apparel tag gun polybag，pallet，strap assortment

Writing Tips

➢ Acknowledging receipt of the buyer's packing requirements
➢ Stating the packing arrangements in detail
➢ Hoping the packing will be satisfactory

Lesson 19

Packing and Shipping Marks

From: Ingrid@Haier.com
To: Edward@Walmart.com
Date: Sep. 6, 20—
Subject: Packing-Washing Machines

Dear Edward,

In reply to your email of Sep. 2 inquiring about the packing of our Washing Machines, we **state** the following:

Our export Washing Machines are packed one set in a **PE bag**, then to a double wall **corrugated carton** padded with **honeycomb** paperboard and bound with double PET straps outside. The **dimensions** are 90cm high, 50cm wide and 60cm long with a **volume** of about 0.27 cubic meters. The **gross weight** is 60kg, the **net weight** is 50kg.

With reference to shipping marks, **in addition** to the gross, net and tare weights on the outer packing, your **initials** WMT, the port of destination and case number will be **stenciled**. Furthermore, **indicative marks** like HANDLE WITH CARE, KEEP DRY, etc, will also be **indicated**.

Should you have any special requirements in packing and shipping marks, please let us know. We will meet your requirement to **the best of our** ability.

Best regards,
Ingrid

NOTES

1. mark：*n.* 标志

   shipping marks 运输标志，装船唛头

   warning marks 警告性标志

   indicative marks 指示性标志

   Warning Marks should also be stenciled on the outer packing.

   警告性标志也应刷在外包装上。

   mark：*v.* 在……上加标志，标上

   Please mark the carton with our initials as per the drawing given.

   请按所给图样给箱子标上我方缩写名称。

2. In reply to...：兹复……，在此答复……

   In reply to your inquiry of Oct. 12，we are now offering you as follows.

   兹答复你方 10 月 12 日询盘，我们在此报盘如下：

   In reply：兹复，此复

   In reply，we are now offering you as follows.

   此复，现报盘如下：

3. state：*v.* 说明，声明

   We believe we have repeatedly stated the importance of packing.

   我们相信我们已经反复说明了包装的重要性。

   Please make us an offer，stating the earliest date of shipment.

   请报盘，并说明最早船期。

   Partial shipment is not allowed as stated in the L/C.

   按照信用证规定，不允许分装。

4. PE bag：塑胶袋

   PE：polyethylene 的缩写，聚乙烯

5. a double wall corrugated carton：双层瓦楞纸箱

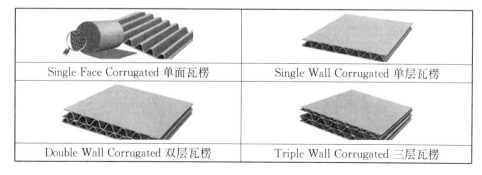

Single Face Corrugated 单面瓦楞	Single Wall Corrugated 单层瓦楞
Double Wall Corrugated 双层瓦楞	Triple Wall Corrugated 三层瓦楞

6. honeycomb paperboard：蜂窝纸板

7. dimension：*n.* 物品的长，宽，高

Please specify the dimensions of the packages.

请说明包件的尺寸。

The carton dimensions are 1124mm（L）×868mm（W）×600mm（H）.

外箱尺寸为高度 11.24 厘米，宽度 8.68 厘米，高度 6 厘米。

8. volume：*n.* 体积，容积

9. cubic meter：立方米

square meter 平方米

10. gross weight：毛重

net weight 净重

tare weight 皮重

gross：*a.* 毛的

gross national product（GNP）国民生产总值

gross domestic product（GDP）国内生产总值

net：*a.* 净的，纯的

Gross for Net 以毛做净

This bar of chocolate weighs 100 grams net.

这一块巧克力净重 100 克。

11. in addition to：除……之外，并且，此外

In addition to Cotton Piece Goods，we have silk fabrics available at present.

除了棉布外，我们目前还有丝绸织品供应。

12. initial：*n.* 起首的字母；initials（pl.）名字的起首字母缩写

如：BBC＝British Broadcasting Corporation 英国广播公司

WTO＝World Trade Organization 世界贸易组织

CCPIT＝China Council for Promotion of International Trade 中国国际贸易促进委员会

13. stencil：*v.* 用模板刷制（唛头）

We will stencil the shipping marks in strict accordance with your instructions.

我们将严格按照你方指令刷制唛头。

Please note that warning marks like "Stow Away From Heat" etc. should be stenciled on the outer packing.

请注意，警告性标志像"远离热源"等应刷在外包装上。

14. indicative marks：指示性标志

 warning marks：警告性标志

15. Handle With Care：小心轻放

16. Keep Dry：保持干燥

17. indicate：*v.* 说明，表明

 Information indicates that the market is advancing.

 有消息表明行情正在上涨。

 We regret being unable to reduce our price to your indicated level.

 我们抱歉不能把价格降到你所指明的水平。

18. to the best of one's ability：尽某人最大努力

 We will settle this problem to the best of our ability.

 我们将尽力解决这个问题。

 We will improve our packing to the best of our ability.

 我们将尽力改进包装。

 to the best of one's ... 就某人最大的……

 To the best of my knowledge，the goods are arriving next week.

 就我所知，货物将于下周到达。

A SUPPLEMENATRY SAMPLE EMAIL

Dear Mr. Well，

We thank you for your packing arrangements. At the same time，please note our shipping marks as follows：

Please mark our initials on the outer packing，under which the port of destination and package number should be indicated. Furthermore，warning marks such as "Fragile"，"This Side Up" etc.，should also be stenciled on the outer packing.

Please arrange shipping marks accordingly and make shipment within the stipulated time.

Best regards，

Stock

EXERCISES

I . Fill in blanks with the appropriate word as below.

> pack, repacked, packing, package, packed

1. Please see to it that the _____ is suitable for a long sea voyage.

2. All the canned fruits and meat are to be _____ in cartons.

3. We _____ our shirts in plastic-lined, waterproof cartons, reinforced with metal straps.

4. It was found upon examination that nearly 20% of the _____ had been broken, obviously attributed to improper _____ .

5. A thorough examination showed that the broken kegs were due to improper _____ for which the suppliers should be definitely responsible.

6. We can meet your requirement to have the goods _____ in wooden cases but you have to bear the extra _____ charges.

7. The goods had been _____ before they were delivered to our customers.

8. Our fountain pens are _____ in boxes of one dozen each, 100 boxes to a carton lined with water-proof paper.

9. When _____ please take into account that the boxes are likely to receive rough handling at this end and must be able to withstand transport over very bad roads.

10. You know that the appearance of the _____ contributes greatly to the sale of the consumer goods.

II . Fill in the blanks with the proper forms of the following expressions.

> in reply to, inquire about, state, with reference to, in addition to, stencil, furthermore, indicate, should, let us know, to the best of our ability

1. _____ your inquiry of Aug. 1st, we are pleased to make you an offer, subject to our final confirmation, as follows.

2. We take this opportunity to write you _____ container service provided by COSCO.

3. Please _____ the shipping marks and warning marks on the outer packing according to our packing requirements.

4. _____ any damage occur during transit, please _____

immediately.

5. We should _____ that your packing must be in exact accordance with Chinese Export Standard.

6. _____, attractive packing will help greatly push the goods.

7. Exploratory investigations have _____ large amounts of oil below the sea bed.

8. _____ your inquiry of Aug. 1st，we are pleased to inform you that the shipping container we provide are of two sizes，namely 10ft and 20ft respectively.

9. _____ protecting the goods，exquisite inner packing will appeal to the prospective buyers.

10. You may rest assured that we will execute your order No. 123 _____ .

Ⅲ. **Translate the following sentences into Chinese.**

1. We do not object to packing in cartons，provided the flaps are glued down and the cartons secured by metal bands.

2. If cartons are used，please supply each item in strong polythene bags to ensure protection from damp.

3. Correct and distinct marking for the outside containers is absolutely necessary.

4. The greatest care must be given to packing and crating，as any damage in transit would cause us heavy losses.

5. You may rest assured that double wall corrugated cartons are shockproof and suitable for long sea voyage.

6. The cases used to pack our recorders are light but strong. They save shipping space and facilitate the storage and distribution of the goods.

7. Honeycomb paperboard buffering packing is eco-friendly and recyclable.

8. Our usual packing for dyed poplin is in bales lined with waterproof paper，each containing 600 yards in single color.

9. In case your shipping marks are required，your order should clearly indicate such marks and should reach us one month before the shipment time.

10. Our cartons for canned food are not only seaworthy，but also strong

enough to protect the goods from possible damage.

Ⅳ. Writing task.

Please refer to Task A1-8 on Page 314.

RECAP

Language Focus	Knowledge Focus
mark	shipping marks
stencil	double wall corrugated cartons
indicate	honeycomb paperboard
in reply to	dimensions, volume, cubic meters
in addition to	gross weight, net weight, tare
to the best of one's ability	PE bag, PET straps
	indicative marks, warning marks

Writing Tips

➢ Acknowledging receipt ofthe buyer's email

➢ Stating the arrangement of inner packing and outer packing

➢ Describing shipping marks

➢ Expressing your willingness and ability to meet the buyer's other requirements

Task 6

Discussing Terms of Payment

Learning Objectives

To be able to write emails negotiating the mode and means of payment

To get familiar with the writing plans，useful sentences and phrases of negotiating payment terms

Lesson 20

Inquiring About Terms of Payment

Inquiring About Terms of Payment

From: bob. miller@dimed. es
To: richard. wang@blues. com
Date: June 8, 20—
Subject: Your price list and payment terms?

Dear Mr. Wang,

Let us reintroduce ourselves as a **Venezuelan dealer** of **food additives.** During our **brief** meeting at the **China Import & Export Fair** (Canton) in May 20—, you kindly presented me a name card and some of your samples. After a close study back home, we are glad to tell you that we find much interest in most of them, and we have **confidence** that your goods will **find a ready market at this end.**

But as I was rather in a hurry then at the fair, there were a few things left not discussed. Would you please send us a price list, stating the payment terms you usually accept for your exports?

We look forward to your prompt reply.

Best regards,
Bob Miller

A Reply to the Above

From：richard. wang@blues. com
To：bob. miller@dimed. es
Date：June 8，20—
Subject：RE：Your price list and payment terms?
Attachments：price list. xls（12K）

Dear Mr. Miller，

We really appreciate your **intention** to push the sale of our products in your country. Thank you very much.

In reply，we'd like to inform you that we generally accept **remittance** of 30% **deposit** by T/T after order confirmation，but before **mass production** and the balance against copy of **B/L.**

Attached is a price list for all the items available for export.

We hope the terms on the list will be acceptable to you and wish to **enter into** business with you soon.

Best regards，
Richard Wang

NOTES

1. payment：*n.* 支付，付款

   payment in advance 预付

   payment by installments 分期付款

   deferred payment 延期付款

   payment on arrival of goods 货到付款

   down payment 定金

   terms of payment/modes of payment/payment terms 支付方式，付款条件

   instruments of payment 支付工具

   pay：*v.* 支付，付款

   How much did you pay for the tickets?

   你买这些票花了多少钱？

   Payment is to be made by a confirmed irrevocable letter of credit payable by draft at sight，to be opened 30 days before the time of shipment and to remain valid for negotiation in China within 15 days after the date of shipment.

   支付用保兑的、不可撤销的凭即期汇票付款的信用证，装运前 30 天开出，装运后 15 天内在中国议付有效。

   国际贸易中常用的付款方式（terms of payment）有：

   Collection 托收，包括：

   (1) D/P（Documents against Payment）付款交单

   (2) D/A（Documents against Acceptance）承兑交单

   Remittance 汇付，包括：

   (1) M/T（Mail Transfer）信汇

   (2) T/T（Telegraphic Transfer）电汇

   (3) D/D（Demand Draft）票汇

   L/C（Letter of Credit）信用证

   国际贸易中常用的付款工具（instruments of payment）有：

   draft，bill of exchange 汇票

   check/cheque 支票

   promissory note 本票

2. Venezuelan：*a.* 委内瑞拉的

   Venezuela：*n.* 委内瑞拉

3. food additives：食品添加剂

4. brief：*a.* 短暂的

5. China Import & Export Fair：中国进出口商品交易会，即广交会

6. Canton：*n.* Guangzhou 的旧称

7. present：*v.* 给予，提交，提供，出示

   He presented the report to his colleagues at the meeting.

   他在会上向同事们提交了这份汇报。

   presentation：*n.* 给予，提交，提供，出示，讲话

   On D/A terms，all drafts must be accepted（承兑）by the drawees upon presentation.

   在承兑交单条件下，所有汇票都必须在提示时予以承兑。

8. find a ready market：畅销，有好销路

   You can find a ready market for Chinese green tea here.

   你们可在此地为中国绿茶找到好销路。

9. at this end：在此地，在我地

   at our end 在我地

   at your end 在你地

10. intention：*n.* 意图，意愿，意向，动机

    I've no intention of changing my plans just to fit in with his.

    我不想为了适应他的计划而改变我的计划。

    intend：*v.* 打算，计划

    These goods are intended for the Middle East market.

    这些货物是专为供应中东市场的。

11. remittance of 30% deposit by T/T：电汇全部货款的 30%作为订金

    remittance：*n.* 汇款；汇付

    make/send remittance for ＋ 金额

    We have sent remittance for USD500 to cover the advertising expenses.

    我们已将 500 美元的广告费汇出。

    remit：*v.* 汇寄，汇款

    We have already remitted your commission by check.

    我们已将你方佣金以支票汇出。

12. deposit：*n.* 订金；押金；存款

    Please send us your proforma invoice for 30% deposit.

    请寄来你方形式发票以便我方预付 30%货款。

    A ￡50 deposit is required when ordering，and the balance is due upon delivery.

订货时需要交 50 英镑的订金，货到后结清余款。

It is common to ask for the equivalent of a month's rent as a deposit.

要求交一个月的房租作押金是很常见的。

The amount of yuan on deposit jumped two-thirds in the third quarter.

人民币存款在第三季度跃升 2/3。

v. 付订金

We would like you to deposit 30% of the total amount.

我们希望你方预付 30% 货款作为订金。

13. mass production：大批量生产，大货生产

14. balance：*n.* 余额，余下的部分

    The balance of 20% will be remitted after a successful test run.

    20% 的余额将在试运行成功后汇付。

    We have supplied most of your order; the balance will follow after the holidays.

    我们已供应你方所订的大部分货物；剩余部分将在假日后交货。

15. B/L：Bill of Lading 提单

16. enter into：开始，达成，建立等

    to enter into an agreement 达成协议

    to enter into business relations 建立业务关系

SUPPLEMENTARY SAMPLE EMAILS

Dear Sophie，

We confirm the price you revised. Thank you for your efforts.

As for payment，we propose T/T against copy of shipping documents. Is that O. K. ?

Thanks and best regards，
Amy

Dear Amy，

We agree to T/T payment. But as this is our first deal，we require 50%
deposit before delivery and the balance against copy of shipping
documents. Please understand.

Best regards，
Sophie

EXERCISES

Ⅰ. **Fill in the blanks with the right word or words and then put them into Chinese.**

1. We have _____ (entered into，entered) a provisional agreement on
   the technological transfer.

2. When you make the offer，will you please _____ (inform，state)
   the earliest time of shipment?

3. We need an agent in that country to help us to _____ (push the sale
   of，push sale with) our products.

4. We appreciate the _____ (confidence，confidential) you have
   placed in us in the past and look forward to further dealings with you.

5. Should the Christmas Bear be of _____ (interest，interesting) to
   you，please let us know.

6. Our brand of silk shirts has entered the market and we are sure that
   they will _____ (find a good market，find good market) _____
   (in your end，at your end) .

7. The end-users have no _____ (intention，interest) of importing the
   machines.

8. We refer to our L/C No. 305 covering 2,000 m/t steel shipped on 3rd
   October. The shipping documents were _____ (presented，
   present) to us yesterday.

9. Our usual terms of payment are 30% deposit by T/T before production and the
   _____ (balance，balancing) against copy of B/L，or by L/C at sight.

10. Your request for T/T _____ (payment，pay) has been
    considered and we accept it for this order.

Ⅱ. Translate the following sentences into Chinese.

1. Payment is to be made against sight draft drawn under a confirmed, irrevocable, divisible and transferable Letter of Credit without recourse for the full amount.

2. As agreed, the terms of payment for the above order are D/P sight draft or 30 days D/A.

3. We would suggest that for this particular order you let us have a T/T. On receipt of the remittance, we shall ship the goods on the first available steamer.

4. We have accepted your bill and we now have the documents. We shall collect the consignment as soon as it arrives in Bonn and honor your draft at maturity.

5. The documents will be presented to you by the Citi Bank against your acceptance of the draft.

Ⅲ. Translate the following sentences into English.

1. 请尽快报盘，说明包装、规格、可供数量、支付方式等。

2. 这类货十分流行，相信在你地也定会畅销。

3. 既然你们已经同意了我们的支付条款，我们将与厂家联系下一步的装运事宜。

4. 对这笔交易，我们建议以即期信用证付款。

5. 请先支付样品费，下单后将从货款中扣除。

Ⅳ. Writing task.

Please refer to Task A1-9 on Page 325.

RECAP

Language Focus	Knowledge Focus
pay, payment present, have confidence in .../ that ... remittance, remit find a ready market, at this end, enter into	mode of payment, means of payment T/T, deposit, B/L China Import & Export Fair

Writing Tips

- ➢ Requiring 30% deposit and balance against copy of B/L to ensure safety in payment
- ➢ Expressing thanks to a new customer whether or not his or her emails will bring about business
- ➢ Giving replies to all issues covered in customers' emails respectively

Lesson 21

Request for Easier Terms of Payment（1）

Request for Easier Terms

From: samuel. collins@falcon. com
To: emily. song@tyarts. com
Date: May 10, 20—
Subject: easier terms of payment

Dear Emily,

We are writing to inform you that our L/C No. BRC990 **covering** our Order No. QD356 has been opened through **NatWest.** The advising bank should be sending you an advice shortly.

We have been dealing with you on an L/C basis for years. This has become a **financial** burden. We believe we have **proved trustworthy** business partners to each other after these years of satisfactory cooperation. So we should think that we **deserve** some easier terms of payment, say, T/T against copy of shipping documents.

As we will be sending another order within the month, could you please confirm that you agree to the new terms of payment?

Best regards,
Samuel Collins

Request Granted

| From: emily. song@tyarts. com |
| To: samuel. collins@falcon. com |
| Date: May 10, 20— |
| Subject: RE: easier terms of payment |

Dear Samuel,

Thank you for your email of today, informing us of the opening of the L/C No. BRC990.

Thanks to the efforts from both sides, the cooperation between us has developed very satisfactorily. **With a view** to encouraging future business, we are pleased to accept your proposal for payment by T/T for future deals instead of L/C by draft **drawn at sight**.

We believe this modification to payment terms will be more **conducive** to the expansion of trade between us.

Best regards,
Emily Song

NOTES

1. easy terms：易于接受的条件

   easy：*a.*（价格/报盘等）易于接受的

2. covering：*prep.* 包括的，涉及……的；*a.* 有关的

   We attach a catalogue covering the main items suppliable at present.

   兹随附一份目前可以供应的主要商品的目录。

   the covering L/C 有关信用证

3. NatWest：（英）National Westminster Bank 国民西敏寺银行

4. financial：*a.* 财政的，财务的；金融的；资金的

   financial difficulties/success 资金上的困难/成功

   chief financial officer（CFO）首席财务官

   finance：*n.* 财务，理财；金融

   corporate/personal/public finance 公司/个人/公共理财

   finance department 财务部

   finance company/house 金融公司

   finance：*v.* 为……提供资金，资助

   The local authority has refused to finance the scheme.

   当地权力机构拒绝为该项目提供资金。

5. prove：*v.* 证明，证实，显示（一个结果）

   The dispute over the song rights proved impossible to resolve.

   对这首歌著作权的争议，结果是不可能解决的。

6. trustworthy：*a.* 值得信赖的

7. deserve：*v.* 应该得到

   They certainly deserved to win that match.

   他们应该赢得这场比赛。

8. shipping documents：装船单据

9. grant：*v.* 给予；同意

   We normally grant a 3% discount for orders over 5,000 dollars.

   对于超过 5000 美元的订单，我们通常给予 3%的折扣。

   She granted their request/wish.（正式）

   她同意了他们的请求。

10. thanks to：由于，多亏

    The company was able to continue trading thanks to a loan from the bank.

    多亏银行的贷款，这家公司才得以继续经营。

11. with a view to：为了……

These measures have been taken with a view to increasing the company's profits.

采取这些措施是为了提高公司的利润。

12. modification：*n.* 修改，改正

This draft contract needs further modification.

这份草拟合同需要进一步修改。

modify：*v.* 修改，改正

The L/C contains quite a few errors. You need to modify them.

信用证有不少错误，你需要改正它们。

13. draft drawn at sight：开立的即期汇票

draw：*v.* 开具汇票

draw a draft on sb，draw on sb 向某人开汇票

We agree to draw（a draft）at sight instead of at 30 days after sight.

我们同意开具即期而非 30 天的汇票。

We have drawn on you through the Bank of China for the invoice value of the consignment.

我们已经通过中国银行开出汇票，按发票金额向你们索款。

We have drawn on you at 60 days for USD12,000 against your trial order.

对你们的试订货,我们已向你方开出金额为 12000 美元 60 天期见票付款的汇票。

14. conducive：*a.* 有利的，有帮助的

This will not be conducive to the development of trade between us.

这对我们双方的贸易发展是没有好处的。

A SUPPLEMENTARY SAMPLE EMAIL

Dear Mr. Wang,

Please make the 36 samples as described below.

If acceptable，I will wire you ＄150 US dollars，and you will one-day mail the samples to me.

The ＄150 US dollars will be credited to my account when I re-order larger volumes.

Looking forward to your early reply.

Best regards,
Amy

EXERCISES

Ⅰ. **Fill in the blanks with the proper forms of the following expressions.**

> prove, deserve, thanks to, draw, on... basis
>
> with a view to, agree to, modification, conducive, covering

1. _____ the economy of scale （规模经济） in our manufacturing, it has been possible to reduce our prices, which are now lower than those garments of similar quality.

2. We are anticipating the prompt shipment and are desirous of establishing a regular connection for the future if this first consignment _____ to conform to the sample supplied.

3. We have _____ on you at 60 days and passed the draft and shipping documents to our branch.

4. After a careful study of your draft contract, we find a few _____ would be necessary.

5. Tony _____ our special thanks for all his efforts.

6. We believe you will _____ the customer's remark on their goods: "The superior performance and the material used justify their slightly higher prices".

7. The pricing for this model is _____ a cost-plus.

8. We shall be pleased to submit a detailed scheme which we hope will be _____ to encouraging business.

9. We will grant you 5% commission _____ initiating business in this line.

10. We thank you for L/C No. 235 _____ the 200 sets of Seven Star microwave ovens.

Ⅱ. **Translate the following sentences into Chinese.**

1. We assume you will settle this outstanding amount by banker's draft in USD, and hope to receive payment soon.

2. Exporters sometimes send the documentary bill direct to a bank in the importer's country, but more usually deal with their own bank, who arrange for the bill to be presented to the foreign buyer by their branch or correspondent abroad.

3. We regret that at the moment we can not meet in full my acceptance,

which is due for payment on August 15.

4. Shipping documents and our draft for acceptance have been passed to the Citibank N. A，HK.

5. As usual，we are drawing on you at 30 days for the value of the goods in favor of the Chase（大通银行）and trust you will accept the draft upon presentation.

Ⅲ. Translate the following sentences into English.

1. 对于外商的订货，我们一般要求保兑的，不可撤销的信用证支付。

2. 信用证方式是我方习惯做法。然而，对目前这笔交易，我们同意你方 D/P 付款的建议，以利你方推销产品。

3. 我们认为在装运前以电汇方式支付是这笔交易唯一可行的办法。

4. 由于所涉及的额外保费较少，因此我们不要求你方修改信用证，而将从应付你方的佣金中扣除。

5. 由于在过去两年来我们在生意上的往来完全令人满意，我们十分乐意做此更改，即装运后电汇支付。

Ⅳ. Writing task.

Please refer to Task A6 on Page 330.

RECAP

Language Focus	Knowledge Focus
easy terms，financial burden covering，prove，deserve trustworthy partners thanks to，with a view to，be conducive to	L/C by draft drawn at sight
Writing Tips	
Asking for easier payment terms： ➢ Confirming or placing an order ➢ Proposing easier payment terms ➢ Justifying your proposal by showing mutual trust and goodwill	Agreeing to easier payment terms： ➢ Appreciating efforts in cooperation ➢ Giving serious consideration to the customer's proposal ➢ Agreeing to easier payment terms in order to facilitate future business

Lesson 22

Request for Easier Terms of Payment （2）

Request for Easier Terms

From： ben. clark@. ysfh. com
To： richard. wang@eipp. com. cn
Date： Sept. 25, 20—
Subject： terms of payment

Dear Richard,

Attached please find our P. O. #206 for 5,000 tons of chemical fertilizers.

As to payment terms, we wonder if you could grant us **D/P** terms. As one of the leading importers of chemicals in Manila, Philippines, we have had no difficulties in **meeting our obligations** and have always **settled our account** promptly. If you need **references**, we will be glad to supply them to you.

We look forward to your confirmation of our first order, and hope it will mark the beginning of our pleasant business relations in the future.

Best regards,
Ben Clark

Request Rejected

| From: richard. wang@eipp. com. cn |
| To: ben. clark@. ysfh. com |
| Date: Sept. 26, 20— |
| Subject: RE: terms of payment |

Dear Ben,

Thank you for your P. O. #206 of September 25 for 5,000 tons of chemical fertilizers. We have considered your request for payment by D/P and regret that we can't grant the terms you asked for.

We hope you will understand that the urgency of your order left us with **insufficient** time to make the usual status enquiries and we therefore **have no choice but to follow** our usual practice with new customers, i. e. payment by sight L/C. Maybe after several smooth and satisfactory transactions, we can consider other easier terms.

We look forward to your confirmation and regular dealings.

Best regards,
Richard Wang

NOTES

1. chemical fertilizers：化肥

2. D/P：＝Document against Payment 付款交单

   D/P at sight 即期付款交单

   D/P at 60 days after sight 见票后 30 天付款交单，常用 60 days D/P

3. meet our obligations：如期偿还债务

   meet：*v.* 支付

   We believe you will meet our draft on presentation.

   我们相信你方在汇票提交时付款。

   obligation：*n.* 义务；债务

   The sellers are under an obligation to complete the delivery of the goods within the contracted time of shipment.

   卖方有责任在合同规定的交货期内完成交货。

4. settle our account promptly：迅速结账

   settle：*v.* 解决；结算

   You are requested to settle your account quarterly.

   请按季度结账。

5. reference：*n.* （资信）证明书；备询人，资信征询公司

   Banker's Reference：银行资信证明书

   reference bank 备询银行，参考银行

   If it is required，we can provide first class reference.

   如果需要，我们可提供最好的资信证明。

   The ABC Company has given us your name as reference.

   ABC 公司举出贵方名字作为资信征询人。

   Would you kindly send us the name of a bank to whom reference can be made?

   请告知可供我们作资信征询的银行的名称。

6. reject：*v.* 拒绝

   The British government is expected to reject the idea of state subsidy for a new high speed railway.

   预计英国政府不会考虑为修建一条新的高速铁路提供国家补贴的设想。

7. insufficient：*a.* 不够的，不足的

8. status inquiry：这里指资信询查

   status：*n.* 情况，状态

   credit/financial/ credit and financial status 资信状况

Please advise us of the status of the goods ordered.

请告知所订货物的情况。

9. We have no choice but to follow our usual practice.

我们只得按我方惯例办。

have no choice but to . . . : 除……外别无他法，不得不……

As our stocks are running low，we regret we have no choice but to decline your order.

由于我们的存货正在减少，我们不得不谢绝你方订货。

follow：*v.* 按照执行

We hope you will strictly follow our shipping instructions.

希望你方严格按照我们的装运要求办理。

10. payment by sight L/C：以即期信用证方式支付

by 表示支付的方式，如 to pay by collection 用托收方式支付；payment by check 用支票支付

in 表示支付的货币，如 to pay in Canadian dollar 用加元支付；payment in euro 用欧元支付

We usually pay by T/T or D/P.

我们通常用电汇或付款交单方式支付。

Do you accept payment in Renminbi?

你们接受人民币付款吗?

A SUPPLEMENTARY SAMPLE EMAIL

Dear Mr. Chen，

As this is our first deal，we'd like to make clear our payment terms first，i. e. O/A 45 days.

Please understand. This is our usual practice with all customers.

If you agree，we can come to details of the business.

Looking forward to your early reply.

Best regards，

Jenny

EXERCISES

Ⅰ. Fill in each of the following blanks with a word chosen from the list given.

> order, grant, suppliers, satisfactory, by L/C,
> terms, favorable, time, on T/T basis

Dear Ms. Wen,

We are pleased to learn from your email that you have been able to ship our _____ in good _____ but we are surprised that you still demand payment _____ . After many years of _____ trading we feel that we are entitled to more _____ terms. Most of our _____ are doing business with us _____ and we should be grateful if you could _____ us the same _____ .

We are looking forward to your favorable reply.

Best regards,

Willa White

Ⅱ. Translate the following sentences into Chinese.

1. As usual, our terms of payment are still by T/T, 40% in advance, and 60% paid within one week after B/L copy.
2. Provided you fulfill the L/C terms, we will accept the drafts drawn under the L/C.
3. We've made your remittance of CAD3,000 for payment of the 20% of freight due.
4. We should be grateful if you could grant the credit asked for.
5. While we would like to offer you more time to clear the balance, our own financial position makes this impossible. Therefore we must ask you to settle the account within the next fortnight.

Ⅲ. Translate the following email into Chinese.

Thank you so much, Tom.

Since it's the first time we are dealing with you, we will pay you 30% in advance and the balance once you finish production. If I pay you 100% in advance and then you come up with issues later on, I will not be able to manage the situation. I had experiences from other suppliers like this before and that's the reason I don't want to repeat it again...

If you can accept it, we can work together or else... it's fine. We will look into another opportunity.

Regards,

Daniel

IV. Writing task.

Please refer to Task A7 on Page 331.

RECAP

Language Focus	Knowledge Focus
meet obligations settle account have no choice but to follow usual practice	D/P payment by sight L/C bank reference status inquiry

Writing Tips

Rejecting proposal for easier payment terms:

➢ Taking a cautious approach to the payment terms when dealing with new customers

➢ Rejecting a customer's request in a courteous manner

➢ Explaining reasons of refusal

➢ Expressing willingness to agree to easier payments for orders in the future

Task 7

Discussing Terms of Insurance

Learning Objectives

To be able to write emails negotiating the insurance coverage, amount, premium etc.

To get familiar with the writing plans, useful sentences and phrases of negotiating insurance terms

Lesson 23

About Insurance

From: peter. li@126. com
To: lila. bright@yatex. com
Date: Nov 18, 20—
Subject: insurance matters

Dear Lila,

In regard to insurance, we would like to inform you of the following:

All Risks

Generally we **cover** WPA &. War Risk **in the absence of definite** instructions from our clients. If you desire to cover all risks, we can provide such coverage at a slightly higher **premium.**

Breakage

Breakage is a special risk, for which an extra premium will have **to be charged.** The present rate is about . . . ‰. But please note the cover is subject to a **franchise** of 5%. In other words, claims are payable only for the part of the loss that is over 5%.

Value to be **insured**

We note that you wish us to insure shipments to you for 110% of the invoice value. We agree to this, as it's our **usual practice** to cover insurance for 10% above the invoice value.

We trust the above info will **serve your purpose** and we await further news from you.

Best regards,
Peter Li

NOTES

1. insurance：*n.* 保险

   insurance amount 保险金额，保值   insurance premium 保险费，保险费率

   insurance policy 保险单   insurance certificate 保险凭证

   insurance company 保险公司   insurance coverage 保险范围

   insurance clause 保险条款

   "投保"的动宾搭配通常有：

   cover/effect/arrange/take out insurance 投保，办理保险

   insurance 一词有下列介词可以搭配：

   insurance on 保险的标的物，如：

   insurance on 1,000 sets electric fans 为 1000 台电风扇投保

   insurance for 保险金额，如：

   insurance for 110% of the invoice value 按发票金额的 110%投保

   insurance against 保险险别，如：

   insurance against All Risks and War Risk 投保一切险和战争险

   insurance at 保险费，如：

   insurance at a premium of 5‰ 按 5‰的保险费投保

   insurance with 保险公司，如：

   insurance with PICC 在中国人民保险公司投保

   We have covered insurance on your order with PICC for 110% of the invoice value against All Risks and War Risk.

   我们已在中国人民保险公司对你们的订货按发票金额的 110%投保了一切险和战争险。

2. in regard to：关于，至于

   We have already written to you in regard to this matter.

   关于此事，我们已写信给你了。

   in regard to，regarding，with regard to，as regards 都做"关于"解。

   regarding：*prep.* 关于，至于

   Regarding payment, we would like to pay by an irrevocable sight letter of credit.

   至于付款，我们想以不可撤销的即期信用证付款。

   Please let us have all necessary information regarding your products for export.

   请告知所有关于你们出口产品的必要信息。

With regard to your letter of May 6，we regret we cannot comply with your wishes.

关于你方 5 月 6 日的来信，很遗憾我们不能满足你的要求。

As regards the balance，we will advise you of the position in a few days.

关于余数，将于不日内告知。

3. All Risks：一切险。按照中国人民保险公司 1981 年 1 月 1 日修订的《海洋运输货物保险条款》规定，海洋运输保险的基本险别分为：平安险（Free from Particular Average，F. P. A.）；水渍险（With Particular Average 或 With Average，W. P. A. 或 W. A.）；一切险（All Risks，A. R.）

4. generally：*adv.* 通常，一般地

These goods are generally shipped in bulk.

此货通常散装装运。

5. cover：*n.* ＝insurance cover 保险

Does your policy provide adequate cover against breakage?

你们的保单提供足够的破碎险吗?

cover：*v.* 保险，投保

We wish to cover the goods against All Risks.

我们想投保一切险。

You're requested to cover War Risk in addition to All Risks.

除一切险外，请加保战争险。

Insurance is to be covered by the buyers.

由买方办理保险。

This insurance policy has covered us against All Risks and War Risk.

这份保单给我们保了一切险和战争险。

We usually cover 110％ of the invoice value.

我们通常投保发票金额的 110％。

6. in the absence of：没有，在没有……的情况下

We cannot ship the goods in the absence of your L/C.

没有你方信用证，我们不能装运此货。

7. definite：*a.* 明确的，确切的

You must be more definite about the packing method.

你方必须把包装方法说得更明确一些。

8. coverage：*n.* 保险；承保险别；保险范围（包括险别、保值、保险起讫地等）

What types of coverage do you usually underwrite?

你们公司通常承保什么险？

If the business is concluded on CIF terms，what coverage will you take out?

如果以 CIF 价成交，你们将投保什么险？

9. premium：*n.* 保险费

extra premium＝additional premium 额外保费

10. breakage：*n.* 破碎险，一般附加险的一种

根据海洋运输货物保险条款（OMCC，即 Ocean Marine Cargo Clause），中国人民保险公司承保的附加险有一般附加险和特殊附加险两种。

一般附加险（general additional risk）有：

theft，pilferage and non-delivery（T. P. N. D.）偷窃提货不着险

fresh water and/or rain damage（FWRD）淡水雨淋险

shortage 短量险	intermixture and contamination 混杂沾污险
leakage 渗漏险	clash and breakage 碰损破碎险
taint of odour 串味险	sweat and heating 受潮受热险
hook damage 钩损险	breakage of packing 包装破碎险
rust 锈损险	

特殊附加险（special additional risks）有：

war risk 战争险	strikes 罢工险
aflatoxin 黄曲霉素险	failure to deliver 交货不到险
on deck 舱面险	import duty 进口关税险
rejection 拒收险	

flame risk extension clause（F. R. E. C.）货物出口到香港（包括九龙）或澳门，存仓火险责任扩展条款

11. charge：*v.* 收取费用；记账

We charge them RMB￥5,000 for storage.

我们向他们收取存储费 5000 元。

Shall we charge the flowers to your account?

我们可以把这些花记到你的账上吗？

n. 费用

There is an additional charge for sending shipments by air.

空运货物要追加费用。

If the material is found faulty，we will replace it free of charge.

如果发现材料有缺点，我们将免费更换。

12. rate：*n.* 本课＝insurance premium rate （保险）费率

    rate 还有"价格"的意思

    What's the going rate for this type of machine tool?

    这种机床的现价是多少？

13. franchise：*n.* 免赔率（额）；相对免赔率（额）

    deductible franchise：绝对免赔率（额）

14. insure：*v.* 保险

    We normally insure this item against All Risks and TPND.

    这种货我们通常投保一切险和偷窃、提货不着险。

    This insurance policy insures us against All Risks.

    本保险单为我们投保了一切险。

    We usually insure for 10％ above the invoice value.

    我们通常按发票金额的 110％投保。

    Do you insure against FWRD on this item?

    这种货你们投保淡水雨淋险吗？

15. usual practice：＝customary practice 惯例

    It is our usual practice to cover insurance for 110％ of the invoice value against WPA and War Risk.

    我们的惯例是按发票金额的 110％投保水渍险和战争险。

16. serve your purpose：使你达到目的

    serve：*v.* 帮助达到；当作

    Agency serves a useful function for both sellers and buyers.

    代理对买卖双方都起到很大的作用。

    The judge said that the fine would serve as a warning to other motorists who drove without due care.

    法官说这次罚款对不谨慎驾驶的人来说，是一个告诫。

A SUPPLEMENTARY SAMPLE EMAIL

Dear Mr. Black,

Attached is our CFR quotation for Hand Tools and we are sure you will find our prices workable. Regarding insurance, please note the following:

—We usually insure the goods sold on CIF basis with our underwriter, the People's Insurance Company of China (PICC) for 110% of total invoice value against All Risks and War Risk as per the Ocean Marine Cargo Clauses of the PICC of January 1, 1981.
—If a higher percentage or broader coverage is required, the extra premium will be for buyers' account.

As to the PICC, we wish to inform you that the PICC is a state-owned company with agents in practically all the major cities and seaports in the world. It is renowned for settling claims promptly and equitably. As far as we know, the rates they quote are among the most competitive in the industry. If you have further questions, please let us know.

We look forward to receiving orders from you.

Best regards,
Tomy Zhao

EXERCISES

Ⅰ. Fill in the blanks with the proper forms of the following expressions.

in the absence of, serve your purpose, in regard to, usual practice subject to, generally, rate, charge, await, inform

1. It's regarded as a _____ to pay 20% in advance in such deals.
2. This risk is _____ an additional premium, which should be borne by you.
3. We are _____ your shipping instructions.
4. Any increase in the _____ of freight is to be for buyers' account.
5. The extra premium will _____ to your account.

6. _____ insurance, we would like to have the shipment covered against All Risks at your end.

7. We'll cover our requirements elsewhere _____ any further information from you.

8. We wish to _____ you that we've taken out insurance with PICC under Open Policy.

9. _____ speaking, the People's Insurance Company of China Ocean Marine Cargo Clauses provide coverage of three basic risks and some additional risks.

10. I'm sure this material will _____ .

II. Supply the missing words in the blanks and translate the email into Chinese.

Dear Mr. Bright,

Regarding the question of insurance, we wish to state _____ for transactions concluded on CIF _____ our usual practice _____ to cover All Risks and War Risk for 110% of the invoice _____ . If you wish to cover other _____ that are under the Ocean Marine Cargo Clauses of the People's Insurance Company of China, we may do so _____ your behalf, but the _____ premium should be _____ by you.

The Risk of Breakage required in your letter is _____ fact included in All Risks. Therefore, it is not _____ to cover it separately.

Please contact us if you need any further information.

Best regards,

III. Translate the following sentences into Chinese.

1. Insurance is to be covered by buyers.

2. The insurance covers only WPA and War Risk. If additional insurance coverage is required, the buyer is to bear the extra premium.

3. If you wish to insure the cargo for 130% of the invoice value, the premium for the difference between 130% and 110% should be for your account.

4. Please effect insurance for your account of RMB13,200 on the goods against All Risks, from Shanghai to Los Angeles.

5. In compliance with your request, we have covered the shipment against All Risks for 110% of the invoice value with the Pacific Insurance

Company.

6. For goods sold on CIF basis insurance is to be covered by us for 110% of the invoice value against All Risks based on the warehouse to warehouse clause.

7. The risk covers the damage caused by breakage that occurs in transit.

8. Our insurance company can only entertain claims for losses that are in excess of 5% of the whole lot as the goods are covered with a franchise of 5%.

9. As you will be placing regular orders with us, we suggest that we take out an open policy for approximately $50,000 worth of product annually.

10. The rate for insurance would be 3‰ of the invoice amount.

Ⅳ. Translate the following sentences into English.

1. 如果没有你们的明确指示，我们将按一般惯例投保水渍险和战争险。

2. 如你方愿意投保破碎险，我们可以代为办理。

3. 请将装运给我们的货物投保水渍险和战争险。

4. 请按发票金额的 110% 投保一切险。

5. 至于第 345 号合约项下货物，我们将自行办理保险。

6. 我们已将你方订货按发票金额的 110% 向中国人民保险公司投保了一切险。

7. 我们可以提供此种保险，但保费略高。

8. 额外保费由你方支付。

9. 至于索赔，我们的保险公司只接受超过实际损失 5% 的部分。

10. 很遗憾，我们不能接受这一索赔，因为你们的保险没有包括破碎险。

RECAP

Language Focus	Knowledge Focus
cover insurance on... for ... against ... with ... at ...	FPA, WPA, All Risks, additional risks
insure... for ... against ... with ... as per ...	premium, premium rate insured value, insurer, the
cover, coverage	insured
in regard to, charge	PICC, OMCC
	franchise

Writing Tips

➢ Explaining insurance terms in detail，including the insurance company，the coverage，insured value，premium rate，insurance policy and other particulars

➢ Itemizing points to be covered in an email by adding subheadings

➢ Highlighting important points by underlining

Lesson 24

Asking for Additional Coverage

Asking for Additional Coverage

From: charles. wood@sandr. com
To: mingnan@mingnan. cn
Date: Mar. 30, 20—
Subject: L/C opened for S/C No. A205 and insurance

Dear Bill,

Regarding S/C No. A205 covering 3,000 **speakers**, we would like to inform you that we have established with the Bank of China in London a confirmed, irrevocable L/C No. AB2234 **amounting to Stg.** £61,500 with **validity** until 15th May.

Please **see to it that** the above-mentioned goods are shipped before the 15th of May and insured against All Risks for 150% of invoice value. We know that according to your usual practice, you insure the goods only for 10% above invoice value, therefore, the extra premium will be **for our account.**

Please arrange the insurance **as per** our request and in the meantime we await your shipping advice.

Best regards,
Charles Wood

Insurance Covered

From: mingnan@mingnan. cn
To: charles. wood@sandr. com
Date: Apr. 20, 20—
Subject: insurance covered for S/C No. A205

Dear Charles,

We are pleased to inform you that we have covered the above shipment against All Risks for 150% of the invoice value, i. e. , **GBP**92, 250. The policy is being prepared accordingly and will be **forwarded** to you by the end of this week together with our **debit note** for the extra premium.

For your information, we are making arrangements to ship the 3, 000 speakers by s. s. "Red Star" sailing on/about the 28th of April.

Best regards,

Bill Zhou

NOTES

1. additional coverage：额外的保险

2. speaker：*n.* 音箱，扬声器

3. amount to：合计，共计；等于

   Their investment amounts to ＄10m.

   他们的投资总额达一千万美元。

   Your reply amounts to a refusal of our request.

   你方答复等于拒绝了我们的请求。

4. Stg. £61,500：61500 英镑

   Stg. 是英镑 Pound Sterling 的简写；£是英镑符号

5. validity：*n.* 有效期

   We have to point out that shipment must be made within the validity of our L/C.

   我们强调一点，必须在我们信用证有效期内装船。

   valid：*a.* 有效的

   The offer is valid for 5 days.

   此报盘有效期五天。

6. see（to it）that...：务请注意（做到），确保，设法使，留意做到

   that 从句中要用一般现在时。

   Please see that all the goods against Order No. 125 are packed in cartons.

   务请注意订单 125 号项下的所有货物需用纸箱包装。

   We will see to it that we send you a full range of samples by DHL.

   我们会用敦豪快递寄去全套样品。

7. for our account：由我们支付的

   for one's account：＝for account of sb 由……支付

   The demurrage is for account of the exporter.

   滞期费由出口商支付。

   "由……支付/负担" 的常用表达方式还有：

   at one's cost/expense

   to be borne by sb.

   to be charged to one's account 等

8. as per：根据，按照

   as per our request：按我方要求

   As per our earlier discussion, the shipment should be completed before Nov. 15.

按照我们先前的讨论（结果），装运需在 11 月 15 日前完成。

9. GBP：＝the Great Britain Pound 英镑，是英镑的国际货币代码

10. the policy：指 insurance policy 保险单

11. forward：v. 寄送，运送

Two sample books have been forwarded by courier.

已快递两本样品本。

The 50 tons of iron nails will be forwarded in a few days.

50 吨铁钉不日内运出。

forwarder，forwarding agent 货运代理

12. debit note：借记通知

credit note 贷记通知

A SUPPLEMENTARY SAMPLE EMAIL

Dear Mr. Tian，

The quotation you gave us is on a CIF basis. As we are in an open cover agreement with our underwriter，we prefer that you send us a CFR quotation.

However，we would also be interested to know what benefits we are likely to get if insurance is to be covered at your end.

Best regards，
Sophie King

EXERCISES

Ⅰ. Fill in the blanks with the proper forms of the following expressions.

inform, establish, cover, accordingly, forward

1. We now _____ you that we've loaded the goods onto S. S. "Peace".

2. We have received your letter and have amended the contract _____ .

3. We'd like to inform you that we've _____ the consignment to

Shanghai.

4. After the license is approved, we'll _____ an L/C in your favor.

5. We have received your L/C No. M237 _____ the said goods. But on perusal, we find some discrepancies in it.

II. Correct the mistakes in the following sentences.

1. If you wish to cover the insurance to table-cloths against All Risks at 130% of the invoice value, you should be borne by the additional premium for the difference between 130% and 110%.

2. Please insure on the cargo against F. P. A. to our account.

3. We hope to receive the policy at £5,750 for our September shipment within the next few days.

4. The cargo sold on CFR basis shall be effected insurance by the buyers.

5. As contract No. 9927 stipulated, insurance is to be affected against 120% of the invoice value.

III. Supply the missing words in the blanks and translate the email into Chinese.

Dear Winnie,

We have received your letter of January 24 _____ us to insure your order _____ an amount of 30% _____ the invoice value.

_____ it is our usual _____ to _____ shipments for the invoice value _____ 10%, we are prepared to _____ with your request _____ getting _____ for 130% of the _____ value. But the extra _____ will be _____ your account.

Best regards,

Sherry

IV. Translate the following sentences into English.

1. 应你方要求已代为标题货物向中国人民保险公司投保一切险，保额 3200 英镑，保费由你方支付。

2. 若货物受损，你方可在货物到达后 30 天内向当地保险公司提出索赔，我们相信他们会迅速予以办理。

3. 中国人民保险公司是一家大型国有企业，享有理赔迅速，处理公正的声誉，并在全世界各主要港口及地区设有代理机构。

4. 对于按 CIF 价成交的货物，我们通常向中保按照发票金额的 110% 投保一切险和战争险，根据中保 1981 年 1 月 1 日制订的海洋运输货物保险条款办理。

5. 如系 CIF 条款，卖方应负责投保销售确认书中规定的全部险别并支付保险费。

RECAP

Language Focus	Knowledge Focus
amount to see to it that... for one's account forward	additional coverage Stg. £, GBP debit note
Writing Tips	
Asking for additional coverage: ➢ Referring to the goods for shipment ➢ Stating requirements on insurance ➢ Asking for additional coverage ➢ Instructing how the extra premium is to be paid	Covering insurance as requested: ➢ Advising the buyer of insurance arrangement as requested ➢ Sending insurance policy and debit note for extra premium

Task 8

Concluding a Transaction

Learning Objectives

To be able to write emails placing orders and confirming orders

To be able to make out the purchase order, Proforma invoice and sales contract

To get familiar with the writing plans, useful sentences and phrases of closing a deal

Lesson 25

Sending a First Order

From: Franz@tse.com
To: Sissi@rsm.com
Date: Sep. 6, 20—
Subject: order for Cotton Prints
Attachments: P. O. No. SR-1919. pdf (28K)

Dear Sissi,

Thank you for your email of 3rd Sep. sending us **patterns** of **cotton prints.** We find both the quality and prices satisfactory and are pleased to attach our **Purchase Order** No. SR-1919 for 10,000 yards.

We would like to **stress** the importance of quality. Please note that the quality of your delivery should be in accordance with that of the sample cuttings you sent us. We expect to find a good market for these prints and hope to place further and larger orders with you **in the near future.**

Our usual terms of payment are **Cash against Documents** and we hope they will be acceptable to you. Meanwhile should you wish to make inquiries concerning our **financial standing,** you may refer to our bank:

BANQUE DE FRANCE
PARIS-BASTILLE
3 bis place de la Bastille
75004 PARIS
FRANCE

Please send us your Sales Contract in duplicate.

Best regards,
Franz

NOTES

1. pattern：*n.* 图案，花稿

2. cotton prints：*n.* 印花布

3. Purchase Order：购货单，客户订单，简写为 P. O. 、P/O

   order：*n.* 订单；所订的货

   initial/first order 首笔订单，第一笔订单

   trial order 试订单

   fresh/new order 新订单

   duplicate order 重复订单

   repeat order 续订单

   to accept/entertain an order 接受订单

   to decline/refuse an order 拒绝订单

   to fulfill/perform/carry out an order 执行订单

   to complete/finish an order 完成订单

   place an order with sb. for sth. 向某人订购某种货物

   We are pleased to place a trial order with you for 100 overhead projectors.

   我们高兴地向你方试订 100 台投影仪。

   We will place larger orders with you for Good Boy Brand Children's Bicycles.

   我们将向你方大量订购好孩子牌儿童自行车。

   Your order will be shipped no later than June this year.

   你方订货将不迟于今年 6 月装运。

   order：*v.* 订购

   We are prepared to order 2,000 footballs from you.

   我们打算向你方订购两千只足球。

   If you order immediately，we can probably collect that much.

   如你方立即订购，我方也许能收集到此数量。

4. stress：*v.* /*n.* 强调

   We'd like to stress the importance of the user-friendliness of the software.

   我们想强调一下软件容易操作的重要性。

   In their last letter they have stressed that the quality of their products is the best in this line.

   在上一封信中，他们强调说他们产品的质量在同类中是最好的。

5. in the near future：在不久的未来

   Owing to the advance in the cost，we shall have to raise our prices in the near future.

由于成本上涨，我们不久将提高价格。

6. Cash against Documents：交单付现，简写为 CAD

7. financial standing：财务状况

As to our financial standing and credit，we refer you to our bank.

关于我公司的资信情况，请向我方银行了解。

A SUPPLEMENTARY SAMPLE EMAIL

Dear Yang，

We are pleased to let you know your samples have passed our evaluation. We are now placing an order with you for the following：

Model 01：10000pcs@USD3/pc

Model 02：14000pcs@USD4.5/pc

Other terms remain the same as what we've discussed in previous emails.

Please establish a P/I for our approval.

With best regards，

Morris

EXERCISES

Ⅰ. **Fill in the blanks with variations of the words "regard" or "result".**

1. In _____ to S/C No. 1378，please ship the goods without delay.

2. We know nothing _____ the market conditions there.

3. As _____ your suggestion，we shall revert to it later.

4. You should be responsible for the loss _____ from the delay in opening the relative L/C.

5. As a _____ of our close cooperation，substantial business has been concluded to our mutual satisfaction.

Ⅱ. **Fill in the blanks with the proper forms of the following expressions.**

satisfactory，in the near future，attach，stress，
in accordance with，note，expect，should，concerning，refer to

1. We hope very much to find a _____ solution to the problem.

2. Please _____ a curriculum vitae （简历）to your letter of application.

3. We _____ our offer of June 1 for 1,000 Fuji Digital Cameras.

4. We would like to _____ the importance of an appealing logo（商品标识）.

5. They _____ the consumers' growing demand for quicker service.

6. We hope more business can be concluded _____ .

7. We _____ that there will be a lot of applicants for this job.

8. Our goods are packed strictly _____ international packing standards.

9. _____ you ever need anything，please don't hesitate to contact me.

10. I've had a letter from the tax authorities _____ my tax payments.

Ⅲ. Translate the following sentences into Chinese.

1. Should your price be found competitive，and delivery date acceptable，we intend to place a large order with you.

2. We look forward to placing further orders with you，and trust that you will make every effort to meet our requirements.

3. As we believe we can sell large quantities in this market，we give you a repeat order for 1,000 doz. .

4. Please keep us posted of the developments in your market.

5. We will persuade our manufacturer to accept this order for an earlier shipment as requested by you.

6. Attached is our Order♯08 with full instructions covering shipping and packing.

7. We look forward to your confirmation of our order and your affirmative reply to our new arrangement of payment.

8. We need these goods urgently and have to request you to send the S/C at once.

9. We would do our best to push the sale on your behalf if you are disposed to entertain our commission rate.

10. Sales can be done in a mode you like，either on consignment or through placing orders with you.

Ⅳ. Translate the following sentences into English.

1. 如果你方能供应一级核桃仁，我们准备购买 50 公吨，即期装运。

2. 兹随附一份试购订单，如果货物达到我们预期的质量，不久将续订。

请立即办理这一订单为盼。

3. 如果你方能设法减价，比方说 2%，我们准备再向你方订购 500 台三星（Samsung）微波炉。

4. 如果这第一份订单执行得令人满意，我们会再向你方订购。

5. 货物品质优良，包装精美，一定会在美国市场受到欢迎。

Ⅴ. **Writing task.**

Please refer to Task B5 on Page 335.

RECAP

Language Focus	Knowledge Focus
order（*v.* /*n.*）	cotton prints
place an order with sb. for sth.	Purchase Order（P. O，P/O）
stress	pattern
in the near future	CAD
refer to the bank	financial standing

Writing Tips	

➢ Confirming quality and price

➢ Sending a first order，stating order number and goods ordered

➢ Stressing what the buyer concerns，i. e. quality，timely shipment，etc.

➢ Stating the payment terms

➢ Asking for S/C

Lesson 26

Confirming an Order

From: Aurora@sb. com
To: Philip@ft. com
Date: Sep. 19, 20—
Subject: order confirmation

Dear Philip,

We are pleased to receive your order of 18th Sep. for tablecloth and welcome you as one of our customers.

We confirm supply of 10,000 dozen tablecloth at the prices stated in your email and will arrange for delivery by **the first available steamer** upon receipt of your L/C. We feel confident that when the goods **reach** you, you will be completely satisfied with them at the prices offered.

The **draft contract** is being **drawn up** and will be **submitted** to you for approval as soon as it is ready. We hope the **conclusion** of this deal will **pave the way for** further friendly cooperation between us and **mark** the beginning of a happy working relationship.

Best regards,
Aurora

NOTES

1. the first available steamer：第一艘便轮

2. reach：*v.* 到达；达成

   We are taking all necessary steps for the opening of the L/C and hope it will reach you in a week or so.

   我们正采取一切措施开立信用证，希望它一周左右抵达你处。

   We hope we can meet each other half way and reach an agreement.

   我们希望咱们各让一半达成协议。

3. draft contract：合同草案，草约

   draft：*n.* 草稿，草案，初稿

   They asked us to check the（first）draft of the contract.

   他们要求我们审查一下合同的初稿。

   draft：*v.* 起草，草拟（同下文的 draw up）

   Draft a proposal for the project and we can discuss it at the meeting.

   请为该计划草拟一个方案，我们开会时讨论。

4. draw up：准备，起草，草拟

   We will have the contract drawn up for signature tomorrow.

   我们将把合同拟好，以便明天签字。

   "起草合同"还可以说：to draft/make out/prepare a contract

5. submit：*v.* 提交，提供

   You must submit your application before January 1st.

   你必须在 1 月 1 日之前提交申请。

   They desired that the dispute be submitted for arbitration.

   他们要求把争端提交仲裁。

   Please submit specifications，preferably with illustrations.

   请提供规格，最好有插图。

6. conclusion：*n.* 完成；商定，结论

   We look forward to the conclusion of this business.

   我们希望达成这笔交易。

   We have come to the conclusion that it is not the time to discuss this subject now.

   我们得出结论认为现在不是讨论这个问题的时候。

   conclude：*v.* 完成；得出结论

   We are glad to have concluded this transaction with you.

   我们非常高兴已和你方达成了这笔交易。

   "达成交易"的说法还有：to close/finalize/complete a deal

7. deal：*n.* 交易

We are pleased to have been able to finalize this deal with you.

我们很高兴能最终和你方达成这笔交易。

This deal is concluded to our mutual satisfaction.

交易满意地达成。

"一笔交易" 还可说 a transaction

8. pave the way for：为……铺平道路

We hope your first order will pave the way for our future dealings.

我们希望你方第一个订单将为我们今后的交易铺平道路。

Scientists hope that data from the probe will pave the way for a more detailed exploration of Mars.

科学家希望这次探索获得的数据将为进一步探索火星铺平道路。

9. mark：*n.* 标志

We hope the first transaction between us will be the mark of the beginning of our good business relations.

我们希望第一笔交易将成为我们之间良好业务关系开始的标志。

mark：*v.* 标志着，意味着，代表着

The signing of the treaty marked a major milestone on the road to European Union.

该条约的签订，是通向欧洲联盟道路上的一个里程碑。

A SUPPLEMENTARY SAMPLE EMAIL

Hi，Greta！

We have received your Order No. 123 of Aug. 1st with thanks.

We confirm supply of 10000 Seagull Brand Digital Cameras at USD60 per set CIF Los Angeles for shipment in October. Our terms of payment are 30% deposit by T/T and balance against copy of B/L.

Attached please find the approved P. O. No. 123 with our signature. We expect your T/T to start production.

Please feel free to let us know if you have any other requirements.

Best Regards，
Robert

EXERCISES

Ⅰ. Fill in the blanks with proper forms or variations of the words given below.

inquire, advantage, interest, receive

1. If you find our products of _____ to you, please let us have your specific inquiry.

2. Your quotation sheet for Bamboo Ware together with the pamphlets has been _____ with thanks.

3. We look forward to _____ your orders at the new prices and urge you to take _____ of the special discount.

4. We are writing to you to _____ about the current price of your microscopes.

5. We have received a number of _____ from our trade connections here for your new products.

6. We may do business on the basis of L/C at 60 days sight with bank _____ borne by us.

7. We thank you for your order which is now _____ our attention.

8. The garments on display at the fair were attractive; their style, in particular, _____ the visitors very much.

9. We hope that, by our joint efforts, the business between us will be promoted to our mutual _____ .

10. We regret that the goods you are _____ for are out of stock at present.

Ⅱ. Fill in the blanks with the proper forms of the following expressions.

confirm, state, available, upon receipt of, confident
reach, draw up, submit, approval, pave the way for

1. We hope our offer is satisfactory and a mutually beneficial agreement can be _____ .

2. We are enclosing a copy of our draft contract for your _____ .

3. We _____ having sold you 10,000 sets of Gree Air Conditioners.

4. The goods you asked for are out of _____ because of the huge demand.

5. We should _____ that quality is of utmost importance in your fulfillment of our orders.

6. We will _____ a pamphlet for your reference before our discussion.

7. We feel _____ that we can meet your requirements and come to terms in our mutual interest.

8. We hope this negotiation will _____ our future cooperation.

9. We will be only too pleased to send you our lowest quotations _____ your specific inquiries.

10. We will _____ the contract according to the terms agreed upon.

Ⅲ. Translate the following sentences into Chinese.

1. We are glad to have booked you order for 50 tons of Groundnuts.

2. Thank you for duplicating your order of Oct. 12 for 10,000 dozen Pillow Cases.

3. We note with pleasure that you have decided to purchase from us 1,000 metric tons of Soya Beans on the basis of our offer, to be delivered in one shipment before the end of December.

4. After examination, we find the shipment of high standard and are satisfied with the quality supplied by you.

5. Although the prevailing quotations are somewhat higher, we will accept the order on the same terms as before with a view to encouraging business.

6. We are well experienced in this line and can place orders with you in large quantities if your prices are attractive enough.

7. We think that it would be in your interest to have this deal concluded.

8. It is understood that a letter of credit in our favor covering the above-mentioned goods will be established soon.

9. We are very pleased to confirm having sold to you 100 tons of News Print.

10. We thank you for all the efforts you've made toward closing a deal.

Ⅳ. Translate the following sentences into English.

1. 我们很高兴地确认已从你方买进 50 公吨红小豆，10 月或 11 月份船期。

2. 兹确认你方 1234 号订单，希望尽快开来信用证。

3. 兹确认已售给你方一万只斯伯丁（Spalding）篮球，请告包装要求。

4. 合同草本正在草拟，即将寄出。

5. 由于双方共同努力，我们达成了交易，希望这是我们之间贸易的良好开端。

V. Writing task.

Please refer to Task A8-1 on Page 322.

RECAP

Language Focus	Knowledge Focus
conclude a transaction close/finalize/complete a deal reach, draw up, submit pave the way for, mark	the first available steamer draft contract

Writing Tips

➢ Appreciating buyers' order
➢ Confirming the ordered items and terms
➢ Reinforcing buyers' confidence in the purchase by quality warranty
➢ Drafting the contract for approval

Lesson 27

Sending a Proforma Invoice

Sending an Order

From: Fitzwilliam@Jan. com
To: Elizabeth@Austin. com
Date: Sep. 6, 20—
Subject: P/O for Cashmere Coats
Attachments: P/O No. FT-106. pdf (1. 4M)

Dear Elizabeth,

Thanks for your quotation sheet and samples. Both the price and quality are satisfactory. We now place **a trial order** for 1000 pieces.

For your information, Women's Cashmere Coats are in great demand in Toronto and prices are much high. But the customers here are very selective. Therefore, we must stress the importance of quality and design. If these coats are of superior quality and modern design, we are sure they will **have a good market** in Toronto.

Attached is our **P/O** No. FT-106. Please send us your **P/I** as soon as possible.

Best regards,
Fitzwilliam

Sending a Proforma Invoice

| From: Elizabeth@Austin.com |
| To: Fitzwilliam@Jan.com |
| Date: Sep. 8, 20— |
| Subject: P/I No. PAP-109 for P/O No. FT-106 |
| Attachments: P/I No. PAP-109. pdf (1. 2M) |

Dear Fitzwilliam,
Thank you for your P/O No. PAP-109 and your efforts.

We confirm having booked your order for 1000 pieces of Women's Cashmere Coats. You may rest assured that our products are of excellent quality and **exquisite workmanship.** We trust they will enjoy fast sales at your end.

Attached is our P/I. No. PAP-109. Please **sign** it back and arrange 30% deposit as soon as possible so that we may make production.

Thank you in advance for your cooperation.

Best regards,
Elizabeth

ATTACHMENT

CAMELLIA GARMENTS CORPORATION

Room 2901, Shangri-La Mansion, 209 Donghai Road, Qingdao 266000,
P. R. CHINA
TEL: 0532-88761006   FAX: 0532-88761007

PROFORMA INVOICE

TO: MAPLE TRADING CO., LTD.   INVOICE NO.: PAP-109

    129 QUEEN ST., TORONTO, CANADA   INVOICE DATE SEP.6, 20—

TERMS OF PAYMENT: BY T/T WITH 30% DEPOSIT, 70% AFTER RECEIPT OF
                     FAXING COPY OF B/L
PORTOF LOADING: QINGDAO, CHINA
PORT OF DESTINATION: TORONTO, CANADA
TIME OF DELIVERY: WITHIN 30 DAYS AFTER RECEIPT OF 30% DEPOSIT

Marks and Numbers	Description of goods	Quantity	Unit Price	Amount (CIF TORONTO)
MAPLE TORONTO NO. 1-100	ART. NO. 1-101 WOMEN'S CASHMERE COATS 1-102 WOMEN'S CASHMERE COATS 1-103 WOMEN'S CASHMERE COATS	600 PCS 200 PCS 200 PCS	USD100.00/PC USD90.00/PC USD90.00/PC	USD60,000.00 USD18,000.00 USD18,000.00
			TOTAL AMOUNT:	USD96,000.00

TOTAL VALUE: SAY U. S. DOLLARS NINETY-SIX THOUSAND ONLY

BENEFICIARY: CAMELLIA GARMENTS CORPORATION
                 RM2901, SHANGRI-LA MANSION, 209 DONGHAI ROAD,
                 QINGDAO 266000, P. R. CHINA
ADVISING BANK: BANK OF CHINA, QINGDAO BRANCH
                 160 ZHONGSHAN ROAD, QINGDAO, CHINA
A/C NO.:   668763211866129

                        CAMELLIA GARMENTS CORPORATION
                 RM2901, SHANGRI-LA MANSION, 209 DONGHAI ROAD
                          QINGDAO 266000, P. R. CHINA

NOTES

1. trial order：试订单

   We are glad to send you our trial order for 10，000 dozen embroidered table cloth.

   我们高兴地寄去我方关于一万打绣花桌布的试订单。

   If your price is reasonable，we will place a trial order with you.

   如你方价格合理，我们将向你方试订。

2. cashmere coats：羊绒大衣

3. have a good market：找到好销路，有个好市场

4. P/O：Purchase Order 买方订单，客户订单，订购单

   As the market is advancing，we recommend you send us your P/O soon.

   因市价正在上涨，我们建议你方速寄买方订单。

5. P/I：Proforma Invoice：形式发票

   常见发票种类还有：

   Commercial Invoice 商业发票

   Customs Invoice 海关发票

   Consular Invoice 领事发票

6. book sb's order：接订，接受某人订货

   We are pleased to book your order for 1,000 Mu Lan Brand Motorcycles.

   我们高兴地接受你方 1000 辆木兰牌摩托车的订货。

   比较：book sth. with sb.＝place an order with sb. for sth. 向某人订货

   We are going to book 10，000 cases of Sprite with the Coca-Cola Company for this event.

   为这次活动，我们打算向可口可乐公司订购一万箱雪碧。

7. exquisite workmanship：工艺精良，工艺也可以叫 craftsmanship

8. sign... back：签字并退回，会签。相当于 counter-sign（详解见 Lesson 28）

A SUPPLEMENTARY SAMPLE EMAIL

Dear Mr. Churchill,
We are very pleased having concluded this transaction.

Kindly find our P/I attached in excel file, and sign it back if everything is OK.

The total volume is only 22CBM. Please add a few items to fully fill a 20GP, i. e. 27. 5CBM. Volume calculation formula has already been inserted

Please inform us as soon as 30% deposit has been made by T/T so that we may make arrangements for production.

Best regards,
Macadam

EXERCISES

I. **Fill in the blanks with the most suitable word from the four choices given.**

1. We are pleased to inform you that the first shipment proves _____ .
   A. satisfy   B. satisfied   C. satisfactory   D. satisfaction
2. We confirm _____ your order No. 789 for 10,000 dozen women's blouses.
   A. to have received   B. having received
   C. to receive   D. receiving
3. If your prices are found _____, we intend to _____ a large order with you.
   A. accept, put   B. acceptable, place
   C. accept, allow   D. acceptable, admit
4. As the goods are out of stock, we are unable to _____ your order.
   A. admit   B. place   C. receive   D. entertain
5. We assure you that we will ship the goods _____ the least possible delay.
   A. for   B. at   C. without   D. with
6. Please sign and return one copy to us _____ our record.

A. for   B. at   C. by   D. with

7. The L/C terms should be _____ exact conformity _____ the stipulations in our S/C.

  A. in，of   B. in，with   C. with，for   D. with，of

8. We believe the goods will reach you _____ due course.

  A. in   B. with   C. at   D. for

9. We will certainly keep your quotation sheet _____ file for future reference.

  A. on   B. in   C. at   D. for

10. The buyer shall open an irrevocable L/C _____ a bank acceptable to the seller.

  A. at   B. in   C. with   D. for

Ⅱ. Translate the following sentences into Chinese.

1. Should you be able to reduce your price by 2%，we could probably place an order with you.

2. All products should strictly conform to Chinese export standards.

3. While we appreciate your order，we feel it necessary to point out that the prices have already been increased to USD100 per dozen.

4. As the goods are out of stock at present，we have to decline your order.

5. Please make sure that our order is executed without any delay.

6. We hope the goods under your order No. FT-118 will reach you in perfect condition.

7. In case an order amounts to EUR5，000，we'd allow a special discount of 3%.

8. We are pleased to inform you that our clients are quite satisfied with your first shipment.

9. We are glad having concluded 10，000 pairs Double Happiness table tennis bats.

10. We hope the first deal will bring us more transactions in future.

Ⅲ. Translate the following sentences into English.

1. 我们对你方样品非常满意，现向你们首次订购1000台。

2. 如果你方产品质优价廉，我们相信它们在美国会有一个好市场。

3. 我们想强调价格和包装的重要性。

4. 因我方大豆目前缺货，抱歉不得不谢绝你方订单。

5. 如你方价格适中，我们将大量订货。

6. 我们向你方保证，我们货物的质量一定与样品一致。

7. 我方玩具熊猫需求甚旺，建议你方速下订单。

8. 兹随附我方形式发票 126 号，请查收。

9. 敬请寄来你方形式发票以便我方办理 30％预付款。

10. 兹告知我方同意电汇的付款方式，但你方需预付 50％货款。

Ⅳ. **Writing task.**

Please refer to Task A1-10 on Page 325.

RECAP

Language Focus	Knowledge Focus
book sb's order exquisite workmanship	Proforma Invoice (P/I) trial order
Writing Tips	
Sending an Order： ➢ Approving price and quality ➢ Sending P/O ➢ Stressing the importance of quality and design. ➢ Asking for P/I ➢ Looking forward to future orders	Sending a Proforma Invoice： ➢ Appreciating P/O ➢ Confirming the order ➢ Sending P/I ➢ Expressing confidence in quality and sales ➢ Asking for payment

Lesson 28

Counter-signature

Sending a Sales Contract

From: Vivian@Lee. com
To: Laurence@Olv. com
Date: Aug. 18, 20—
Subject: Order No. 128
Attachment: S/C No. ZC-108. pdf (1. 4M)

Dear Laurence,

We have booked your Order No. 128 for 250W Poly Solar Panels and are sending you herewith our Sales Contract No. ZC-108 **in duplicate**. Please sign and return one copy to us for our file.

It is understood that a letter of credit in our favor covering the above-mentioned goods will be established immediately. We wish to **point out** that the **stipulations** in the relevant credit should strictly **conform** to the terms stated in our Sales Contract in order to avoid subsequent amendments. You may rest assured that we shall effect shipment **with the least possible delay** upon receipt of the credit.

We appreciate your cooperation and look forward to receiving your further orders.

Best regards,
Vivian

Counter-signature

| From: Laurence@Olv. com |
| To: Vivian@Lee. com |
| Date: Aug. 19, 20— |
| Subject: RE: Order No. 128 |
| Attachment: S/C No. ZC-108. pdf (1.4M) |

Dear Vivian,

We have duly received your Sales Contract No. ZC-108 covering the 50 sets of 250W Poly Solar Panels that we have **purchased** from you. Attached please find the **duplicate** with our counter-signature. We trust the conclusion of this **transaction** marks the good beginning of pleasant business relations between us.

The relative L/C has been established with the Standard Chartered Bank, New York, in your favor. We believe it will reach you **in due course.**

Please see to it that the goods are shipped within the time stipulated in the L/C. Any delay in shipment will undoubtedly **involve** us in no small difficulties.

Thank you in advance for your cooperation.

Best regards,
Laurence

NOTES

1. counter-signature：*n.* ＝ countersignature 或 counter signature 会签，副署签名

   Attached please find the duplicate contract with our countersignature.

   兹附上我方会签的一份合同，请查收。

   countersign：*v.* 会签，副署

   Attached please find the duplicate contract countersigned by us.

   兹附上我方会签的一份合同，请查收。

2. contract：*n.* 合同

   Sales contract 销售合同，缩写为 S/C

   Sales Confirmation 销售确认书，售货确认书，缩写为 S/C

   Now everything is settled and we expect to have the contract ready for signature within a day or two.

   现在一切都已解决，合同可望在一两天内准备好由双方签字。

   Attached you will find our Sales Contract No. 123 in duplicate of which please countersign and return one copy to us for our file.

   兹随附我方销售合同 123 号一式两份请查收，请会签并退回一份以便我方存档。

   We are pleased to send you herewith our Sales Confirmation No. 123 in three originals.

   高兴地附上我方销售确认书 123 号三份正本。

   contract：*v.* 订立合同；承包

   We are pleased to contract with you for 1,000 Toy Pandas.

   我们高兴地和你方订立 1000 只玩具熊猫的合同。

   It is utterly important that shipment should be effected before the contracted deadline.

   在合同规定的期限内完成装运是至关重要的。

3. 250W Poly Solar Panel：多晶硅太阳能电池板

4. in duplicate：一式二份

   "一式……份"的说法有：

   一式二份：in duplicate, in two copies, in two fold

   一式三份：in triplicate, in three copies, in three fold

   一式四份：in quadruplicate, in four copies, in four fold

   duplicate：*n.* 一式两份中的任一份；副本

   Please return the duplicate for our records.

请退回一份，以便我方存档。

I lost the original form so they sent me a duplicate.

我丢失了表格正本，所以他们给我寄了一份副本。

duplicate：a. 完全相同的

As the wool carpets enjoy fast sales in our market，we are glad to place a duplicate order with you.

由于羊毛地毯在我市场旺销，我们高兴地向你方重复订购。

duplicate：v. 重复，复制

As our clients are quite satisfied with your products，we will duplicate our last order.

因我方客户对你方产品相当满意，我们将按上次订单重复订购。

Can you duplicate this document for me?

能不能为我复制这份文件?

5. for one's file：供某人存档

   for one's record：供某人存档

   Please return the duplicate for our file.

   请退回副本以便我方存档。

   The buyer is requested to sign and return one copy of this sales contract for the seller's file immediately after receipt of the same.

   买方在收到销售合同后，应立即会签并退回一份供卖方存档。

   相同结构的其他短语还有：

   for one's reference 供某人参考

   for one's information 供某人参考

   for one's perusal 供某人详阅

   for one's consideration 供某人考虑

6. It is understood that：不言而喻……，应该……

   It is understood that the relevant L/C is to be opened one month before the date of shipment.

   不言而喻，有关的信用证应于装船前一个月开出。

7. in our favor：以我方为受益人的（详解见 Lesson 31）

8. point out：指出

   We wish to point out the importance of sincerity in doing business.

   我们希望指出诚信在生意中的重要性。

   We have to point out that your price is much on the high side.

我们必须指出你方价格偏高。

9. stipulation：*n.* 规定

The stipulations in the relevant credit should be in strict accordance with the terms stated in our S/C.

有关信用证的规定应与我方销售合同的条款严格相符。

The transaction is concluded on the stipulation that L/C（should）be opened 30 days before the time of shipment.

这笔交易是以在装船前 30 天开出信用证为条件达成的。

stipulate：*v.* 规定

The contract stipulates payment by 30 days L/C.

合同规定付款条件为 30 天期信用证。

The L/C stipulates that shipment（should）be made not later than the end of August.

信用证规定装运不能迟于 8 月底。

10. conform：*v.* 符合，一致

It is necessary that the specifications should conform to the requirements of the customer.

规格与客户的要求相符是十分必要的。

The quality of the goods must strictly conform to the sample.

货物的质量必须严格与样品一致。

conformity：*n.* 符合，一致

in conformity with 与……一致

This is not in conformity to/with our arrangement.

这与我们的安排不符。

Before buying a pram，make sure that it is in conformity with the official safety standards.

购买婴儿车之前，要确保它符合官方的安全标准。

11. avoid：*v.* 避免

We wish to avoid putting you to extra expenses.

我们想使你方避免额外的花费。

Please cross out Art. No. 102 in order to avoid misunderstandings.

请将货号 102 划掉，以免引起误解

12. subsequent：*a.* 以后的

13. amendment：*n.* 修改（详解见 Lesson 33）

14. with the least possible delay：＝without any delay 立即，马上

We shall effect shipment with the least possible delay upon receipt of the credit.

一俟收到信用证我们将立即安排装运。

15. duly：*adv.* 适当地；及时地；预期地

Please return one copy of the contract to us duly completed with your signature.

请签署本合同后寄回一份。

We hope the shipment will duly reach you and will be to your entire satisfaction.

我们希望这批货物及时抵达你方并令你方完全满意。

16. purchase：*v.* 购买（正式）

We intend to purchase from you a large quantity of sesame oil.

我们打算从你方购买大量香油。

The museum is trying to raise enough money to purchase a painting by Van Gogh.

这家博物馆正试图筹集足够资金，以买进梵高的一幅画。

purchase：*n.* 购买（正式）；购买的东西

We will make large purchases of digital players to fill the local demand.

我们将大量购买数码播放机，以满足当地的需求。

This product may be frozen. If required，freeze it on the day of purchase.

该产品可以冷冻。如需要，可在购买当天冷冻。

How do you wish to pay for your purchases?

你想怎样支付所购物品？

Purchase Contract 购货合同，订购合同

Purchase Confirmation 购货确认书，订购确认书

Purchase Department 采购部

purchasing power 购买力

17. transaction：*n.* 交易

We regret transaction cannot be concluded at your bid, as it is far below our cost.

我们抱歉无法按你方递价达成交易，因其远远低于成本。

The commission granted for this transaction is 3% as stipulated in our S/C.

按照我方销售合同的规定，这笔交易的佣金是 3%。

transact：*v.* 完成交易

We are prepared to transact business only on these terms.

我们只按这些条件交易。

Our representative has full authority to transact negotiations on this matter.

我们的代表完全有权就此事进行谈判。

18. in due course：＝at the due time 在适当的时候，如期地

Please be assured that the goods will reach you in due course.

请放心，货物将如期抵达。

The relative L/C will be established in due course.

有关信用证将按时开出。

19. involve：*v.* 使陷于，使卷入，牵涉

We hope this delay will not involve you in any inconvenience.

我们希望此次耽搁没有给你方带来任何的不便。

The extra insurance premium involved will be forthe buyer's account.

所造成的额外保险费用由买方负担。

In addition to visible trade，which involves the import and export of goods，there is also invisible trade，which involves the exchange of service between nations.

除了涉及货物进出口的有形贸易，还有涉及国家之间劳务交换的无形贸易。

SUPPLEMENTARY SAMPLE EMAILS

Dear Jimmy，

Thank you for your order No. 209 of June 6th for 20,000 dozen "Welo" Brand Animal Plush Toys. Attached is our S/C No. TD209 of which please counter-sign and return one copy to us for our file.

We'll arrange production upon receipt of your 30% deposit by T/T.

Any request for further assistance or information will receive our immediate attention.

Best regards,
Clinton

Hi Clinton,

Please see the counter-signed S/C No. TD209 in attached pdf file.

We are possible to arrange 30% deposit by this week. Please let me know when you've received it.

Best regards,
Jimmy

EXERCISES

Ⅰ. Fill in the blanks with the proper forms of the following expressions.

> duly, purchase, duplicate, in due course, conform to
> see to it that, delay, involve, avoid, assure

1. Please _____ L/C terms are in strict accordance with the stipulations in our S/C.
2. Please return the _____ with our counter-signature for our records.
3. Your Order of June 6th has been _____ received.
4. Please note that any _____ in shipment will undoubtedly place us in an awkward position.
5. As the amount _____ is less than STG1,000, we will accept Documents Against Payment.
6. In order to _____ or reduce significant losses to a business, emergency managers should work to identify and anticipate potential risks, hopefully to reduce their probability of occurring.
7. We are pleased to confirm having _____ from you 10,000 Racing Bikes.
8. We have instructed our bank to open the covering L/C and hope it will reach you _____ .
9. We can _____ you that you will be entirely satisfied with the superior quality and attractive design of our products.
10. The quality of the goods should strictly _____ that of the sample.

Ⅱ. **Translate the following sentences into Chinese.**

1. We confirm having booked your order for 10,000 sets of Whirlpool（惠而浦）washing machines.

2. It is understood that the terms in the L/C should in exact accordance with the stipulations in the S/C.

3. We will make shipment with the least possible delay upon receipt of your confirmation.

4. You may rest assured that goods will reach you in time and will prove satisfactory to you.

5. To avoid anything missing，we submit our draft contract for your perusal.

6. We are pleased to have put through this business with you.

7. We have received with thanks your quotation of Jun. 1st and are pleased to send you the following order，which we trust will receive your best attention.

8. Please supply the goods in strict conformity with the particulars given，any deviation from which will be at your own risks，unless agreed by us.

9. We shall be grateful for prompt delivery as the goods are needed urgently.

10. We thank you for giving us a trial and promise that your order will be dealt with promptly and carefully.

Ⅲ. **Translate the following sentences into English.**

1. 你公司6月1日关于一万个户外折椅（Outdoor Folding Chair）的订单已收到。兹随附第346号销售确认书，请回签一份以便存档。

2. 我已接受你方85号订单订购货号1002号印花布10万码。请告颜色搭配并按合同规定的条款开立以我方为抬头的有关信用证。

3. 我们得悉上述货物的有关信用证即将开出。请放心，一俟收到你方信用证，我方将尽早安排第一艘可以订得舱位的轮船装运。

4. 你方毛毯在我地很畅销，我方客户想向你方按上次订单重复订货。

5. 我们已收到向你们购进两万打Calvin Klein男式衬衣的合同SDG0306号。

Ⅳ. **Writing task.**

Please refer to Task A8-2 on Page 323.

RECAP

Language Focus	Knowledge Focus
in duplicate, duplicate for one's file, in due course conform to, in conformity with stipulate, purchase, transaction, involve	Sales Contract (S/C) in duplicate counter-signature

Writing Tips	
Sending a Sales Contract: ➢ Sending a S/C ➢ Asking for counter-signature ➢ Stressing the conformity of L/C terms with S/C ➢ Assuring buyers of timely delivery ➢ Looking forward to future orders	Counter-signature: ➢ Appreciating S/C ➢ Counter-signing the S/C ➢ Advising the seller of the opening of L/C ➢ Stressing the importance of timely delivery ➢ Expressing thanks

Lesson 29

A Specimen of Sales contract

SALES CONTRACT（ORIGINAL）

Contract No.：ZV109　　　　　　　　　Date：Sep. 19，20—

Signed at：Nanjing，China

Sellers：ZEST Outdoor Sports（Jiangsu）Import & Export Corporation

　　　　18-7 Dasifu Road，Qinhuai District，Nanjing 210000，China

Buyers：Pacific Trading Co.，Ltd

　　　　118 Green Road，New York，U. S. A.

This Sales Contract is made by and between the Sellers and the Buyers whereby the Sellers agree to sell and the Buyers agree to buy the undermentioned goods according to the terms and conditions stipulated below：

1.

Name of Commodity	Quantity	Unit Price	Total Amount
Canvas Folding Chairs with Wooden Frame	6,000 pieces	USD10. 00 per piece CIF New York	USD60,000. 00

2. Packing：One piece in a box，10 boxes to a carton

3. Shipping Marks：

PTC

New York

No. 1-600

4. Time of Shipment：During November，20—，allowing partial shipments and transshipment.

5. Port of Shipment：Shanghai，China.

6. Port of Destination：New York，U. S. A.

7. The Sellers are allowed to load **5% more or less** and the price shall be calculated according to the unit price.

8. Insurance: To be covered by the Sellers for 110% of the invoice value against All Risks and War Risk as per the relevant Ocean Marine Cargo Clauses of the People's Insurance Company of China. If other coverage or an additional insurance amount is required, the Buyers must have the consent of the Sellers before shipment, and the additional premium is to be borne by the Buyers.

9. Terms of Payment: The Buyers shall open with a bank acceptable to the Sellers an irrevocable Letter of Credit at sight to reach the Sellers 30 days before the time of shipment specified, valid for negotiation in China until the 15th day after the aforesaid time of shipment.

10. Commodity Inspection: It is mutually agreed that the **Certificate of Quality** issued by the **State General Administration for Quality Supervision and Inspection and Quarantine** of P. R. China at the port of shipment shall be taken as the basis of delivery.

11. **Discrepancy** and Claim: Any claim by the Buyers on the goods shipped shall be filed within 30 days after the arrival of the goods at the port of destination and supported by a survey report issued by a surveyor approved by the Sellers. Claims in respect to matters within the responsibility of the insurance company or of the shipping company will not be considered or entertained by the Sellers.

12. **Force Majeure:** If shipment of the contracted goods is prevented or delayed in whole or in part due to Force Majeure, the Sellers shall not be liable for non-shipment or late shipment of the goods under this Contract. However, the Sellers shall notify the Buyers by fax or email immediately and furnish a certificate issued by the China Council for the Promotion of International Trade attesting such event or events.

13. **Arbitration:** All disputes arising out of the performance of or relating to this Contract shall be settled amicably through negotiation. In case no settlement can be reached through negotiation, the case shall then be submitted to the **Foreign Economic and Trade Arbitration Commission** of the **China Council for the Promotion of International Trade,** Beijing, China, for arbitration in accordance with its Rules of Procedure. The award of the arbitration is final and binding upon both parties.

THE SELLERS	THE BUYERS
林新明	*Armand Duval*
Chief Executive Office	*President*

ZEST Outdoor Sports（Jiangsu）
Import & Export Corporation
China National Light Industrial Products
Import & Export Corporation
18-7 Dasifu Road，Qinhuai District
Nanjing 210000，China

Pacific Trading Co.，Ltd
118 Green Road，New York，
U. S. A.

NOTES

1. Canvas Folding Chairs with Wooden Frame：木质扶手帆布折叠椅

2. 5％ more or less：5％的溢短装

    more or less clause 溢短装条款

    Please insert the wording "5％ more or less allowed" in the quantity clause.

    请在数量条款中插入"允许溢短装 5％"的字句。

    You are required to add "more or less clause" to the covering L/C.

    我们要求你方在有关信用证中加上溢短装条款。

3. Certificate of Quality：质量检验证书

4. State General Administration for Quality Supervision and Inspection and Quarantine of P. R. China：简称为 AQSIQ，国家质量监督检验检疫总局

5. discrepancy：*n.* 不同，不符

    There is some discrepancy in numbers.

    在数字上有一些不符。

    Such small discrepancies between the products and the sample are normal and permissible.

    这种产品与样品之间的些微不同是在正常的允许范围之内。

6. Force Majeure：不可抗力，人力不可抗拒

    In the event of Force Majeure，we shall not be held responsible for the late delivery or non-delivery of the goods.

    如果发生不可抗力事件，我方将不为延期交货或未交货而承担责任。

7. arbitration：*n.* 仲裁

    In case negotiation fails，the dispute should be submitted to arbitration.

如果协商不能解决，争议将被提交仲裁。

arbitration clause 仲裁条款

arbitration committee 仲裁委员会

voluntary arbitration 自愿仲裁

compulsory arbitration 强制仲裁

arbitrate：*v.* 仲裁

to arbitrate a dispute：仲裁一项争议

arbitrator：*n.* 仲裁人

arbitral：*a.* 仲裁的

arbitral award 仲裁裁决

8. Foreign Economic and Trade Arbitration Commission：对外经济贸易仲裁委员会

9. China Council for the Promotion of International Trade（CCPIT）：中国国际贸易促进委员会

EXERCISES

Ⅰ. Translate the following Sales Contract into Chinese.

Sales Contract

Sellers：Shanghai Oriental
Import & Export Corporation
128 Huangpu Road，Shanghai，China
Buyers：Brothers Grimm Co.，Ltd.
26 Sunlight Ave.，Hamburg，Germany

No.：FSO126
Date：Aug. 1，20—
Signed at：Shanghai

The undersigned Sellers and Buyers have agreed to close the following transaction according to the terms and conditions stipulated below：

1.

Name of Commodity	Specification	Quantity	Unit Price	Total Amount
Green Tea	First Grade	1,000 kgs	USD20.00 per kg CFR Hamburg	USD20,000.00

（The Sellers are allowed to load 5% more or less and the price shall be calculated according to the unit price.）

2. Packing：500 grams in a tea box，100 boxes to a carton lined with damp-proof paper.

3. Shipping Marks：At Sellers' option

4. Time of Shipment：During September/October，20—.

5. Loading Port and Destination：From China ports to Hamburg.

6. Insurance：To be effected by the Buyers.

7. Terms of Payment：By confirmed, irrevocable, transferable, divisible L/C with transshipment and partial shipments allowed, and with 5% more or less in quantity and value permissible, payable at sight and valid in China till the 15th day after shipment.

General Terms and Conditions

1. The Buyers shall establish the covering Letter of Credit before August 15，20—，failing which the Sellers reserve the right to rescind this Contract without further notice, and lodge a claim for direct losses sustained, if any.

2. Quality/Quantity Discrepancy：In case of quality discrepancy, claim should be raised by the Buyers within 30 days after arrival of the goods at the port of destination; while for quantity discrepancy, claim should be raised by the Buyers within 15 days after arrival of the goods at the port of destination. It is understood that the Sellers shall not be liable for any discrepancy of the goods shipped due to causes for which the Insurance Company, Shipping Company, other transportation organization or Post Office is liable.

3. The Sellers shall not be held liable for failure or delay in delivery of the entire lot or a portion of the goods under this Confirmation in consequence of any Force Majeure incidents.

4. The Buyers are requested to countersign and return one copy of this Sales Confirmation immediately after receipt of the same. Objection, if any, should be raised by the Buyers within 5 days after receipt of this Confirmation, in the absence of which it is understood that the Buyers have accepted the terms and conditions of the Sales Confirmation.

Sellers：   Buyers

李姜慧   *Alain Delon*

General Manager   *Chairman*

Shanghai Oriental I/E Corp.   Brothers Grimm Co. ，Ltd.

Import & Export Corporation   26 Sunlight Ave. ，

128 Huangpu Road，Shanghai，China   Hamburg, Germany

Ⅱ. Fill in the contract form in English based on the give information.

卖方：山东物产进出口公司 （Shandong Native Produce Imp/Exp Corporation）

买方：法国福斯食品公司

成交时间：20—年 9 月 2 日

交易内容：

100 公吨花生米，20—年产大路货（FAQ 20— crop），每公吨成本、运费加保险费到福斯（FOS SUR MER）价格 600 美元，双层麻袋装，每袋净重 100 公斤。船期为 20—年 10 月由青岛到福斯。由卖方根据中国保险条款按发票金额的 110%投保水渍险和偷窃提货不着险。装船唛头由卖方选定。付款条件是在装船前一个月开出以卖方为受益人的不可撤销的信用证，凭即期汇票付款。

CONTRACT

No.

Sellers：

Buyers：

This Contract is made by and between the Buyers and the Sellers, whereby the Buyers agree to buy and the Sellers agree to sell the under mentioned commodity according to the terms and conditions stipulated below：

Commodity：

Specifications：

Quantity：

Unit Price：

Total Value：

Packing：

Shipping Marks：

Insurance：

Time of Shipment：

Port of Shipment：

Port of Destination：

Terms of Payment：

Done and signed in _____ on this _____ day of _____ ， _____ .

Ⅲ. Fill in the contract form in English based on the emails exchanged between the buyers and sellers.

CONTRACT

No.

Sellers：

Buyers：

This Contract is made by and between the Buyers and the Sellers， whereby the Buyers agree to buy and the Sellers agree to sell the under mentioned commodity according to the terms and conditions stipulated below：

Commodity：

Specifications：

Quantity：

Unit Price：

Total Value：

Packing：

Shipping Marks：

Insurance：

Time of Shipment：

Port of Shipment：

Port of Destination：

Terms of Payment：

Done and signed in _____ on this _____ day of _____ ， _____ .

Email 1

From: Aaron _ Wu@tyarts. com

To: Claudia@Claven. com

Date: June 2, 20—

Subject: establishing business relations

Attachments: photos

Dear Miss Claudia Venegas,

We are writing to reintroduce ourselves as Shandong Tianyi Arts &. Crafts I/E Co. , Ltd. . We are glad to have met you at the Canton Fair where you took some interest in our products.

We are a manufacturer and exporter of Arts &. Crafts, including decorations, ornaments, promotions and Christmas items, etc. . Most of our products are exported to American and European markets. Because our factory is located in the Free Trade Zone, we enjoy some favorable policies from the government. Therefore we can provide more competitive prices than other suppliers.

We hereby send you some photos of our products for your reference. Should any of them be of interest to you, please let us know.

Best Regards,

Aaron Wu

Shandong Tianyi Arts &. Crafts I/E Co. , Ltd

65 Hongkong West Road, Qingdao 266071, China

Tel: 86-532-82748906

Fax: 86-532-82748909

Email: inquiry@tyarts. com. cn

Website: www. tyarts. com

Email 2

From: Claudia@Claven. com

To: Aaron _ Wu@tyarts. com

Date: June 3, 20—

Subject: DSA302 and DSA303

Hello, Aaron!

We thank you for your letter and photos. We are interested in items DSA302 and DSA303, but we need you to send samples. Our FedEx account is 19623186-2.

Awaiting your prompt reply.

Best regards

Claudia Venegas

Claven Stationery S. A. 20 Masquire Place

Paris, France

Tel: 33-1-62368126

Fax: 33-1-62368129

E-mail: claudia@claven. com

Website: www. claven. com

Email 3

Dear Claudia,

Thanks for your prompt reply.

We have sent the samples to you today. We guess you will receive them in three days.

But we have to mention that the design is for one of our previous customers. Please inform us of your own design when you send us orders.

Sincerely,

Aaron Wu

Email 4

Hello, Aaron!

Once again thanks for your message. Just yesterday we received your samples. Thanks and we will work on the order and get back to you.

My best regards,

Claudia Venegas

Email 5

Dear Claudia,

Good morning!

In your previous email you agreed to work on the order and get back to me, but so far we haven't received your order.

Do you still need these picture frames? If so, we can guarantee the best quality and the most competitive prices, because we have our own factory with advanced equipment. We also have a long and stable relationship with wood suppliers, and we can get the best prices. So we know how to cut cost without affecting the quality & delivery date.

We are sure our first deal will be successful!

Sincerely yours,

Aaron

Email 6

Hello, Aaron!

Our designs are ready. We have sent them to you today by courier.

Will you please quote us your best prices for items DSA302 and DSA303? We need $1 \times 20'$ container to begin with. Please also state your terms of payment.

Please reply as soon as possible.

Claudia Venegas

Email 7

Dear Claudia,

Thank you for your prompt reply. The following is our quotation for the quantity of $1 \times 20'$ container:

DSA302: USD3. 30/piece FOB Ningbo

DSA303: USD3. 33/piece FOB Ningbo

Each one in a shrink pack, 20 pieces packed in a double-layer corrugated carton (dimensions: 51. 5 cm $\times$ 61. 5 cm $\times$ 33 cm) .

Payment by sight L/C or T/T. In case of T/T, we need 30% deposit before production, 70% after faxing copy of B/L.

We believe the above is acceptable.

Awaiting your favorable reply.

Yours,

Aaron

Email 8

Dear Aaron,

We confirm your offer of yesterday. The quantities for our order are:

DSA302: 3000 pieces

DSA303: 3000 pieces

We prefer to pay by T/T and we agree to your T/T terms.

When is your best delivery date?

Please also tell me how many pieces you usually pack per carton and per inner box.

Best regards,

Claudia Venegas

Email 9

Dear Claudia,

The prices we offered is for picture frames packed in cartons of 20 pieces each, without inner box. However, if you insist on inner boxes, they are subject to a cost of 9 cents each.

The following is our T/T remittance routine:

Bank: Bank of China, Qingdao Branch

36 Zhongshan Road, Qingdao, China

In favor of: Shandong Tianyi Arts & Crafts I/E Corp.

Address: 65 Hongkong Road, Qingdao, China

A/C No.: 653123687231612

Our delivery date will be 20 days after we receive your 30% deposit.

Please reply soon, stating the port of destination.

Best regards,

Aaron

Email 10

Hi, Aaron!

We accept the 9 cents extra cost for inner boxes.

Our port of destination is Nice.

Please prepare a sales contract for us to sign.

Best regards,

Claudia

RECAP

Language Focus	Knowledge Focus
discrepancy arbitration	more or less clause, certificate of quality, AQSIQ Force Majeure discrepancy, arbitration, CCPIT

Writing Tips

Formatting a contract:
➢ Headlining the contract
➢ Telling names of involved parties, contract number, date and place of the contract
➢ Stipulating main clauses in the body part, including goods description, quality standard, quantity, unit price, packing, shipment, insurance, payment terms, etc.
➢ Stipulating general terms and conditions, including Force Majeure, claims, compensation, arbitration, etc.
➢ Stipulating final clauses, including contract languages, validity and signature

PART THREE

EXECUTING A CONTRACT

Task 9

Handling Payment Issues

Learning Objectives

To be able to write emails asking for paying the deposit, the balance or the contract value by T/T or L/C

To be able to check the L/C terms and write emails asking for amendment to L/C

To get familiar with the writing plans, useful sentences and phrases of payment

Lesson 30

Urging Establishment of L/C

| From: Sevener. Collins@elecon. com |
| To: Christty. Zhang@artcras. com |
| Date: May 20, 20— |
| Subject: Urging for L/C for Our S/C No. SD9806 |

Dear Christty,

With regard to the 4, 500 Electric Toasters **under** the **subject** Sales Confirmation, we would call your attention to the fact that the date of shipment is **drawing near**, but so far we still have not received your **relevant L/C.** You are requested to open the covering L/C immediately so as to enable us to make **punctual** shipment of your order.

In order to avoid subsequent amendment, please see that your L/C clauses are **in exact accordance with** the terms of our S/C.

Your prompt attention to this matter will be much appreciated.

Best regards,
Sevener Collins

NOTES

1. urge：*v.* 催促；强调，坚决主张

As the duration of their license is short，buyers urge you to hasten the shipment.

由于许可证期限短，买方催促你们赶快装船。

We urge that attention should be directed to increasing the turnover.

我们主张应集中精力扩大营业额。

We urge the importance of closer cooperation.

我们强调密切合作的重要性。

2. establishment of L/C 开立信用证

开立信用证可以说 establish an L/C，open an L/C，也可以说 issue an L/C。前两者的主语既可以是开证申请人，也可以是银行，to issue an L/C 只能用于银行开证。

We shall open/establish an L/C as soon as the contract is signed.

一签订合同我们就开立信用证。

We have arranged with the bank to issue an L/C in your favor.

我们已与银行洽商开立以你方为受益人的信用证。

3. Electric Toaster 电动烤面包机

4. under：*prep.* 在……（类别、书目、文书等）项下的

Books on Cecil Beaton will probably be under Art or Photography rather than Drama.

关于塞西尔·比顿的书很可能是在艺术或摄影类书目下，而非戏剧类。

The goods under our S/C No. XP09 have been loaded onto S. S. "Eagle".

我方 XP09 号销售合同项下的货物已装到"小鹰"号轮上。

5. subject：*n.* 标题，事由

the subject Sales Confirmation：标题（中、所列）的销售确认书

the subject goods：标题（中、所列）货物

6. draw near：快到，接近

The selling season is drawing near.

旺销季节快到了。

As Christmas draws nearer the shops start to get unbearably crowded.

随着圣诞节越来越近，商店开始变得拥挤不堪。

7. so far：到目前/那时为止，还可以说 as of now

We haven't heard from you so far.

到目前为止我们尚未收到你方来信。

Everything is in order so far.

迄今诸事顺利。

8. relevant L/C：相关的信用证

还可以说 covering L/C，relative L /C

9. enable sb. to do sth：使某人能够做某事

Establishment of L/C in time will enable us to effect prompt shipment per S. S "Dadu".

及时开证才能使我们尽快装"大都"号轮。

10. punctual：*a.* 准时的

He is punctual in paying her bills.

她按期付款。

We are looking for enthusiastic applicants who are reliable and punctual.

我们寻求那些热情的竞聘者，可靠并准时。

11. in exact accordance with . . . : 与……完全相符，与……完全一致

To avoid any possible complaint，we wish to make it clear that the goods supplied to our Order No. 051 must be in exact accordance with the samples in both quality and design.

为避免任何可能的异议，我们想说明供给我们的第 051 号订单的货物在品质和设计上必须与样品完全一致。

We regret to inform you that your shipment is not in accordance with the samples.

很遗憾，你方的船货与样品不相一致。

in accordance with 是正式的说法，通常情况下用 in accord with

The project is completely in accord with government policy.

该项目完全符合政府政策。

"与……一致；符合"还可以说：

be in conformity with . . .

be in compliance with. . .

be in line with. . .

be in agreement with. . .

A SUPPLEMENTARY SAMPLE EMAIL

Dear Alphy

We have received your email of December 20th regarding the P. O. ♯TS780 for the 2nd lot of 20,000 yards and 3rd lot of 30, 000 yards All Cotton Printed Shirting. We have got the goods ready in accordance with the provisions in the contract.

Please open the Letter of Credit in time so as to enable us to book the shipping space on M. V "Prince", a direct steamer sailing on 15th February to your port; otherwise the date of shipment has to be deferred to the end of this month. We hope you will make the best use of your time to rush your L/C.

Looking forward to your favorable reply.

Best regards,
Rocky

EXERCISES

Ⅰ. Fill in the blanks with the proper forms of the following expressions.

with regard to, subject, call one's attention to the fact that, draw near, so far, relevant, enable, avoid, see that, in exact accordance with

1. We've just received your letter of Feb. 15th and the brochure for the _____ machines.
2. _____ our email of June 25th for 1500M/T Tin Foil Sheets, _____ we have no definite information from you about delivery time.
3. We shall be very much obliged if you will effect shipment as soon as possible, thus _____ us to catch the brisk demand at the start of the season.
4. I realize the inconvenience our oversight must be causing you and will _____ we do everything possible to _____ any further delay.
5. We should like to _____ the delay in your opening of the L/C has

caused us great inconvenience.

6. If you send us the _____ details, we will be happy to suggest what specific model suits you.

7. As the Christmas Day is _____, please expedite your shipment.

8. We think it advisable for you to pay attention to the quality of your products, which must be _____ the stipulations set forth in the contract.

Ⅱ. Make a correction in each of the following.

1. As the goods of your order No. 112 <u>has</u> been ready for shipment for
   A
   quite some time, it is imperative that you <u>take</u> immediate action to
   B
   <u>have</u> the relative L/C <u>opened</u> the soonest possible.
   C   D

2. <u>To avoid</u> delay in shipment, please <u>see to it</u> that the credit <u>should open</u> at
   A   B   C
   the beginning of next month, <u>allowing</u> partial shipment.
   D

3. <u>With regards to</u> your Order No. 101, the <u>relevant</u> L/C hasn't arrived
   A   B
   here. We would, therefore, ask you to <u>give</u> this matter your
   C
   immediate <u>attention</u>.
   D

4. <u>Due to</u> unforeseen difficulties, we find it <u>impossible</u> to make shipment
   A   B
   before June 30 and would appreciate <u>you extend</u> the shipment and
   C
   <u>validity</u> of your L/C No. 005.
   D

5. <u>Should</u> you <u>are</u> able to reduce your price <u>by</u> 3%, we can probably
   A   B   C
   come to <u>terms</u>.
   D

Ⅲ. Translate the following sentences.

A. from English into Chinese

1. As stipulated in our S/C No. 762, the relevant credit should reach us

not later than the end of November.

2. Please see to it that the L/C stipulations are in exact accordance with the terms of the contract.

3. We can fulfill your order only on receipt of an irrevocable letter of credit.

4. In order to avoid any further delay, please make sure that the L/C instructions are in precise accordance with the terms of the contract.

5. We would be grateful if you would expedite establishment of the L/C so that we can ship the order on time.

B. from Chinese into English

1. 我方相信你方会确保信用证立即开立。

2. 你方信用证必须在本月底前开到，以便我方将货物装下月 10 日开往你港的直达轮。

3. 我方已收到你方 5 月 3 日电邮，获悉你方已经开立以我方为受益人的信用证。

4. 交货期日益临近，但至今我们未收到你方有关发货的消息。

5. 按照你方要求，我们很高兴接受你方以即期付款交单方式交货。

Ⅳ. **Writing task.**

Please refer to Task A1-11 on Page 327.

RECAP

Language Focus	Knowledge Focus
under，subject	establishment of L/C
enable sb. to do sth.	types of L/C
make punctual shipment	the terms of our S/C
be in exact accordance with	subsequent amendment

Writing Tips

➢ Identifying the covering S/C and the date of shipment.
➢ Stating the problem of non-receipt of L/C
➢ Urging for the buyer's action to open L/C immediately
➢ Giving instructions so as to enable the buyer to avoid subsequent amendment to L/C

Lesson 31

Advising Establishment of L/C

From: Christty. Zhang@artcras. com
To: Sevener. Collins@elecon. com
Date: May 21, 20—
Subject: L/C for S/C No. SD9806 has been opened

Dear Sevener,

This is to inform you that we have now opened an irrevocable L/C No. 302820 **in your favor** against the subject S/C for **CAD**3, 330 (Say Canadian Dollars Three Thousand Three Hundred and Thirty Only) **with** the Royal Bank of Canada, Quebec, to remain valid for **negotiation** in China until 10 Oct. .

You're **authorized** to draw at 30 days sight on the **opening bank** for **full invoice** value after shipment. Before **accepting** the draft, the bank will require you to **produce** the following documents:
1) One copy of CIF Vancouver invoice;
2) Bills of Lading in triplicate;
3) Insurance Policy/Certificate in duplicate;
4) Canada **Customs Invoice.**

We **anticipate** your first **consignment** next month.

Best regards,
Christty

NOTES

1. This is to ...：一般用于正式场合，再如：

   This is to certify that Mr. David Lue has accomplished a three-month course on E-commerce here and has achieved satisfactory academic results.

   兹证明 David Lue 先生在我处完成了三个月的电子商务课程，并取得了满意的成绩。

2. in one's favor：＝in favor of sb 以……受益人

   We will instruct our bankers to open an L/C in your favor upon receipt of your confirmation of this order.

   收到你方关于此项订货的确认后，我方即将要求银行开出以你方为受益人的信用证。

   Our L/C opened in favor of Johnson & Sons was confirmed by Midland Bank.

   我们开给 Johnson & Sons 的信用证是由 Midland Bank 保兑的。

3. CAD：Canadian dollar 加拿大元

4. with the Royal Bank of Canada：由加拿大皇家银行（开立）

   在某银行开信用证，用介词 with 或 through。

   We have opened an L/C with HSBC.

   我们已通过汇丰银行开立了信用证。

5. negotiation：*n.* 议付；谈判；磋商

   As the L/C allows us only five days for negotiation of the document，which is far from enough，we'd appreciate it very much if you could extend the negotiation period to 15 days.

   信用证只允许我们有五天的时间议付单据，这显然是不够的，因此请将议付有效期延长到 15 天。

   The agreement was reached after a series of difficult negotiations.

   该协议是经过一系列艰苦谈判之后达成的。

   After our repeated negotiations，we have succeeded in closing the business.

   经过我们再三磋商，最终达成交易。

   negotiate：*v.* 议付；谈判

   The exporters must present shipping documents when they negotiate payment with the bank.

   出口商向银行议付时，必须呈递装船单据。

The strike was caused by the management's refusal to negotiate with the unions.

这次罢工是由于管理层拒绝与工会谈判而引起的。

negotiable：*a.* 可议付的；可商量的；可转让的

A check that is not negotiable cannot be exchanged for cash and must be paid into a bank account.

一张不可议付的支票是不能兑换成现金的，只能支付到某个银行账户上。

Everything is negotiable at this stage. I'm ruling nothing out.

一切都还好商量。我并没有把话说死。

The bill of lading is non-negotiable.

该提单是不可转让的。

6. authorize：*v.* 授权，批准

We authorized my bank to pay the agent ＄1,000.

我们授权银行向代理支付了 1000 美元。

We are authorized to settle the claim on the spot.

我们被授权当场料理这项索赔。

7. opening bank：issuing bank 开证行

8. full invoice value：100％ of the invoice value 发票全额

9. accept：*v.* 承兑（票据）

acceptance：*n.* 承兑（票据）

You're requested to accept the draft drawn on you.

我们要求你们承兑向你们开具的汇票。

We will immediately present the draft for acceptance.

我们将立即呈递汇票以供承兑。

10. produce：*v.* 出示；提出

Cargoes will be examined and released when you produce the certificates issued by the authorities concerned.

当你出示有关主管机关签发的证件，货物将查验放行。

When you lodge a claim，you must produce your proofs of the statement including the necessary documents.

当你提出索赔时，必须提出说明的证据包括必要单据。

11. Canada Customs Invoice：加拿大海关发票

12. anticipate：*v.* 盼望，期待

We anticipate an increase in demand for the articles.

我们预期对这种货物的需求会增加。

13. consignment：*n.* 一批运送的货

Large consignments are arriving from our neighbouring countries.

大量的货正从邻国运到。

A SUPPLEMENTARY SAMPLE EMAIL

Dear Thirten，

Your email of April 12 has been received. The L/C in your favor has already been opened and sent.

We are attaching a photostatic copy of our Documentary Credit No. 7612 dated April 10 covering the following two specific sales confirmation：

S/C No. 1261 USD3421 hardwares
S/C No. 1262 USD5213 toys
Total：USD8,634

Please verify this matter with your bank.

Best，
Mortty

EXERCISES

Ⅰ. Fill in the blanks with the proper forms of the following expressions.

> inform，open，in your favor，with，negotiate，
> authorize，draw，produce，anticipate，accept

1. This is to _____ you that Mr. Smart _____ to take orders or to collect accounts on our behalf.

2. The relative L/C was opened _____ the Bank of China _____ as early as in May 20，20—.

3. We _____ concluding this transaction with you in the near future.

4. Please _____ on us for the amount due and attach the shipping documents to your draft.

5. Please arrange within a week when I may call on you to discuss my request. I will _____ some evidence supporting my statements.

6. As arranged，we have _____ your bill for $ 2000.

7. Congratulations on your newly _____ business in this city. We hope it will mark the beginning of our close cooperation in the future.

8. We're looking for a new contract at the moment. Everything is _____ at this stage.

Ⅱ. **Fill in the blanks with correct prepositions and then translate them into Chinese.**

1. We will draw _____ you _____ the invoice value with the draft accompanied _____ shipping documents.

2. To cover the shipment，we request you to establish an L/C _____ favor of our Shandong Branch _____ an American bank.

3. _____ view _____ the large amount involved _____ this transaction，we hope you will agree _____ our request _____ installment payment.

4. _____ reference to your email of May 30，we now attach the shipping documents covering the first consignment to Messrs Clintons and Sons Co.

5. Our sales agent _____ your end will be pleased to attend _____ your requirements.

6. The L/C must reach us not later _____ October 30 and remain valid _____ negotiation _____ 15 days _____ the date of shipment.

7. Our L/C is always payable _____ shipping documents.

8. We are grateful _____ your having offered us the information about your local markets.

9. As the buyers are _____ urgent need of the goods，we anticipate your early shipment.

10. We would like to stress that you must present the shipping documents _____ the validity of the credit.

Ⅲ. **Translate the following sentences into English.**

1. 按合同要求，货物装运后我们随附了这批货物的全套不可转让装运单据，请查收。

2. 欣告以你方为受益人的第 58 号信用证已由中国银行电开，请查收。

3. 我方将及时开证，相信你方会采取一切必要措施按期装船。

4. 我们已收到你方第 QD001 号发票，并愿意承兑支付你方见票 30 天期的汇票。

5. 按你方 7 月 1 日的来电要求，我们已指示纽约花旗银行（Citibank New York）开一张以你方为抬头人，价值 26000 英镑的信用证。

Ⅳ. **Writing task.**

Please refer to Task B6 on Page 335.

RECAP

Language Focus	Knowledge Focus
This is to inform you that... open an L/C with... to remain valid for negotiation in... until ... accept，produce，anticipate， authorize consignment	in your favor，CAD opening bank，full invoice value accept the draft Bills of Lading in triplicate Canada Customs Invoice Insurance Policy/Certificate

Writing Tips

➢ Advising the seller of the opening of the covering L/C and other particulars
➢ Calling the seller's attention to drawing documentary time draft for buyer' acceptance
➢ Listing required documents
➢ Expressing expectation for the first consignment

Lesson 32

A Sample L/C

ZCZC BSDDF1 0002090643
P3 SDAAOC
SWIFT BSDDF1 0002090643
99 E N 701 99 S

BASIC HEADER F 01 BKCHCNBJA500 9690 630741
APPL. HEADER O 700 1747000208 TDOMCATTBMTL 4242 982370 0002090647 N
                              ＋ TORONTO DOMINION BANK MONTREAL
                              ＋QUEBEC CANADA
         （BANK NO：8020006） ＋MONTREAL，CANADA
：MT：701 ------------- ISSUE OF A DOCUMENTARY CREDIT -------------

SEQUENCE OF TOTAL	：27：1/2
FORM OF DOCUMENTARY CREDIT	：40A：IRREVOCABLE
DOCUMENTARY CREDIT NUMBER	：20：LC5041757119
DATE OF ISSUE	：31C：150208
APPLICABLE RULES	：40E：UCP LATEST VERSION
DATE AND PLACE OF EXPIRY	：31D：150315 NEG BANK
APPLICANT	：50C：C AND G LINGERIE (1998) INC.，MONTREAL，QUEBEC H2S 3L5
BENEFICIARY	：59：SHANDONG GARMENTS IMP. AND EXP. CORP. 70 XIANGGANG ROAD，QINGDAO THE PEOPLE'S REP OF CHINA 266071
CURRENCY CODE，AMOUNT	：32B：CAD32453.60
PERCENTAGE CREDIT AMOUNT TOLERANCE	：39A：5/5
AVAILABLE WITH...BY...	：41D：AVAILABLE WITH ANY BANK BY NEGOTIATION
DRAFTS AT...	：42C：DRAFT AT SIGHT
DRAWEE	：42D：OURSELVES

PARTIAL SHIPMENTS : 43P: PARTIAL SHIPMENTS ALLOWED

TRANSSHIPMENT : 43T: TRANSHIPMENTS ALLOWED

LOADING/DISPATCH/TAKING/FROM : 44A: THE PEOPLE'S REP. OF CHINA

FOR TRANSPORTATION TO... : 44B: MONTREAL, QUE., CANADA

LATEST DATE OF SHIPMENT : 44C: 150220

DOCUMETNS REQUIRED : 46A:

DOCUMENTS

COMMERCIAL INVOICE IN TRIPLICATE

CANADA CUSTOMS INVOICE OF DEPARTMENT OF NATIONAL REVENUE/
CUSTOMS AND EXCISE IN TRIPLICATE

PACKING LIST IN TRIPLICATE

FULL SET OF CLEAN ON BOARD MARINE/OCEAN BILLS OF LADING **TO
ORDER** BLANK **ENDORSED** MARKED FREIGHT PREPAID **NOTIFY** C AND G
LINGERIE (1998) INC. AND DATED LATEST FEBRUARY 20/2015.

INSURANCE POLICY OR CERTIFICATE COVERING MARINE RISKS, ALL
RISKS, FOR 110 PERCENT OF THE INVOICE VALUE

CHARGES : 71B: ALL **BANKING CHARGES**
OUTSIDE CANADA ARE FOR
APPLICANT'S ACCOUNT

PERIOD FOR PRESENTATIONS : 48: DOCUMENTS TO BE PRESENTED
WITHIN 15 DAYS
AFTER DATE OF SHIPMENT BUT
WITHIN CREDIT VALIDITY

CONFIRMATION INSTRUCTION : 49: WITHOUT

INSTRUCTION TO BANK : 78:

NEGOTIATING BANK TO AIRMAIL (1) DRAFT(S) AND COMPLETE SET OF
DOCUMENTS (2) REMAINING DOCUMENTS BY NEXT MAIL TO US ON
RECEIPT OF DOCUMENTS IN ORDER AT OUR COUNTER WE SHALL PAY A
DEPOSITORY OF NEGOTIATING BANK'S CHOOSING

ADVISE TROUGH BANK : 57A: CIBKCNBJ2—
BANK OF CHINA SHANGDONG BRANCH

TRAILER

MAC: 4678C676 CHK: 982922E807BA

NNNN

ZCZC BSDDF1 0002090643

P3 SDAAOC

SWIFT BSDDF1 0002090643

99 E N 701 99 S

BASIC HEADER F 01 BKCHCNBJA500 9690 630741
APPL. HEADER O 700 1747000208 TDOMCATTBMTL 4242 982370 0002090647 N
　　　　　　　　　　　　　　+ TORONTO DOMINION BANK MONTREAL
　　　　　　　　　　　　　　+QUEBEC CANADA
　　　(BANK NO: 8020006)　+MONTREAL, CANADA
: MT: 701　·············· ISSUE OF A DOCUMENTARY CREDIT ···············
SEQUENCE OF TOTAL　　　　　　　: 27: 2/2
Documentary Credit Number　　　: 20: LC5041757119
DESCRPT OF GOODS/SERVICES　　　: 45B:

　　16/84　PCT　COTTON/POLYESTER　WOVEN　SATIN　FLEECE, LADIES
　　SLEEPWEAR, S/C 20SGC5102
　　1020 PCS PYJAMA STYLE 1539 AT CAD8. 90 PER PC.
　　240 PCS NIGHT SHIRT STYLE 1540 AT CAD5. 40 PER PC.
　　600 PCS HOUSECOAT STYLE 1541 AT CAD8. 90 PER PC.
　　964 PCS PYJAMA STYLE 1542 AT CAD8. 90 PER PC.
　　420 PCS NIGHT SHIRT STYLE 1543 AT CAD6. 40 PER PC.
　　240 PCS NIGHT SHIRT STYLE 1544 AT CAD5. 00 PER PC.
　　480 PCS HOUSECOAT STYLE 1545 AT CAD8. 90 PER PC.
　　C. I. F. MONTREAL
ADDITIONAL CONDITIONS: 47B:
　　SPECIAL CONDITIONS
　　CONTAINER SHIPMENT ALLOWED
　　INSURANCE TO BE COVERED BY SHIPPER
　　SHIPMENT ONLY ON ANY ONE OF THE FOLLOWING FOUR **SHIPPING LINES**
　　IS ACCEPTABLE
　　1. MITSUI　O. S. K. , 2. SEALAND, 3. AMERICAN　PRESIDENT　　4. KASE
　　SHIPPING ENTERPRISE LTD.
　　BENEFICIARY'S CERTIFICATE ADDRESED TO ISSUING BK CONFIRMING
　　THEIR ACCEPTANCE AND/OR NON-ACCEPTANCE OF ALL **AMENDMENTS**
　　MADE UNDER THIS LC QUOTING THE RELEVANT AMENDMENT NO. ,
　　IF THIS LC IS NOT AMENDED SUCH STATEMENT IS NOT REQUIRED.
　　ALL DOCUMENTS CALLED FOR UNDER THIS CERDIT, EXCEPT THOSE
　　WHICH THE CREDIT SPECIFICALLY STATES CAN BE 'COPIES', MUST BE
　　CLEARLY MARKED ON THEIR FACE AS 'ORIGINAL' .
　　A **DISCREPANCY HANDLING FEE** OF CAD80. 00

IS PAYABLE BY THE BENEFICIARY ON EACH DRAWING PRESENTED WHICH DOES NOT STRICTLY COMPLY WITH THE TERMS AND CONDITIONS OF THIS VREDIT AND HAS TO BE REFERRED TO THE APPLICANT.

T. T. REIMBURSEMENT：UNACCEPTABLE

TRAILER
MAC：233E646C　　CHK：50198DC6F8D2

NNNN

NOTES

1. Toronto：多伦多
2. Montreal，Quebec：加拿大魁北克省的蒙特利尔市
3. documentary L/C：跟单信用证
   常见的信用证种类有：
   Irrevocable L/C 不可撤销的信用证
   Sight L/C 即期信用证
   Usance/time/term L/C 远期信用证
   Documentary L/C 跟单信用证
   Transferable and divisible L/C 可转让/可分割信用证
   Revolving L/C 循环信用证
   Reciprocal L/C 对开信用证
   Back to back L/C 背对背信用证
   Standby L/C 备用信用证
4. UCP：abbr. 跟单信用证统一惯例与实务
   全称 Uniform Customs and Practice for Documentary Credits
   UCP 是国际商会出台的一套非官方出版物，其目的是有效地促进信用证结算业务的发展。
5. applicant：*n.* 开证申请人
6. beneficiary：*n.* 受益人
   常见的信用证涉及的各银行有：
   opening/ issuing bank 开证行
   advising bank/ notifying bank 通知行
   negotiating bank 议付行
   accepting bank 承兑行

paying bank/drawee bank 付款行

confirming bank 保兑行

reimbursement bank/ reimbursing bank 偿付行

7. percentage credit amount tolerance：信用证金额浮动允许范围

8. drafts at sight：即期汇票

9. drawee：*n.* 付款行/ 受票人

   drawer：*n.* 出票人

10. commercial invoice：商业发票

    常见的跟单信用证单据种类有：

    packing list 装箱单

    weight and measurement certificate 重量和尺码证明

    certificate of origin 原产地证

    Generalized System of Preference Certificate of Origin FORM A

    普惠制产地证格式 A（GSP FORM A）

    marine/ocean bills of lading 海运提单

    insurance policy or certificate 保险单或保险凭证

11. Canadian customs invoice of department of national revenue/ customs and exercise 加拿大海关提供的加拿大海关发票

12. to order：空白抬头，凭指定

    to order of sb/to sb's order 凭某人指定

    A negotiable B/L is made out to order instead of to a named consignee.

    可转让的提单制成凭指示，而不是指定的收货人。

13. endorse：*v.* 背书，批准

    The Insurance Policy is issued in duplicate and blank endorsed.

    保单签发一式两份，空白背书。

    Our relative application for Import License has been endorsed.

    我们对进口许可证的申请已被批准。

    endorsement：*n.* 背书，批准

    endorsement in blank 空白背书

    endorsement in full 记名背书

    endorser *n.* 背书人

14. notify：*v.* 通知

    The bank will notify the exporters of the L/C by telephone.

    银行将电话通知出口商信用证开到。

The shipping company notified us to take delivery of the goods.

船公司告知我们提货。

15. banking charges：银行费用

16. period for presentations：交单期

17. confirmation instruction：保兑指示

18. woven satin fleece：织缎绒

19. shipping lines：船公司

20. amendment：*n.* 修改

21. discrepancy handling fee：不符点处理费

22. reimbursement：*n.* 偿付，赔偿，退还

    claim reimbursement 索偿，要求付款

    tax reimbursement for export 出口退税

    T. T. reimbursement is not allowed.

    不允许电索。

    reimburse：*v.* 偿付，赔偿，退还

    The opening bank will reimburse the negotiating bank the amount of the credit after receipt of the documents in order.

    开证行在收到齐备无误的单据后将偿付议付行信用证的金额。

EXERCISES

Ⅰ. **Write out the name of the following parties involved in the above L/C.**

   1. Opening Bank：

   2. Applicant：

   3. Beneficiary：

   4. Advising Bank：

   5. Negotiating Bank：

   6. Paying Bank：

Ⅱ. **Answer the following questions according to the above L/C.**

   1. What does "SEQUENCE OF TOTAL" in the L/C stand for?

   2. What kind of credit is this? (Documentary or non-documentary? Time or sight?)

   3. When is this credit issued?

   4. When and where does this credit expire?

   5. What is the total amount of the L/C?

6. What commodities does this credit cover?

7. What are the trade terms?

8. Are partial shipments and transshipments allowed?

9. What is the port of loading?

10. What is the port of destination?

11. When is the latest date of shipment?

12. Is there any special condition on shipping lines?

13. What documents are required under this L/C?

14. How is insurance covered under this L/C?

15. What will happen if there is a discrepancy in shipping documents?

Ⅲ. Translate the following L/C stipulations into Chinese.

1. The Irrevocable Documentary Letter of Credit is available with any bank by beneficiary's drafts on us for full invoice value at sight.

2. Full set of clean on board ocean marine Bills of Lading issued to order of shipper blank endorsed marked "Freight Collect" and notify accountee.

3. All other banking charges outside Korea are for the account of beneficiary.

4. About 300,000 yards of 65% Polyester, 35% Cotton Grey Lawn as per Proforma Invoice No. S-0578 mention to be indicated on commercial invoice, CFR Montreal.

5. Documents must be presented to negotiating bank or paying bank within 15 days after the on board date of Bills of Lading, but within validity of letter of credit.

6. Commercial Invoice signed by the beneficiary specifying the nature of the goods, unit price, total price and payment conditions.

7. Draft(s) drawn under the credit must be negotiated within the validity of the credit.

8. Original certificate of origin delivered should be signed by the chamber of commerce.

9. All certificates required under this L/C must be dated prior to shipment date.

10. The negotiating bank is authorized to confirm the credit hereto.

RECAP

Language Focus	Knowledge Focus
SEQUENCE OF TOTAL DATE AND PLACE OF EXPIRY AMOUNT AVAILABLE WITH...BY... DRAFTS AT..., LOADING/DISPATCH/ TAKING/FROM FOR TRANSPORTATION TO... CONFIRMATION INSTRUCTION DESCRPT OF GOODS/SERVICES	documentary L/C，UCP applicant, beneficiary, opening bank, advising bank，paying bank percentage credit amount tolerance drafts at sight drawee，to order period for presentation reimbursement CURRENCY CODE

Lesson 33

Asking for Amendment to L/C

From: Curran. Wang@acrtas. com

To: Beth. Rice@bricon. com

Date: May 23, 20—

Subject: Please amend L/C No. LC403/0683/19DD

Dear Beth

We have just received your L/C No. LC403/0683/19DD against our P. I. No. QC03/10/20DD. We regret to say that we have found some **discrepancies** upon checking it with our P/I. In order to **ensure** timely shipment, please **amend** the L/C as follows:

1) The name of the beneficiary should **read** "Qingdao Guangda Textiles Import and Export Corporation" instead of "Shandong Textiles Import and Export Corporation";

2) Please insert the word "about" before the quantity and amount in your L/C;

3) Please delete your request for insurance policy/certificate.

As the time of shipment is approaching, please make the necessary amendments **the soonest possible** so that we can effect shipment in time.

Best regards
Curran

NOTES

1. amendment to/of an L/C：对信用证的修改

   amendment：*n.* 修改

   We attach amendment advice No. QD003 to L/C No. CR-57. Please find it in order.

   兹附上第 CR-57 号信用证的第 QD003 修改通知书，请查收。

   amend：*v.* 修改

   Please amend your L/C to allow partial shipments and transshipment.

   请修改信用证允许分批装运和转船。

2. discrepancy：*n.* 差异，不符点

   The seller is liable for the refund of the extra cost due to the discrepancy in weight.

   由于重量差异而多收的货款，卖方应负责退还。

3. ensure：*v.* 保证；确保

   It seems that they cannot ensure the safe arrival of the ordered goods.

   看来他们不能保证订货安全到达。

   They ensure that they will deliver the goods in June.

   他们保证 6 月份交货。

   Close cooperation will ensure smooth execution of your contract.

   密切合作将确保你方合同的顺利执行。

4. read：*v.* 读作；内容是

   We confirm your fax of the 10th，which reads as follows：

   现确认你方 10 日传真，内容如下：

   Please amend the price clause to read "CFR London".

   请将条款更改为 CFR London。

   The thermometer is reading 40℃.

   温度计显示 40 度。

5. insert：*v.* 插入，填入

   I've filled in the form，but you still need to insert your bank details and date of birth.

   我已经填好表格，但你还需要填上有关银行的详细情况和出生日期。

6. delete：*v.* 删除；取消

   They insisted that all the expletives were deleted from the article.

   他们坚持删掉条款中的所有虚词。

   We hope you will delete the clause.

   希望你方取消这一条款。

7. the soonest possible：最快的；尽快地

Please give us the soonest possible reply. 尽快回复。

As the market price is going up，we would recommend you to accept the offer the soonest possible.

鉴于行市上涨，我们建议你们尽早接受报盘。

A SUPPLEMENTARY SAMPLE EMAIL

Dear Ellen，

L/C No. WSD162 issued by the Bank of New South Wales has duly arrived. On perusal，we find that transshipment and partial shipment are not allowed.

Please amend your L/C to read："Partial shipment and transshipment allowed". We hope you will see to it that the amendment is sent without delay.

Best，
Koran

附信用证修改通知书

WestLB（Europa）A. G.

P. O. BOX 2230

3000 CE Copenhagen

The Denmark   IRREVOCABLE DOCUMENTARY CREDIT

Cable Stanchart Telex 24108（SCBR NL）Telephone（010）4365322	OUR REFERENCE FLS-JHLC01	DATE OF ISSUE JULY 27TH，2015
THIS IS AN OPERATIVE AMENDMENT OF CREDIT INSTRUMENT	DATE OF EXPIRY：SEPTEMBER 15TH，2015 PLACE OF EXPIRY：IN CHINA	
Documents to be presented within 15 days after the date of issuance of the transport document（s）but within the validity of the credit.		
APPLICANT F. L. SMIDTH & CO. A/S 77，Vigerslev Alle，DK-2500 Valby Copenhagen Denmark Fax：(01) 20 11 90	BENEFICIARY GOLDEN SEA TRADING CORP. 8TH FLOOR，JIN DU BUILDING，277 WU XING ROAD， SHANGHAI，CHINA	
ADVISING BANK Bank of China 23，Zhongshan Dong Yi Lu，Shanghai P. R. of China	THIS AMENDMENT IS TO BE CONSIDERED AS PART OF THE ABOVE CREDIT AND MUST BE ATTACHED THERETO	

DEAR SIR （S）：

THE LETTER OF CREDIT REFERENCED ABOVE IS AMENDED AS FOLLOWS：

* The place of expiry： In China，in stead of 'at our counter'；

* The address of applicant is 77，Vigerslev，Alle，DK-2500 Valby，Copenhagen，Denmark，in stead of 'DK-2600…'

* The name of the goods is YE803 26' and TE600 24'，in stead of YE803 24' and TE600 26'.

* Delete the clause "1/3 original B/L…"

* 3/3，not 2/3 original clean shipped on board marine bill of lading are required .

* The S/C number should be JH-FLSSC01，instead of FLS9711.

* Transshipment is allowed anywhere，instead of 'Transshipment is allowed only in Hong Kong'.

ALL OTHER TERMS AND CONDITIONS REMAIN UNCHANGED

YOURS FAITHFULLY

WestLB （Europa） A. G.

ADEL   **JONG**

G. Den Adel （A570）   W. E. de Jong （A573）

SUBJECT TO UNIOFORM CUSTOMS AND PRACTICE FOR DOCUMENTARYCREDITS （2007 REV. ） I. C. C. PUBLICATION NO. 600

EXERCISES

Ⅰ. Fill in the blanks with the proper forms of the following expressions.

> against，regret，upon，approach，the soonest possible
> ensure，amend，read，effect，timely

1. We'll send you 10 cases by air freight to _____ delivery to you before May 30.

2. All the products that you require is in stock and can reach your destination _____ .

3. We _____ to say that there is a discrepancy in colors between the received materials and the sample.

4. Payment is to be made _____ sight draft drawn under a confirmed

irrevocable L/C for the full invoice value.

5. We have to inform you that the name of the commodity in your L/C No. 515 should be _____ to read "metal sheets" as contracted.

6. The name of beneficiary should _____ "Shandong Chemicals I/E Company".

7. Since the selling season is _____ and our customers are in urgent need of your products, please ship them by the first available vessel before May 31.

8. Please send one dozen Timely alarm clock radios by Air-Express _____ .

9. You can rely on us to _____ the shipment well before your required schedule.

10. _____ inspecting the contents of the cases, we found that the total contents had been short-delivered by 20 pieces.

Ⅱ. Fill in the blanks with prepositions and then translate them into Chinese.

1. Please note that the credit is available _____ documentary draft _____ 60 days sight.

2. To cover our shipment, we request you to open an irrevocable L/C in favor of our Shandong Branch _____ the contracted amount _____ an American bank.

3. We will draw sight D/P _____ your order.

4. In international trade, when payment is made _____ a documentary L/C, the negotiating bank will be reimbursed as long as the opening bank finds the shipping documents _____ order.

5. Please delete "fresh water damage" _____ the L/C.

Ⅲ. Translate the following sentences into English.

1. 因为你方信用证规定了最迟装运期和有效期为同一个时间，我们在装运后没有足够的时间办理单证结汇。

2. 请从信用证中删去此条款："所有银行费用由受益人支付"。

3. 请将信用证中"运费到付"修改为"运费预付"。

4. 请注意你方信用证修改通知书应在本月底前到达我处，并在数量前加上"about"字样。

5. 请把单价从 RMB0.90 元增加到 RMB0.95 元，并把总额相应增加到 RMB42,000 元。

Ⅳ. Writing task.

Please refer to Task A1-12 on Page 327.

RECAP

Language Focus	Knowledge Focus
upon checking... with ... amend... to read "..." should read "..." instead of " ... " insert，delete ensure，the soonest possible	amendment to L/C discrepancies about

Writing Tips

➢ Identifying the L/C No. and S/C No.
➢ Pointing out the discrepancies
➢ Listing the discrepancies and suggestions of amendment
➢ Asking for early amendment so as to enable the seller to make timely shipment

Lesson 34

Urging Balance Payment

Urging Balance Payment by T/T

From: Eric. Zhou@163. com

To: Matt. Roker@icloud. com

Date: 23 Feb 20—

Subject: Balance Payment

Dear Matt,

Hope this email finds you well.

As arranged in our Proforma Invoice #208, the balance (70% of the whole amount) should be paid by T/T against the copy of B/L. However, we haven't got the **balance** payment yet.

Our shipping agent just informed us that the goods will be arriving at your port in a couple of days. So, please **expedite** the balance payment so that we can **release** the original B/L to you.

We would appreciate your kind cooperation to avoid unnecessary port charges caused by the potential delay.

Please send by email the **evidence of remittance** when you finish your payment.

Regards,
Zhou

A Reply to the Above

From：Matt. Roker @icloud. com
To：Eric. Zhou@163. com
Date：25 Feb 20—
Subject：bank receipt

Dear Eric，

Sorry for the one week delay in payment. And I apologize for our late reply.

Our remittance was made for USD15,600 today，and the **bank receipt** is attached as requested. Please confirm when you've got the money and send me the original B/L.

Best wishes，
Matt

NOTES

1. Hope this email finds you well. ：见信安好

2. balance：*n.* 差额，余额，余数

   the balance 70％＝the rest 70％＝the remaining 70％：70％的余款部分

   Our terms are 50％ cash with order，and balance to be paid within 30days.

   我们的条款是订货时付 50％现金，其余在 30 天内支付。

   balance payment 支付余款   bank balance 银行余额/存款余额

   credit balance 贷方余额   Balance Sheet 资产负债表

3. expedite：*v.* 加快进展；迅速完成

   Please do you utmost to expedite the establishment of the L/C so that we may execute the order within the prescribed time.

   请尽力加快开立信用证以便我方在规定时间内执行订单。

4. release：*v. /n.* 释放，发布

   The new trade figures have just been released.

   新的贸易数字刚刚公布。

   express release bill of lading 电放提单   delivery release 发货通知

   freight release 放货通知，船货放行单   press release 新闻发布/新闻稿

5. port charges：港口费用，这里指 demurrage charge 滞期费

6. evidence of remittance：汇款证明。

   客户的电汇水单：advice for customer

7. bank receipt：银行水单，即汇款后银行给的留底凭条

   也叫 bank slip

A SUPPLEMENTARY SAMPLE EMAIL

Dear Mr. Grind，

Thank you for your order for cotton sheets. Regarding 4,500 pcs，the cost is as follows：
    Commodity：all cotton bed sheets（woven）ART＃6302
    Quantity：4,500pcs
    Unit price：at USD5.76/pc FOB Qingdao Port
    Total amount：USD25920.00

We have your check for USD20,000 which we will hold until you remit the balance of USD5920. The rest of the cotton sheets will then be dispatched.

Your immediate attention will be much appreciated.

Yours truly,

Eric

EXERCISES

Ⅰ. Fill in the blanks with the proper forms of the following expressions.

> balance, remit, apologize, expedite, release,
> receipt, delay, evidence, charges, against

1. The National Bureau of Statistics is scheduled to _____ CPI figures on June 15.

2. As agreed upon, we have _____ you the full amount of the goods by T/T.

3. As the deadline of shipment is approaching, we require you to _____ shipment of our order No. 102.

4. Upon _____ of your email request, we contacted the factory at once for your specifications required.

5. "I am truly sorry this happened, and I _____ for the inconvenience".

6. Please prepay 30% of the total amount to us, and then kindly remit us the _____ before the delivery.

7. A recent survey found that some people are worried about becoming card slaves, a term used to refer to people pay only the minimum amount _____ their credit card debt every month.

8. _____ suggests that the global recession has resulted in significant setbacks in the employment levels.

9. After a few days' _____ the shop refunded my money at last.

10. Recently he has offered the system for120 dollars, plus shipping and handling _____, at alibaba. com.

Ⅱ. **Translate the following sentences into Chinese.**

1. If you have any questions, please feel free to ask me via telephone or email.

2. Please make some modifications to the design in accordance with the feedback information from our headquarters in New York.

3. We will make remittance for USD2800 to cover the expenses.

4. Please transfer the remaining US $ 1500 repairing charge to the following a/c. To show our sincerity, we are willing to reduce our price to the lowest US $ 1480.

5. When the goods purchased by us are ready for shipment and the freight space booked, you let us know and we will remit the full amount by T/T.

Ⅲ. **Translate the following sentences into English.**

1. 你方还有一笔款已到期，请尽快安排支付。

2. 关于货款的到账时间，请跟踪网上发布的信息。

3. 请放心我们一定在货到时支付余款。

4. 已快递你方我公司最新样品图样，待取得跟踪单号后，将上传你方。

5. 请放心我们将尽可能加速样品复制。

Ⅳ. **Writing task.**

Please refer to Task A8-3 on Page ＊＊＊.

RECAP

Language Focus	Knowledge Focus
balance	balance payment
expedite	copy of B/L, original B/L
release	port charges
against the copy of B/L	evidence of remittance
	bank receipt
Writing Tips	

➢ Reminding the buyer of the 70% balance payment by T/T being unpaid

➢ Urging again for immediate payment of the rest for seller's releasing the original B/L

➢ Stressing the buyer's prompt action to avoid unnecessary port charges involved

➢ Asking for the evidence of remittance

Task 10

Handling Shipment Issues

Learning Objectives

To be able to write emails urging for shipment and advising the buyer of shipment

To get familiar with the writing plans, useful sentences and phrases of shipment

Lesson 35

Urging Shipment

From: Mats Johnson (mats@qpt. biz)
To: Bill Liu (wanli@public. qd. sd. cn)
Date: April 16, 20—
Subject: Expecting shipment of P/I. No. 3496

Dear Mr. Liu,

With reference to our previous emails, we wish to call your attention to **the fact that** up to the present moment no news has come from you about shipment under the subject contract.

As you have been informed in one of our previous emails, the users are **in urgent need of** the goods contracted and are in fact **pressing** us for assurance of **timely** delivery.

Under the circumstances, it is impossible for us to **extend** our L/C No. 389 again which expires on 21st August, and we are **obliged** to **remind** you of the matter once again.

We hope you will let us have your **shipping** advice by email **without fail**.

Best regards,
Mats Johnsson

NOTES

1. the fact that：……的事实，that 引导的是同位语从句

   Please don't neglect the fact that there's also a big difference in the quality of the goods they supply.

   请不要忽略这个事实，即他们提供的货物质量大有不同。

2. be in need of：需要……

   be in urgent/bad/dire need of 急需……，相当于 be urgently/badly in need of

   Our clients in South Africa are in urgent need of the goods for the coming shopping season.

   销售季节临近，我们南非的客户急需这批货物。

   be in no need of 不需要……

   We are in no need of the off-grade products.

   我们不需要这种等外品。

3. the goods contracted：合同项下货物

4. press sb. to do sth.：催促某人做某事

   The bank are pressing/urging us to pay off the debt.

   银行催着我们还清贷款。

   Customers are pressing us for an early reply.

   客户催促我们早日给予答复。

5. timely：*a.* 及时的，适时的；*ad.* 及时地，适时地

   The timely loan saved the company from going bankrupt.

   这笔及时的贷款使公司免于倒闭。

   The question was not timely raised.

   问题没有及时提出。

6. extend：*v.* 延长，宽延；扩展

   We propose that you extend the L/C to Oct. 30 to avoid the possible delay in shipment.

   为避免延误装运，建议你方将信用证延至 10 月 30 日。

   We shall be grateful to you if you can extend your offer for two days.

   你方如能将报盘延长两天，我们不胜感激。

   We agree to extend the area of sole agency to cover Vancouver in addition to Montreal.

   我们同意将独家代理的地区除了蒙特利尔外还扩展到温哥华。

7. expire：*v.* 到期，（期满）为止，（到期）失效

表示该含义的词还有：mature，terminate，be due 等

This L/C expires on Aug. 6.

该信用证 8 月 6 日到期。

The Agency Agreement terminated fruitlessly.

代理协议无果而终。

The Insurance Policy will mature tomorrow.

该保险单明天到期。

The note/bill will be due in 60 days.

此票据 60 天到期。

date of expiry＝maturity 到期日

8. be obliged to do：不得不做……，被迫做……

Having signed the contract，they are obliged to pay off their debts within two years.

签订了合同之后，他们就必须在两年之内还清贷款。

9. remind：*v.* 提醒

Please remind me of my appointment with Mr. Lewis in case I forget.

请提醒我与刘易斯先生的约会，以免我忘记。

We would like to remind you that shipment of our order No. 56 is rapidly becoming overdue.

我们愿提醒你方，我方第五十六号订单的装运期很快就要逾期了。

Regarding your order No. 12，we would remind you to open the covering L/C.

关于你方第十二号订单，我们提醒你方开立信用证。

10. shipping advice：装船通知

11. without fail：务必，一定

We will ship the goods next week without fail.

我们一定在下周装运货物。

Be there by ten o'clock，without fail!

你一定要在 10 点之前到那儿!

A SUPPLEMENTARY SAMPLE EMAIL

Dear Mr. Malones，

We wish to call your attention to our Order No. 5691 covering 4 pcs scraper set with wooden handle，for which we sent to you about 30 days ago an irrevocable L/C-expiration date 31 October.

As the season is rapidly approaching，our buyers are badly in need of the goods. We shall be very much obliged if you will effect shipment as soon as possible，thus enabling them to catch the brisk demand at the start of the season.

We would like to emphasize that any delay in shipping our booked order will undoubtedly involve us in no small difficulty.

We thank you in advance for your cooperation.

Best regards，
Tommy Li

EXERCISES

Ⅰ. Fill in the blanks with the proper forms of the following expressions.

call your attention to，remind，in urgent need of，press sb for，timely extend，expire，be obliged to do，under the circumstances，without fail

1. I'm going away next week so _____ I wouldn't have time to start and finish the job.
2. We'd like to _____ to the fact that payment has been overdue for two weeks.
3. We've been _____ them _____ a reply，but so far we haven't heard from them at all.
4. The goods are shipped today and we believe they can reach you _____ .
5. If desirable to both parties，they can renew the contract one month

before it _____ .

6. On receipt of your amendment we shall arrange shipment _____ .

7. Please ship the goods as soon as possible as our buyers are _____ them.

8. As the supplier has breached the contract，we _____ make purchase from elsewhere.

9. The bank has said it cannot _____ its loans to this company any further.

10. We are writing again to _____ you that the amount still owing is USD80,000.

Ⅱ. Give the correct meaning of the word "reference" in the following sentences.

1. We named your bank as a **reference** for our credit investigation.

2. Our new designs will be sent to you for **reference.**

3. With **reference** to your inquiry of 6th January，I am glad to offer as follows.

4. Attached please find a **reference** of Tung Hing Co. ，which should be treated confidentially.

5. **Reference** is made to our email dated 8th March，20—.

Ⅲ. Translate the following sentences into English.

1. 按照合同，货物应于本月底之前装运。然而，如果你方能安排早一点儿交货，我们不胜感激。

2. 我们急需石油，请你方将标题合同项下 50000 吨月内装完。

3. 我们提请你方注意，信用证 5 天后到期，而至今我们未收到任何有关装运的消息。

4. 我们十分抱歉迟交了贵方订货，请接受我们的歉意。

5. 我们保证今后将及时处理你们所有的订货，不会再有延迟装运发生。

6. 如果你们不能在 6 月份完成装运，我们将有权取消合同。

7. 因为合同规定的装运期马上就到了，请立即告知有关装运的信息。

8. 因制造商迟迟没有交货，装船期不能确定，因此我们未及时给你方回复，对此深为抱歉。

9. 我方已同山东外运公司（Sinotrans）联系并预定"和平轮"舱位，该轮预计 5 月 8 日开航。

10. 圣诞节将至，由于我方客户急需此货，请将你方装运期提前至 11 月 30 日。

Ⅳ. **Writing task.**

Please refer to Task B7 on Page 336.

RECAP

Language Focus	Knowledge Focus
in urgent need of, press sb. for...	timely delivery
extend, expire	validity of L/C
remind, be obliged to, without fail	expiry date of L/C

Writing Tips

➢ Referring to P/I No.
➢ Stating the problem of non-receipt of shipping news
➢ Stressing the urgency and expiry date of L/C
➢ Requesting timely delivery
➢ Asking for shipping advice

Lesson 36

Shipping Advice

From: Bill Liu (wanli@public. qd. sd. cn)
To: Mats Johnson (mats@qpt. biz)
Date: April 19, 20—
Subject: shipping advice for P/I No. 3496
Attachment: PL ♯ PI3496. pdf (12K); IN ♯. EH3496. pdf (5K); B/L ♯BLA0033. pdf (15K)

Dear Mats,

We are pleased to inform you that the following goods under Proforma Invoice No. 3496 have been shipped on S. S. Commander **due to sail** for London on April 20. Please find the details as follows:

    Commodity: **Combination Pliers** UF-990 & **Scrapers** TS-012

    Quantity: 200 cartons

    Amount: USD16868. 00

    Name of vessel: Commander

    Voy. No. : H-136

    B/L No. : BLA0033

    ETD: April 20, 20—

    ETA: May 10, 20—

    Shipping Agency at port of destination: Damco Solutions Ltd.

                                                84 Uxbridge Road,

                                              Ealing, London W13 8RA

                                              Phone: +44 208 799 2800

                                              Fax: +44 208 090 6201

We hope the said goods will reach you **at the due time.** Attached are copies of Packing List ♯ 3496, Invoice ♯. EH3496 and B/L ♯ BLA0033. We will airmail you original **documents** upon receipt of balance payment. Please cover insurance on your side.

Best regards,
Bill Liu

NOTES

1. advice：*n.* 建议；通知 advise：*v.*

   （1）通知，告知

   通知某人某事，构成 advise sb. of sth.，advise sb to do sth，advise sb. that/when/what/

   whether 等句型

   We are studying your list of commodities and will advise you of our present interest.

   我们正在研究你方的商品目录，并将告知你方目前我们最感兴趣的商品。

   Please advise（us）when you will deliver the goods we ordered.

   请告知，你方何时能交货？

   keep sb. advised of：随时告知某人某事

   We will keep you advised of the stock position.

   我们将随时告知你方存货状况。

   （2）建议；劝告

   We strongly advised our clients to settle the claim through friendly negotiation.

   我们竭力劝客户通过友好协商解决索赔。

   advise（sb.）against：劝……不要，建议……不要

   We advised our customers against making decisions in haste.

   我们劝客户不要草率作决定。

2. shipped... on SS Commander：装上"统帅"号轮

   "由……轮运输"可以表达为：

   shipped by ...   由……轮装运

   shipped per ...   由……轮运出

   shipped ex ...   由……轮运来

   We are pleased to inform you that your order has been shipped per/by S. S. "Queen".

   欣告你方订货已由"皇后"号轮运出。

   20 cartons out of shipment ex/by S. S. "Queen" were found broken.

   由"皇后"号轮运来的货物中有 20 箱破损。

3. due to：（按计划）定于……

   常用短语还有 be scheduled to，如：

   The tax hearing is due to begin next month.

税务问题听证会定于下月召开。

The airplane is scheduled to take off at 9：00 am.

航班定于早上 9 点起飞。

4. sail：*v.* 航行，启航；*n.* 航行

The first available steamer sailing for/to your port has been booked up.

驶往你港的第一艘便轮舱位已满。

He loaded his vessel with another cargo and set sail.

他给自己的船装上另一批货后便启航了。

sailing date 启航期

5. Combination Pliers & Scrapers：钢丝钳和刮刀

Combination Pliers 钢丝钳	Scrapers 刮刀

6. Voy. No. ：voyage number 航次

7. ETD：Estimated Time of Departure 预计离港时间

8. ETA：Estimated Time of Arrival 预计抵达时间

9. shipping agency：又叫 forwarding agency，forwarder 货运代理

10. at the due time：＝in due course 及时地，在适当的时候

All the documents required under the Letter of Credit have been sent to the bank at the due time.

信用证要求的所有单据已及时寄到银行。

11. document：*n.* 单据

shipping documents 运输单据

non-negotiable shipping documents，copy documents 副本单据

original documents 正本单据

documentary：*a.* 附有单据的，跟单的

documentary L/C 跟单信用证

A SUPPLEMENTARY SAMPLE EMAIL

Dear Jason，

Thank you for your email of Aug. 18，20—

We will change to a 40' container HQ at your instructions. Shipping schedule is as follows：
    MB/L：COSU0102418660
    HB/L：BJS072105
    Vessel：YUE JIN
    Voy. No. ：878F
    Route：TAO-LONG BEACH-HUNTINGBURG IN 5555
    1ST SCHEDULE：ETD TAO：AUG. 21，20..
               ETA LONG BEACH：SEP. 2 OR SEP. 3
               T/T：12-13DAYS（total）

We hope that the goods will reach you in perfect condition and look forward to further orders in the future.

Best regards，
Eric

EXERCISES

Ⅰ. Fill in the blanks with the proper forms of the following expressions.

> due，per，on your side，advise，remaining
> at the due time，enable，inform，sail，meet

1. The medical equipments under order No. G012 have been shipped _____ m. v. "Eagle" .
2. We are pleased to inform you that the 3000 dozen Men's Shirts under Sales Confirmation No. TE429 have been loaded onto S. S. "Merry Wind"，which will _____ on 23rd of October for New York.
3. We trust that the full set of original shipping documents will reach you in _____ course.

4. The goods will be ready for shipment in a few days. Will you please open the L/C immediately, so as to _____ us to ship them on time.

5. To our regret, we have to inform you that we cannot _____ your demand for prompt shipment.

6. You will receive notification of the results _____ .

7. We are glad to _____ you that your order No 207 has been shipped already.

8. Please contact our distributor _____ for any further information.

9. We are _____ that a consignment of paint brush will arrive next week.

10. We'll arrange shipment of the _____ goods by the available steamer next month.

Ⅱ. Translate the following into Chinese.

1. As a rule, we deliver all our orders within three months after receipt of the covering L/C.

2. We hope that the goods can be shipped promptly after you get the L/C.

3. Shipment should be made before October; Otherwise we are unable to catch the season.

4. The order is so urgently needed that we must ask you to expedite shipment.

5. We will try our best to advance shipment to September.

6. Please see to it that the goods are shipped per s. s. "SL MICHGAN" sailing on or about October 20th.

7. The goods ordered are all in stock and we assure you that the shipment will be made by the first available steamer in November.

8. It is stipulated that shipment be made before the end of this month. However, we shall appreciate it if you will arrange to ship the goods at an earlier date.

9. We wish to advise you that the goods under S/C No. 278 went forward on the steamer "IWASHIRO" on July 18. They are to be transsshipped at Hong Kong and are expected to reach your port in early September.

10. For the goods under our contract No. 456756, we have booked shipping space on S. S. "LEHOLA" due to arrive in London around 20th May. Please communicate with Estonian Shipping Company Ltd.

Ⅲ. Translate the following sentences into English.

1. 由于驶往你港的这批货数量太少以至于没有船愿意停靠你港，所以我
   们希望合同中能注上"允许转船"字样。

2. 我们遗憾不能按你方的要求于 12 月初装运此货，因为驶往伦敦的直达
   船仅在每月 20 日左右抵达我港。

3. 合同规定一俟货物装船，卖方必须将装船通知发邮件给客户。

4. 100 套柳编花篮（willow flower basket）拟装 5 月 15 日"红星"轮，
   请将信用证展至 5 月底。

5. 你方订单 VG0980 项下的 2000 双草编拖鞋（straw slipper）已由
   VIRTSU 轮运出，预计 10 天后抵达你港。

Ⅳ. Translate the following email into Chinese.

Dear Tommy，

Kindly note your goods have been delivered on 20ᵗʰ Dec.

Vessel：	NYK TERRA 030E
Container / Seal No：	EMCU9730476 / D1293242

Attached please find the shipping docs (Packing list，Invoice，B/L) and arrange balance payment at your earliest. We will send the original docs to you once receive the payment.

Best regards，

Jennie

Ⅴ. Writing task.

Please refer to Task A1-13 on Page 329.

RECAP

Language Focus	Knowledge Focus
shipped on/per/ex/by S. S "…" advise，advice，sail，due to at the due time，original documents	shipping advice Voy. No.，B/L No.，ETD，ETA shipping agency

续 表

Writing Tips

➢ Informing the buyer of the completeness of shipment
➢ Stating name of ship, B/L NO. , Voy. No. , ETD, ETA, shipping agency, etc.
➢ Attaching copies of shipping documents
➢ Asking for balance payment so as to send original shipping documents to the buyer

Lesson 37

Inquiring About Shipment

From: Mats Johnson (mats@qpt. biz)

To: Bill Liu (wanli@public. qd. sd. cn)

Date: May 12, 20—

Subject: Delayed shipment ofP/I No. 3496

Dear Mr. Liu,

As to P/I No. 3496, we haven't been informed so far of the arrival of S. S. Commander, which is expected to be due on May 10th.

The vessel was **carrying** a consignment of Combination Pliers UF-990 &. Scrapers TS-012 for our clients, **shipped B/L** BLA0033. They have informed us that they are in urgent need of this shipment to catch the selling season, and they want to know why the ship has been **delayed.**

Your prompt reply would be appreciated.

Best regards,
Mats Johnson

NOTES

1. carry：*v.* 运送，运载

   carrying vessel 载货船

   The carrying vessel sailed with full cargo yesterday.

   这艘载货船于昨日满载货物启航。

2. Shipped B/L：已装船提单

   B/L：Bill of Lading 提单

   clean B/L 清洁提单

   order B/L 指示提单

   straight B/L 记名提单

   non-negotiable B/L 不可转让提单

   shipped B/L（on board B/L；shipped on board B/L）已装船提单

   through B/L 联运提单

   transshipment B/L 转船提单

   direct B/L 直达提单

   container B/L 集装箱提单

   antedated B/L 倒签提单

3. delay：*v.* /*n.* 耽搁，延期，延误

   We regret our delay in replying to your email.

   我方很抱歉，延迟回复你方邮件。

   This will cause a delay of about 3 days in shipment.

   这将造成船期约三天的延迟。

   Such being the case，we have delayed answering your email.

   在这种情况下，我们就延迟了答复你方的电子邮件。

   If your L/C does not arrive within a week，shipment will be further delayed.

   如你方信用证一周内仍不到达，船期将再次延误。

A SUPPLEMENTARY SAMPLE EMAIL

Hi Meng，

We have been long waiting for your shipping advice for our Order No. 007，but have not received yet. Now 45 days have passed since the latest time of shipment under L/C No. BF909，we would like to know your explanation for non-execution of our order.

We could only accept this order reaching us not later than the end of May. If you fail to meet this deadline，we shall be compelled to cancel this order and get these goods from other suppliers.

We must point out that this delay has caused us very serious inconvenience. Our present stock of starch is exhausted，and we are unable to meet our customers' demands.

Best regards，
Ason

EXERCISES

Ⅰ. **Put the following terms and expressions into English.**

及时装运	客户
载货船	装船通知
已装船提单	班轮
装船唛头	迅速通关
船运集装箱	直达轮

Ⅱ. **Translate the following sentences into Chinese.**

1. The minimum period necessary for the preparation of the goods for shipment is five to six days. We are anxious to serve you but are sure you will see the need for giving us a little more time to meet your requirements.

2. As we mentioned in our previous emails，shipment for the suits you ordered is not possible in less than two months，but we should like to help you and give your order special priority.

3. As the manufacturers cannot get all the quantity ready at the same time, it is necessary for the contract stipulations to be so worded as to allow partial shipments.

4. Owing to the delay in opening the relative L/C, shipment cannot be made as contracted and should be postponed to October.

5. If you wish to have the goods shipped before Christmas it will be necessary to place your order as soon as possible as the demand is very heavy.

6. We have examined the sample and are prepared to place a trial order provided you can guarantee shipment on or before 31st August.

7. As the only direct steamer that calls at our port once a month has just departed, goods can only be shipped next month.

8. As the goods are to be transshipped at Hong Kong, we shall require through B/L.

9. The goods covered by Order No. 123 have been ready for shipment, Please give us specific shipping instructions.

10. As the date of delivery of goods under Order No. 678 is due, please inform us whether the goods are readily prepared.

Ⅲ. **One of the four underlined parts in each of the following sentences is incorrect. Please identify it and make a correction.**

1. We are <u>confident</u> that you will have no difficulty <u>to ship</u> the goods <u>in</u>
        A   B   C

    four <u>lots</u>.
          D

2. <u>Being</u> no direct steamer to your port <u>from</u> Shanghai, the goods <u>against</u>
    A   B   C

    Order No. 267 <u>have</u> been transshipped at Hong Kong.
                  D

3. October shipment <u>is</u> the best we can <u>get</u>, for the manufacturers have a
                        A   B

    <u>heavy</u> backlog <u>at hand</u>.
     C   D

4. The goods you ordered <u>are</u> ready for shipment. Please <u>advise</u> your
                              A   B

    forwarding agent <u>specific shipping arrangements</u>. <u>No error.</u>
                            C   D

5. The goods ordered are all <u>in stock</u> and we assure you <u>that</u> the shipment
         A   B

 will be <u>made by</u> the first vessel "Pacific Ocean", <u>which leaving</u>
     C   D

 Keelung on June 16.

6. <u>Owing to</u> the shipping schedule, it <u>will be impossible</u> for us <u>to ship</u>
  A   B   C

 the goods until the end of January, <u>that</u> please note.
               D

7. <u>Since</u> your design assortment reached us <u>lately</u>, it will be impo ssible
  A   B

 to <u>effect</u> the shipment <u>until</u> August 20—.
   C   D

8. We regret our <u>inability to</u> comply with your request <u>for shipping the goods</u>
      A   B

 in early March, because the direct steamer <u>sailing for</u> Basra <u>call</u> at our port
                 C   D

 only around 15th every month.

9. We regret that our mills are <u>faced</u> difficulty <u>in the course of</u>
           A   B

 printing the design required, and <u>should ask</u> for your consent
              C

 <u>to the postponement of shipment</u> to the end of July.
      D

10. Owing to the delay <u>to open</u> the L/C, shipment can not be made
        A

 <u>as contracted</u> and should be postponed <u>to September</u>. We are sorry for
   B   C

 any inconvenience <u>resulting from</u> this.
        D

RECAP

Language Focus	Knowledge Focus
carry, a consignment of...	carrying vessel, shipped B/L
delay	types of B/L

续 表

Writing Tips

- ➤ Stating the problem of non-arrival of or delay in arrival of the ship
- ➤ Indicating P/I NO, name of commodity, B/L No.
- ➤ Stressing the urgency
- ➤ Asking for explanation of reasons for delay

PART FOUR

SETTLING TRADE DISPUTES

Task 11

Making Claims and Adjustment

Learning Objectives

To be able to write emails making complaints, claims and settling the claims

To get familiar with the writing plans, useful sentences and phrases of claims and adjustment

Lesson 38

Claim for Inferior Quality

A Letter of Claim

From: Emil@hotmail. com
To: Amy@sina. com
Date: July 7, 20—
Subject: Claim for offset printing machines P. O. No. 87-03
Attachments: Pictures of rusted rollers. jpg (2. 5M)

Hi Amy,

We're very glad to inform you that your consignment of the subject goods reached us two weeks ago. Yet **upon their arrival**, we found that there were **rust** spots on some of the rollers. We immediately had them **re-inspected** by our **surveyor**, the Tianjin Entry-Exit **Inspection and Quarantine Bureau.** Attached are their survey report and some photos taken of the rollers, which **evidence** that six out of the 50 rollers are rusted.

Our experts **are of the opinion that** the rust was not scoured off completely before the machines were electroplated. **As a result,** the chrome coating would certainly not hold.

This **mishap** has **put us in no small trouble** because the machines are being **installed** right now, the **test run** is scheduled for late next month, and then they will **be put into regular service.** So we hope that you can give this matter your prompt attention and ship replacements as soon as possible.

Best regards,
Emil

Claims Accepted

From：Amy@sina. com
To：Emil@hotmail. com
Date：July 9，20—
Subject：RE：Claim for offset printing machines P. O. No. 87-03

Hi Emil，

We are sorry to note that the subject goods we have shipped to you are found **defective.** After discussing the case with our **manufacturer，** they have agreed to accept full **responsibility** for the present incident and have promised to ship replacements without delay. They also would like to **convey** their apologies to you and promise that similar mistakes won't happen again.

The new rollers are expected to reach you early next month. Please hold the defective rollers **at our disposal.**

Also we would like to offer you a 5% discount for your next order for the inconvenience brought to you.

We add our apology for the trouble we have caused you and hope that this oversight won't affect the future business between us.

Best regards，
Amy

NOTES

1. claim：*n.*/*v.* 索赔

   lodge/file/raise/put in a claim 提出索赔

   claim against sb. 向某人索赔

   claim on sth. 为某货物索赔

   claim for 为某原因索赔

   claim for 索赔……金额

   I'm afraid we'll have to lodge a claim against you on your last shipment for US＄1,000 for inferior quality.

   恐怕我们必须对你方上批船货向你提出劣质索赔 1000 美元。

2. offset printing machines：胶印机

3. upon their arrival：它们到达以后

   upon/on：*prep.* ＝after 在……之后

   upon receipt of your reply 收到你们的回复之后

   Upon receiving your letter we decided to make an inquiry to our Egyptian suppliers.

   收到你们来信后，我们决定向埃及的供货商询盘。

4. rust：*n.* 锈 *v.* 生锈

5. roller：滚轴

6. re-inspect：*v.* 复验

   We had the goods re-inspected at our own expense.

   我们自费让人对货物进行了复验。

7. surveyor：*n.* 检验员，鉴定人

   surveyor's report，survey report 检验报告

8. Entry-Exit Inspection and Quarantine Bureau：出入境检验检疫局

   State Administration For Entry-Exit Inspection And Quarantine of P. R. China 中华人民共和国国家出入境检验检疫总局，简称为 CIQ（China Inspection and Quarantine 的缩写），隶属于国家质量监督检验检疫总局（AQSIQ）。

9. evidence：*n.* 证据 *v.* 证明

   Have you any evidence for the short-delivery?

   你有什么证据能证明短交吗?

   We can provide a clean Bill of Lading, which evidences that the damage must have occurred during the long sea voyage.

   我们可以提供清洁提单，它能证明货损肯定是发生在长途海运过程中。

10. be of the opinion that . . . : 认为

    We are of the opinion that the underwriters should be held responsible.

    我们认为保险商应承担责任。

11. scour off/away：刷掉

12. electroplate：*v.* 电镀

13. as a result：结果是，因此

    Your packing is not up to export standards，and as a result the packages were broken in the course of transportation.

    你方包装未达到出口标准，结果造成运输途中包件破损。

14. chrome coating：镀铬的外层

15. mishap：*n.* 不幸的意外事故

    A series of mishaps led to the nuclear power plant blowing up.

    一系列不幸的事故导致了核电厂的爆炸。

16. put us in no small trouble：给我们造成很大麻烦

17. install：*v.* 安装

18. test run：试运行

19. be put into regular service：（机器等）投入正常使用

20. replacements：*n.* 替代品

21. defective：*a.* 有毛病的

    defect：*n.* 毛病，缺陷

22. responsibility：*n.* （过错）责任；（工作）责任，职责

    The minister took/accepted full responsibility for the disaster and resigned.

    部长承认对所发生的灾难承担全部责任，并引咎辞职。

    It's her responsibility to ensure the project finishes on time.

    她的职责是保证项目按时完成。

23. convey their apologies：表达他们的歉意

24. at one's disposal：由某人处理

    As to when we should start the negotiations，we're at your disposal.

    至于什么时候开始谈判，我们听你们的。

A SUPPLEMENTARY SAMPLE EMAIL

Dear Jessie,

Unfortunately we got information from our warehouse today that the belts of the bathrobes under PO No. 738612 aren't bound taut enough and the collars aren't fold down, as you can see in attached pictures.

This has to be revised in our warehouse, and we will pass the costs on to supplier on the basis of a claim. Costs will be as follows:

	Costs per piece	Cost for total quantity (1278 pieces)
Fold collar	€ 0.15	€ 191.70
Bound belt	€ 0.30	€ 383.40
Total costs		€ 575.10

We'll send you the corresponding claim next week.

Best regards,
Constanze

EXERCISES

I. Fill in the blanks with the proper forms of the following expressions.

upon, evidence, put, schedule, defective, contact (*n.*),
contact (*v.*), convey, as a result, at sb's disposal

1. We'd like to _____ our congratulations on your successful bid.
2. _____ their return they discovered that their house had been burgled.
3. You can _____ me at 388 9146.
4. If an item is _____ we will repair or replace it at our discretion (自行处理).
5. I don't really know how she got the job, but I suspect her mother's got _____ .
6. The train is _____ to arrive at 8:45, but it's running twenty minutes late.
7. His desire to win an Olympic medal is _____ by his performances throughout this season.

8. We have to let you know that your delay in shipment has _____ us in great trouble.

9. I would take you if I could, but I don't have a car at my _____ this week.

10. The fault is clearly on your part. _____, you should be fully responsible for the loss thus incurred.

Ⅱ. Fill in the blanks with proper prepositions.

1. Upon checking the consignment, we find that the goods are much inferior in quality _____ our sample and also slightly different in shade.

2. We are sorry to have to complain _____ the quality of your delivery of wheat.

3. We thank you for the prompt dispatch of our order but regret to draw your attention _____ the fact that a shortage in weight of 180 kg was noticed after its arrival.

4. We have received your email of July 21 and must straightway apologize for sending you goods _____ inferior quality.

5. We would like to ask you to send us _____ DHL _____ our expense a sample of the defective shirts for our factory to examine.

6. Please hold the damaged goods _____ our disposal until we hear from our insurers.

7. We have to hold you responsible _____ any loss that might result _____ this delay.

8. It was found that nearly 20% of the packages had been broken, obviously attributed _____ improper packing.

9. Regretfully, we find that the bulk of the goods delivered are not up _____ sample.

10. The situation is very clear and we hope you will see your way _____ making a prompt settlement.

Ⅲ. Translate the following sentences.

A. from English to Chinese

1. This is to remind you that the time of shipment has long been overdue; yet up to this date we still haven't received your advice of dispatch of the cameras.

2. We are receiving urgent requests from customers and you will understand that this delay places us in an awkward position.

3. Unfortunately we find that you have supplied goods below the

standards we expected from the samples.

4. We are only prepared to accept the goods if you will reduce the price, say, by 3%.

5. On opening the cases we found that we had received the wrong goods, the shipment apparently being intended for another buyer.

B. from Chinese to English

1. 经检查所收货物之后，我们发现发票所列几项商品未在其中。

2. 约 20 箱中，每箱只装了 100 只碗，而不是装箱单所录入(enter)的 120 只。

3. 很遗憾地告知你方货物短量 100 公斤。

4. 对因此失误给你方和你方客户造成的麻烦，我们必须致以歉意。

5. 你方提出收下错发的货物，对此我们十分感激并将从发票金额中降价 3%，希望你方同意。

Ⅳ. Writing task.

Please refer to Task A1-14 on Page 329.

RECAP

Language Focus	Knowledge Focus
raise/lodge/file a claim against sb. on sth. for... （reasons） re-inspect, at one's disposal, responsibility upon one's arrival, evidence, as a result	claims, survey report, surveyor the Entry-Exit Inspection and Quarantine Bureau defective goods
Writing Tips	
Lodging a claim: ➢ Confirming receipt of goods ➢ Describing the quality problem ➢ Presenting survey report and photos ➢ Asking for prompt settlement	Accepting a Claim: ➢ Expressing regret over the inferior quality ➢ Explaining causes to the problem ➢ Admitting mistakes or oversight ➢ Taking action to satisfy the customer's demand, e. g. by offering discount, sending free replacements ➢ Reassuring the buyer of the quality of future orders

Lesson 39

Claim on Damaged Goods

Claim on Damaged Goods

From：King123@hotmail.com
To：bailu@sina.com
Date：July 7，20—
Subject：Claim on Order No. SI106
Attachments：Pictures of Case No. 8. jpg （1.2M）

Dear Mr. Bai，

We received your consignment of toys this morning(our Order No. SI106). However，on examining the **contents** we found that 20 electric trains on one side of Case No. 8 were badly **dented** and are **unsaleable.** This case had obviously been either dropped or struck by a heavy object. Attached please find the pictures of Case No. 8 and the electric trains **in question.**

As this consignment is urgently needed to complete orders from one of our **major** customers，it is absolutely essential that you ship replacements ASAP.

Your prompt attention to this matter would be appreciated.

Best regards，
King

Claims Rejected

From: bailu@sina. com
To: King123@hotmail. com
Date: July 8, 20—
Subject: RE: Claim on Order No. SI106

Hi King,

We regret to know that on arrival one of the cases of Order No. SI106 **was found** damaged. But I'm afraid to say that all the cases were in perfect condition at the time they were loaded, as is evidenced by our clean Bill of Lading. Therefore it is quite obvious that the damage must have been caused in transit. In this case the **liability** clearly **rests with** either the **shipping company** or the insurance company. As this transaction was closed on CFR basis, we would suggest that you approach them for **settlement of your claim.**

We fully understand your present situation. If you agree, we would like to ship you another 20 electric trains at 3% **off the contracted price.** Please let me know whether this is agreeable to you.

Best regards,
Bai

NOTES

1. damage：*v. /n.* 损坏

   Many goods were badly damaged during the sea voyage.

   许多货物在海运途中受到严重损坏。

   Bad weather has caused serious damage to the crops.

   恶劣天气给庄稼造成了严重损坏。

   damaged：*a.* 被损坏的，受到伤害的

   Both the cars involved in the accident looked badly damaged.

   事故中的两辆轿车都受到严重损坏。

2. contents：*n.* 内装货物；内容；含量

   Now cups say，"caution，contents are hot"．

   现在纸杯上都印着"内有热饮，小心烫口"。

   It's easy to update the content of the Web site.

   更新网页上的内容非常容易。

   This type of milk has a lower fat content.

   这种牛奶的脂肪含量较低。

3. dent：*v.* 使凹陷，瘪

4. unsaleable：*n.* 无法销售的，另拼为 unsalable

5. in question：该，所谈论的

   For shareholders of the company in question，a takeover must be appealing.

   对该公司的股东来说，收购一定会让他们心动。

6. major：*a.* 大的；主要的，重要的

   We are a major distributor of audio and video equipment.

   我们是一家大的音像设备分销商。

   There has been a major change in attitudes towards mergers and acquisitions recently.

   最近对并购的看法发生了重要的转变。

7. be found...：被发现……

   The goods are found defective.

   货物被发现是劣质品。

8. liability：*n.* 责任

   They deny any liability for the damage caused.

   他们拒绝为产生的损失负责。

   liabilities：*n.*（复）负债

The business has liabilities of £2 million.

该公司负债 200 万英镑。

9. rest with：在于，还可以说 lie with

The authority to call an emergency meeting rests/lies with the president.

召集紧急会议的权力在总统。

10. settlement of one's claim：理赔

11. 3% off the contracted price：低于合同价 3%

A SUPPLEMENTARY SAMPLE EMAIL

Dear David,

I have been informed about problems with liquid markers we have got from you. Please kindly check attached pictures and inform me of the following：

1. Why you have shipped to us damaged product. I have checked 300 markers：all of them have same problem.

2. What options you can offer to solve this problem. （our customers refuse to buy this product）

Waiting for your prompt reply.
Bruno

EXERCISES

Ⅰ. Fill in the blanks with the proper forms of the following expressions.

content, major, reject, find, liable, rest,
commit, off, in question, contract（v.）

1. It _____ on us to decide whether to lodge a claim against you or not.

2. 8% _____ the original price is the best we can do.

3. The United States is a _____ influence in the United Nations.

4. Both children have _____ their parents' religion and have become Buddhists.

5. The president said that once he had _____ to this course of action there was no going back.

6. The labor costs _____ are still relatively light.

7. Smith was _____ guilty of the murder.

8. This type of steel has a relatively low carbon _____ .

9. If we lose the case we may be _____ for the costs of the whole trial.

10. It's a pity that the quality of your shipment failed to meet the _____ standard.

Ⅱ. Translate the following sentences.

A. from English into Chinese

1. We were very sorry to receive your complaint that the material you received was not of the quality expected.

2. On going into the matter we find a mistake was indeed made in the packing through a confusion in numbers，and we have arranged for the right goods to be dispatched to you at once.

3. We are therefore entitled to a compensation up to US$1,000.

4. It would not be fair if the loss were totally imposed on us as the liability rests with both parties. We are ready to meet you half way, i. e. , to pay 50% of the loss only.

5. We reserve the right to claim compensation from you for any damage.

B. from Chinese into English

1. 订单 56 号的货物中有两箱到达时发现严重受损。

2. 此箱完整无损，很明显箱内货物的损坏应由发货人负责。

3. 经检验，你方所交花生之水分大大超过了合同规定的最高限度。

4. 经检验，发现 45 号箱所装货物并非我方所订之货物，很显然是你方发错了货。

5. 上海出入境检验检疫局出具的检验报告证明你方短交 500 公斤。

Ⅲ. Translate the following email into Chinese.

Dear Bruno，

First of all，we are so sorry about the quality problem happened in your first trial order. It's an invisible problem caused by gluing, and unfortunately our workers could not find it before packaging. We have met the glue factory and re-trained our workers to avoid future problem.

1. Is it possible for you to check all goods and advise the total quantity of the defects?

2. After checking the pictures, we had urgent meeting and tested a lot of solutions. The best way is: one plastic sticker should be made to cover the defective part with glue on the back. Attached are images FYI.

We will send you immediately few samples. After getting your positive test result, enough quantity of stickers will be sent by air. We will surely pay for your labor cost and other related fees and deduct them from next order value.

Waiting for your comments.

David

RECAP

Language Focus	Knowledge Focus
damage, contents, in question, liability, rest with 3% off the contracted price	major customers, shipping company clean Bill of Lading settlement of claim

Writing Tips	
Lodging a claim: ➢ Describing the damaged goods ➢ Clarifying the responsibility (buyer, seller, shipping company or insurance company) ➢ Putting forward suggestions to solve the problem (discount, replacement, etc)	Rejecting a claim: ➢ Expressing regret over the damage ➢ Figuring out reasons leading to the damage ➢ Refusing claims if it is not your responsibility ➢ Showing understanding ➢ Suggesting what can be done ➢ Expressing willingness to assist in settling the claim

Lesson 40

Complaint About Delay in Delivery

From：Ason@hotmail.com
To：Mengsang@sina.com
Date：May 7, 20—
Subject：Complaint about delay in delivery

Hi Colleen,

Your email of May 5th covers the invoice No. DO602 for the 10 cases Hosiery Underwear, but we much regret to have to inform you that we cannot accept this shipment. For some time past we have been pressing you for the shipment of these goods, and in our last email of May 2nd we informed you that unless this order was already on the way, the parcel would arrive too late for the season and so be of no use to us.

Nevertheless, you have thought **fit** to send the goods, and now this delay has caused us serious **inconvenience**. The only thing we can do to **oblige** you is either to take them on **consignment** and try to sell **retail**, or accept them for next season at an **allowance**, which we leave you to determine.

Kindly let us know your decision as soon as possible.

Best wishes,
Tommy

NOTES

1. complaint：*n.* 投诉，抱怨

   complain：*v.* 投诉，抱怨

   The buyers complain about the excessive moisture of the minerals.

   The buyers complain that the minerals contain too much moisture.

   The buyers complain to the sellers of the excessive moisture contained in the minerals.

   买方对矿石含水量过多表示不满。

   We've received a number of complaints about the poor quality of the goods you deliver.

   我们收到了许多关于你方供货质量差的投诉。

   We find it necessary to make a complaint about the poor quality of your delivery.

   我们认为有必要对你方所交货物的质量之差进行投诉。

2. fit：*a.* 合适的 *n.* 合适 *v.* 适合，吻合，契合

   Cartons are quite fit for ocean transportation.

   纸箱非常适用于海洋运输。

   Some analysts doubt that retail is a good fit for our company.

   一些分析师怀疑零售对我们公司来说是不是一个合适的选择。

   The new design fits well with the local market demands.

   新设计与当地市场需求完全吻合。

   All these have to fit the cultural circumstances.

   所有这些都必须契合当地的文化环境。

3. inconvenience：*n.* 不便

   We apologize for any inconvenience caused by the late arrival of the goods.

   我们为货物晚到造成的一切不便表示歉意。

   inconvenience：*v.* 给……造成不便

   The strike inconvenienced many people.

   这场罢工给很多人造成了不便。

4. oblige：*v.* 施惠于……，帮……的忙；施惠，帮忙，效劳

   We only went to the party to oblige some old friends who especially asked us to be there.

   我们去派对就是为了帮老朋友们的忙——他们特别要求我们一定要去。

   We needed a guide and he was only too happy to oblige.

我们需要一名向导，而他非常乐意效劳。

5. consignment：*n.* 寄售

take them on consignment：以寄售的方式接受他们（指货物）

6. retail：*adv.* 以零售方式

For the defective goods，we try to sell retail.

我们尽量将这些次品零卖。

retail：*n.*

Retail sales grew just 3.8 percent last year.

去年零售额只上升了3.8%。

retail：*v.* 零售

The software retails for $69.

这个软件零售价为69美元。

retailer：*n.* 零售商

retailing：*n.* 零售业

retail business/trade 零售业

retail price 零售价

wholesale：*n.*/*v.*/*adv.* 批发

Warehouse clubs allow members to buy goods at wholesale prices.

仓储式会员店允许会员以批发价购买商品。

The cartoon plush toys wholesale at USD5/pc.

卡通毛绒玩具批发价为每个5美元。

The fabrics are sold wholesale to retailers，fashion houses，and other manufacturers.

这些纺织品被批发给零售商、时装店和其他制造商。

wholesaler：*n.* 批发商

7. allowance：*n.* 折扣；津贴；限额

to sell at an allowance 折价销售

A SUPPLEMENTARY SAMPLE EMAIL

David,

Your last delay is a problem. If you need longer lead time, you should tell us; otherwise, we must ask you to meet your delivery obligations.

We will send you more POs to ship in next 3 months. Please note you don't want to continue to experience problems. We will carefully consider the processing, quality and delivery of these orders, and then discuss how we grow together or slow down our cooperation.

Bruno

···

PONum	LineNum	ItemNum	Field	Factory	Prior ETD
GMI2014-1209	3	BD MAK DE V13	ETD	~~3/22/2014~~	3/13/2014
GMI2014-1209	4	BD MAK DE V13	ETD	~~4/1/2014~~	3/20/2014

EXERCISES

Ⅰ. Fill in the blanks with the proper forms of the following expressions.

compensate, inconvenience, fit, oblige, retail,
consequence, compel, cancel, complain, allowance

1. The free _____ for luggage is 20 kg.

2. He _____ that his boss was useless and he had too much work.

3. We regret that we have to _____ our order because of the inferior quality.

4. Can we ship you extra 3 pcs as the _____ for the damaged goods next time?

5. Please _____ me with a reply as soon as possible.

6. Any delay would cause us no little _____ and financial loss.

7. We consider series MR01 _____ for your market.

8. If you fail to delivery on time, we shall be _____ to turn to other suppliers.

9. Record profits in the _____ market indicate a boom in the economy.

10. We are unable to meet our customers' demands. As a _____ , they have placed orders elsewhere.

II . Translate the following sentences.

A. from English to Chinese

1. We regret that we have to complain about the way in which the consignment just received has been packed.

2. After checking the goods received we regret to have to tell you that you have short-shipped this consignment by 100kg.

3. We have had the case and contents examined by the insurance surveyor，but，as you will see from the enclosed copy of his report，he maintains that the damage was due to insecure packing and not to any unduly tough handling of the case.

4. We have again to claim for the non-delivery of the goods ordered by us for immediate delivery，which you stated were in stock.

5. Upon investigation，we have found that the error occurred in the factory.

B. from English to Chinese

1. 鉴于此，我方只好向你提出索赔，金额共计 50 万日元（Yen）。

2. 我方会采取一切必要措施以防类似事件再次发生。

3. 对由此给贵方造成的不便深表歉意，并同意赔偿贵方损失共计 3,000 英镑。

4. 很抱歉，我方商检机构出具的检验证书证明货物装运时完全达到合同规定的标准，故歉难接受贵方索赔。

5. 损坏系意外事故所致，故请与保险公司联系索赔事宜。

III . Translate the following email into Chinese.

Hi Ason,

We would like to apologize for our delay in delivery and all the inconveniences thus brought to you.

Many reasons caused the situation today：lack of raw material，no available steamer due to long-lasting frog weather at our end etc. As we have got the goods ready，we'll make shipment by the first available steamer and send you the shipping advice before the end of May.

Also we will offer you a 10% discount to compensate the losses due and an extra 5% to your next purchase from us. We promise this won't happen again.

Best regards,

Meng

IV. Rewrite the following sentencesto make them more effective.

1. We have received your email. We have known you are complaining about our delay in delivery.

2. I will explain the reasons for delay in shipment to you now.

3. You'd better file the claim against the shipping company, it is not our responsibility.

4. You must produce evidence in support of your claims.

5. Please lodge the claim on the shipping company for the goods shipped to you for USD1,000.

RECAP

Language Focus	Knowledge Focus
complain (to sb.) of sth	take. . . on consignment
complain about/that. . .	retail
make a complaint about . . .	allowance
inconvenience, retail	

Writing Tips

➢ Referring to order No. and goods in question
➢ Stating delay in delivery
➢ Indicating the serious consequence
➢ Putting forward suggestions to solve the problem, e. g. taking the goods on consignment, selling retail, etc.
➢ Asking for early decision

COMPREHENSIVE
WRITING TASKS

Learning Objectives

To apply the writing techniques of
business emails to a simulated situation
of import and export transactions

Comprehensive Writing Task A（Export Business）

Suppose you are Aaron Wu，the Export Sales Representative of SHANDONG TIANYI ARTS & CRAFTS IMP./EXP.CO.，LTD..Now you are requested to complete the following email-writing Task A1 based on the business with an American Company FALCON ARTWORKS and Tasks A2-A8 based on the business with other importers.

Task A1-1 *Lesson 1*

根据以下信息撰写一篇贵公司的介绍：

山东天意工艺品进出口公司坐落在美丽的海滨城市——青岛。公司成立于 1982 年，有着 30 多年对外贸易经营历史，主要经营各类工艺品的生产和进出口业务，2014 年出口额为 3246 万美元，是山东省主要的编织工艺品制造和进出口公司。

公司在多年的经营活动中建立了稳定的货源供应和销售渠道。在国内，创建了 2 家自属生产企业，占地 2 万平方米，员工总数达到 280 余名，其中专业研发人员 25 名。同时，我公司与省内外 50 多家工艺品生产厂家保持着良好的协作关系。2012 年，自属工厂通过了 SGS 公司的 ISO9001：2000 质量体系认证。2013 年工厂通过了 IKEA 验厂。

公司现经营的商品主要有：装饰品（decorations）、手提包、鞋帽、人造花（果）（artificial flowers and fruits）、仿真首饰（simulation jewelries）、圣诞礼品、工艺美术品、瓷器等多种工艺品和日用工艺品。产品设计新颖，工艺精美。选取玉米壳（corn husk）、麦秸（wheat straw）、纸绳（paper straw）、海草（sea grass）、酒椰（Raphia）、柳条（wicker）等纯天然材料加工而成的编织工艺品远销北美、南美、东欧、东南亚和非洲市场。此外，可承接 OEM 订单，根据客户要求加工产品，设计以及定做包装。多年来，公司以优质的服务、可靠的质量和良好的信誉，赢得了海内外客商的信赖。

随着公司对外贸易的持续发展，我们将不断增强企业竞争力、创造力，打造良好的品牌效应和现代化的企业形象，实现企业稳定、快速的持续发展。

地址：青岛市香港西路 65 号山东工艺品大厦 16—17 层

电话：0086-532-82748906

传真：0086-532-82748909

邮编：266071

Email：inquiry@tyarts.com.cn

公司网页：www.tyarts.com

Task A1-2 *Lesson 3*

　　在今年 4 月份的广交会上，你收到了一张名片，该客户表示对你公司的工艺品感兴趣。广交会后，请你立即撰写一封邮件跟进该客户，请求建立业务关系。

　　该客户的名片如下：

Gary Falcon

Chairman & CEO

Falcon Artworks

PO Box 1234

Houston，TX USA 12345

Tel：1-713-651-6908

Email：Gary@falcon.com

Fagary.falcon@falconnet.com

F A L C O N

Task A1-3 *Lesson 8*

　　美国 Falcon Artworks 公司经理 Gary Falcon 先生给你发来了电邮，询问货号 BDF306、JDF506 和 SDF608 的干花产品价格，打算订购数量分别为 4000pcs，600pcs，5000pcs。现在你根据下列信息给 Gary Falcon 先生写一封电邮报盘，注意最低起订量。

QUOTATION SHEET

Art. No.	Descriptions	Unit Price FOB Qingdao	MOQ	Color
BDF306	Bulk Dried Flower	USD9.90/PC	4000pcs	All colors available
JDF506	Jasmine Dried Flower	USD15.60/PC	800pcs	White
SDF608	Scented Dried Flower	USD1.68/PC	5000pcs	Multi-colored

Task A1-4 *Lesson 12*

你收到了美国 Falcon Artworks 公司经理 Gary Falcon 先生的电子邮件，Gary 接受最低起订量，但认为报价偏高，其他供应商的价格偏低，要求你降价。现在你立即给 Gary 回复一封邮件，说明你方价格的合理性，产品的销售情况，供不应求的现状。为促成交易，你同意降价，价格见附件中的报价单，并催促客户尽快接受报价。

QUOTATION SHEET

Art. No.	Descriptions	Unit Price FOB Qingdao	Quantity	Color
BDF306	Bulk Dried Flower	USD9. 60/PC	4000pcs	All colors available
JDF506	Jasmine Dried Flower	USD15. 20/PC	800pcs	White
SDF608	Scented Dried Flower	USD1. 28/PC	5000pcs	Multi-colored

Task A1-5 *Lesson 14*

你收到了美国 Falcon Artworks 公司经理 Gary Falcon 先生的还盘邮件，Gary 认为价格仍然超出了预算。现在你写一封电子邮件回复 Gary，告知如果他能增加订购数量（总量大约为 1 个 20 尺柜），你可以考虑将价格再降低一些，最低价见报价单，并希望对方尽快接受。

QUOTATION SHEET

Art. No.	Descriptions	Unit Price FOB Qingdao	Quantity	Color
BDF306	Bulk Dried Flower	USD9. 50/PC	5000pcs	All colors available
JDF506	Jasmine Dried Flower	USD15. 10/PC	1000pcs	White
SDF608	Scented Dried Flower	USD1. 20/PC	6000pcs	Multi-colored

Task A1-6 *Lesson 15*

今天你收到美国 Falcon Artworks 公司经理 Gary Falcon 先生的邮件，如下：

Dear Aaron，

We'd like to order 1×20' container of the dried flower Item No. BDF306, JDF506 and SDF608 for a start. Prices and quantities are as indicated in your last email.

Please confirm shipment is to be made before the end of Sept.

Looking forward to your early reply.

Best regards，
Gary

你给 Gary 回复，说明工厂订单过多，9 月底发货有困难，最快船期为 10 月中旬。

Task A1-7 *Lesson 16*

美国 Falcon Artworks 公司经理 Gary 回信，担心 10 月中旬装船可能赶不上圣诞销售旺季，再三要求我方尽力帮助解决。如不能在圣诞节前收到货物将取消订单或由卖方承担所造成的相应损失。

考虑到为了今后更好地合作，使得双方之间的友好关系和贸易关系顺利地长久地发展下去，你在经过不断与工厂、货运代理协商后，确定最快装船时间为 10 月 5 日，并保证能在圣诞节之前，让 Gary 收到货物。现在你根据该情况给 Gary 回信。

Task A1-8 *Lesson 19*

你给美国 Falcon Artworks 公司经理 Gary Falcon 先生写一封电子邮件告知你们的包装方式如下：

干花每束装一个塑料袋，2 束装一个内盒，每 5 盒装一个纸箱，10 箱放一纸托盘上。装船唛头为买方公司名称 FA，目的港休斯敦及批次号（LOT No.）。另外，包装外箱标明毛重、净重及一些警告性标志如"小心轻放"、"保持干燥"。

Task A1-9 *Lesson 20*

美国 Falcon Artworks 公司经理 Gary Falcon 先生来信确认了包装方式，并询问支付方式。现在你给 Gary 回复邮件，告知公司通常采用的支付方式是：在下单后大货生产之前电汇货款的 30% 作为订金，余额用即期信用证，发货前两周天内要求收到 L/C。

Task A1-10 *Lesson 27*

今天你收到了美国 Falcon Artworks 公司经理 Gary Falcon 先生发来的订单。现在要求你：

（1）根据订单填制形式发票；

（2）写一封电子邮件给 Gary，确认订单，随附形式发票，并要求签回。

FALCON ARTWORKS

PO BOX 1234 HOUSTON，TX USA 12345

TEL：1-713-651-6908 FAX：1-713-651-6906

PURCHASE ORDER

P/O No. 1501   DATE：AUG. 8，20..

TO：SHANDONG TIANYI ARTS & CRAFTS IMP/EXP CO.，LTD.

Art. No.	Descriptions	Unit Price FOB Qingdao	Quantity (PCS)	CTNS	Amount
BDF306	Bulk Dried Flower	USD9. 50/PC	500	50	USD4750. 00
JDF506	Jasmine Dried Flower	USD15. 10/PC	1000	100	USD15100. 00
SDF608	Scented Dried Flower	USD1. 20/PC	6000	600	USD7200. 00
TOTAL			7500	750	USD27050. 00

1. SHIPPING MARKS：   FA

                 HOUSTON

              LOT NO. 1501

2. THE FOLLOWING DOCUMENTS MUST BE REQUIRED：

    （1）COMMERCIAL INVOICE

    （2）PACKING LIST

    （3）BILL OF LADING

    （4）CERTIFICATE OF ORIGIN

3. TIME OF SHIPMENT：OCTOBER 5，20..

4. DESTINATION PORT：HOUSTON，USA

SHANGDONG TIANYI ART&CRAFTS IMP. /EXP. CO. , LTD.

16-17F，SHANDONG ARTS&CRAFTS MANSION，65 HONGKONG WEST ROAD

QINGDAO 266071，P. R. CHINA

TEL：86-532-82748906   FAX：86-532-82748909

PROFORMA INVOICE

TO：   FA1501

INVOICE NO. ：   _____

INVOICE DATE：   _____

TERMS OF PAYMENT：   _____

PORT TO LOADING：   _____

PORT OF DESTINATION：   _____

TIME OF DELIVER：   _____

Marks and Numbers	Description of goods	Quantity	Unit Price	Amount (FOB QINGDAO)

Total Amount：

TOTAL VALUE

NAME OF BENEFICIARY BANK：BANK OF CHINA，QINGDAO BRANCH

SWIFT：QDBKCNB086A

NAME OF BENEFICIARY：SHANDONG TIANYI ARTS & CRAFTS IMP/EXP CO. , LTD.

A/C NO. 02-81021188

FAX NUMBER：86-532-82748909

Task A1-11 *Lesson 30*

按照天意公司和美国 Falcon Artworks 公司的约定，发货前一周美国公司应该将信用证开到天意公司。现大货已生产完毕多日，而你们至今尚未收到开立有关信用证的消息。现在你给 Gary 写一封邮件，要求他赶快开立信用证，以免延误交货。

Task A1-12 *Lesson 33*

你收到中国银行发来的信用证通知书及随附信用证。请对照与美国 Falcon Artworks 公司签订的 P/O No. 1501 合同审核该信用证，看是否存在不符点。如存在不符点需要修改，请给 Gary 发邮件，要求其修改信用证。

中国银行
BANK OF CHINA

信 用 证 通 知 书

通知编号：AD98117

日期：2015-09-26

致：Shandong Tianyi Arts and Crafts Imp. & Exp. Corp.

65 Hongkong West Road，Qingdao，China

径启者：

我行收到如下信用证一份：

开证行：Bank of America，Houston

开证日：2015-09-25

信用证号：110 LCI 98546

金额：　USD27，050.00

现随附通知。贵司交单时，请将本通知书及正本信用证一并提示。其他注意事项如下：

本信用证之通知系遵循国际商会《跟单信用证统一惯例》第 600 号出版物。

如有任何问题及疑虑，请与中国银行股份有限公司联络。

电话：0532-82375943

传真：0532-82370006

中国银行股份有限公司

MT：701 ················· ISSUE OF A DOCUMENTARY CREDIT ·················

SEQUENCE OF TOTAL ：27： 1/1
DOCUMENATRY CREDIT NUMBER：20： 110 LCI 98546
DATE OF ISSUE ：31C：150925
APPLICABLE RULES ：40E：UCP LATEST VERSION
DATE AND PLACE OF EXPIRY ：31D：151020 AT OUR COUNTER
APPLICANT ：50C：FALCON ARTWORKS
　　　　　　　　　　　　　　　　HOUSTON，TX USA 12345
BENEFICIARY：59：SHANDONG TIANYI ARTS & CRAFTS IMP/EXP CO.，LTD.
　　　65 HONGKONG WEST ROAD QINGDAO，CHINA
CURRENCY CODE，AMOUNT ：32B：USD 27050.00
AVAILABLE WITH...BY... ：41D：AVAILABLE WITH
　　　　　　　　　　　　　　　　ANY BANK BY NEGOTIATION
DRAFTS AT... ：42C：DRAFTS AT 60 DAYS AFTER SIGHT
DRAWEE ：42D：OURSELVES
PARTIAL SHIPMENTS ：43P：PARTIAL SHIPMENTS PROHIBITED
TRANSSHIPMENT ：43T：TRANSHIPMENT PROHIBITED
PORT OF LOADING/AIRPORT OF DEPARTURE：44E：ANY CHINESE PORT
PORT OF DISCHARGE/ AIRPORT OF DESTINATION：44F：HOUSTON
LATEST DATE OF SHIPMENT ：44C：151005
DESCRPT OF GOODS/SERVICES ：45B：AS PER P/I NO. FA1501
DOCUMETNS REQUIRED ：46A：
DOCUMENTS
　　COMMERCIAL INVOICE SIGNED AND STAMPED BY THE BENEFICIARY
　　IN TRIPLICATE
　　ORIGINAL CERTIFICATE OF ORIGIN IN DUPLICATE
　　PACKING LIST IN TRIPLICATE
　　3/3 ORIGINAL CLEAN ON BOARD MARINE/OCEAN BILLS OF LADING TO
　　ORDER BLANK ENDORSED MARKED FREIGHT PREPAID ＋ 01 COPY
　　NOTIFY APPLICATION
　　INSURANCE POLICY OR CERTIFICATE
　　ADDITIONAL CONDITIONS ：47B：
　　PAYMENT WITH RESERVES ARE NOT ALLOWED WITHOUT OUR
PRIOR AGREEMENT
CHARGES ：71B：
　　ALL YOUR CHARGES FEES ARE TO BE FOR THE BENEFICIARY'S ACCOUNT
NNNN

Task A1-13 *Lesson 36*

美国 Falcon Artworks 公司所订购的货物已于 10 月 5 日装船完毕，信息如下：

船公司：MAERSK LINE

船名/航次：MSC KTRINA/FD14W

提单号：NAB1506A006

集装箱号：BSIU2088018

开船日期：2015-10-06

目的港货代：FIRST PACIFIC LOGISTIC CO.，LTD. HOUTON，USA
TEL：1-713-651-7661 FAX：1-713-651-7662

根据以上信息并结合订单 P/I No. FA1501 的内容，现在你给 Gary 发一个装货通知，并随附相关单据。要求内容完整，信息准确，语言流畅，格式正确。

Task A1-14 *Lesson 38*

美国 Falcon Artworks 公司经理 Gary Falcon 先生发来一封邮件，称 P/I No. FA1501 订单货物已经收到，但是经开箱检查后，发现 Item No. JDF506 干花中有 20 箱有发霉味道（smell of mildew），有些干花甚至开始腐烂（rotting），抱怨货物质量问题，随附了产品检验报告和照片为证，请你做出解释和提出解决办法。

经分析查实，你发现工厂因为赶工期，造成部分干花在干燥过程中没有干透就包装发货了，由此造成了发霉和腐烂问题，确属我方原因。

现在你给 Gary 回复一封邮件，斟酌一下该怎么写，同时提出下个订单补装 20 箱。

Task A2 *Lesson 5*

你在阿里巴巴网站 www. alibaba. com 上得知美国一家名叫 FREEMAN CO.，LTD. 的公司经营羊毛地毯（WOOLEN CARPETS）。现在你给其出口部的 Mr. Panjiyar 写一封电子邮件，询问该产品的规格、颜色、尺寸、质量、包装、装运时间、付款方式及能否现货供应。

Task A3 *Lesson 7*

你收到了德国汉堡一个客户 Anderly 的电邮，向你询购材质为玉米壳、麦秸、纸绳的手工编织的提包。现在你给 Anderly 回复一封电子邮件，表示非常高兴地收到其询盘，并对其所要的产品报盘 FOB，CFR 和 CIF 的最优惠价格，详情见所附报价单。

Task A4 *Lesson 9*

你从阿里巴巴网站上得知澳大利亚的 Safwan Trading Co.，Ltd. 联系人 Mr. Rahaman（email address：groupvision@yahoo.com）询购中国产陶瓷马克杯。现在你给他们写一封电邮，说明消息来源，介绍一下自己的公司，并主动报盘，随附样品图片和价目表。

价目表

Descriptions	Specifications	Unit Price（USD/pc FOB Qingdao）
Porcelain Mug	BT-DY581	6
Porcelain Mug	CX-DY486	4
Porcelain Mug	CX-TZ439	5

Task A5 *Lesson 10*

来自于科威特的 AL HOMAIZI CO.，LTD. 的客户 Jimmy 发来邮件询购 BXC-205 和 BXC-208 号手提包，可这两款手提包现在没货，但你又不想失去生意的机会，于是向他们推荐 ABZ-006 和 AXC-008H 号手提包。现在要求你写一封电邮给 Jimmy，介绍 ABZ-006 和 AXC-008H 号手提包的优势，从款式、时尚、颜色、质量、价格偏高的理由等方面说服客户接受这两款新型的手提包。

Task A6 *Lesson 21*

你刚刚收到老客户 Richard 的邮件如下：

Dear Aaron,

We've been placing regular orders with you for years and our past dealings are always pleasant and satisfactory to both of us.

Yet, the present terms of payment, I'm afraid, have put us in a really difficult financial situation. As you know, our retailers pay us 90 days after receiving your goods, but we have always remitted you money immediately after receiving the copy of B/L.

So this time I'd like to propose a different way of payment, namely, by T/T within 45 days after the arrival of goods. Please understand our difficulties. We will send you the order upon receipt of your confirmation.

Best regards,
Richard

该客户虽与你做业务多年，但前一段时间该客户曾拖欠你货款达80万美元，后经努力磋商才得以收回。现在你考虑一下是否同意该客户来信中所提要求，并写一封电子邮件给予回复。

Task A7 | *Lesson 22*

你刚刚收到新客户 Jill 的邮件如下：

Dear Aaron,

During our short meeting at China Import and Export Fair, we are very impressed by your quality white glass vases.

We introduced ourselves as a chain store dealer in Los Angeles. There is a promising market in America and we intend to purchase a lot 1000 pieces of glass vases for the initial order. Should the items sell well, we'd like to place repeat orders.

For payment，may we suggest T/T on arrival of goods?

Your early reply will be appreciated.

Best regards,
Jill Parker

现在你根据以下信息给 Jill 回复邮件：

1. 新客户惯例是即期信用证；

2. 考虑到订货量大和开发北美市场，同意发货前支付 30％订金，余额可以货到后立即电汇；

3. 要求对方提供资信备询银行。

Task A8-1 *Lesson 26*

你接到了日本樱花株式会社一万件竹编榻榻米的订单如下。现在你给客户 Mr. Tomo 回复一封邮件，确认该订单，并说明销售合同备好后发给他。

PURCHASE ORDER
Sakura Kabuskiki Kaisha

VENDOR # 3216

P. O. NUMBER：0006128
ORDER DATE：6/19/20—

Shandong Tianyi Arts & Crafts Imp. & Exp. Corp.
16-17F，Shandong Arts & Crafts Mansion
65 Hongkong West Road，Qingdao 266071，China

SHIP VIA	ORIGIN	CIF	TERMS
Vessel	China	Nagoya	D/P

ITEM NO.	COMMODITY	SIZE	QTY	UNIT PRICE	AMOUNT
8116811	Bamboo Tatami	60cm×90cm	3,000 pcs	$12.00/pc	$36,000.00
8116812	Bamboo Tatami	90cm×120cm	3,000 pcs	$16.00/pc	$48,000.00
8116813	Bamboo Tatami	120cm×180cm	4,000 pcs	$18.00/pc	$72,000.00
		Order Total：	10,000 pcs		$156,000.00

Requirements：
Material：100% natural bamboo
Technics：Handmade
Feature：Anti-slip，Waterproof and Wrinkle-Resistant
Packing：Each piece in a polybag，then in a box，10 pcs to a carton
Delivery：In May，20—
Payment：By T/T with 30% deposit and balance against copy of B/L

Task A8-2 *Lesson 28*

山东天意工艺品进出口公司与日本樱花株式会社签订了一万件竹编榻榻米的合同，客户订单号 0006128。现在你给 Mr. Tomo 发一封电子邮件，附寄销售合同，请对方签回，并要求对方尽快开信用证，以便安排生产和装运。为进一步合作，你可以发一份日式室内装饰品的目录供对方参考。

Task A8-3 *Lesson 34*

山东天意工艺品进出口公司与日本樱花株式会社签订了一万件竹编榻榻米的合同，客户订单号 0006128。按合同条款规定支付方式是：出货前付清 30% 货款，剩余款凭提单副本付清。上周三你公司已出货寄单并通知对方付款。对方已经安排尾款支付，但现在还没消息。现在你发个邮件给 Mr. Tomo 催一催。

Comprehensive Writing Task B（Import Business）

Suppose you are Jack Zhang, the Import Sales Representative of SHANDONG TIANYI ARTS & CRAFTS IMP./EXP.CO., LTD.. Now you are requested to complete the following email-writing Tasks B1-B7 based on the business with an Indian company JINDAL CRAFTS.

你公司想进口一批印度特色的手工首饰。通过阿里巴巴网站，你找到一家名叫 JINDAL CRAFTS 的印度公司，经比较，认为他们所经营的各种材质的手工首饰，如银质和石质的手镯、项链、耳环等，可能会符合你处客户要求。你想进一步了解一下该公司和其产品。如果质量好、价格公道的话，公司会考虑长期合作。现在要求你根据网站上登记的该公司联系信息（见下图）给该公司发邮件，表达建交愿望。

（JINDAL CRAFTS 公司联系人）

印度公司 JINDAL CRAFTS 给你发来了商品目录，你对其中对 Item No. 382 银质手镯、Item No. 486 项链和 Item No. 686 耳环产品很感兴趣。现在你撰写一封具体的询价邮件，请对方报盘 CIF 青岛价格，各样 500 件，同时索要样品。

Task B3 *Lesson 11*

你收到印度公司 JINDAL CRAFTS 的销售经理 Mr. Manoj Aggarwal 的报盘和空运寄来的样品，对 Item No. 382 银质手镯、Item No. 486 项链和 Item No. 686 耳环产品比较满意，认为款式时尚、工艺精巧，但认为 Item No. 382 @ USD9. 8/PC，Item No. 12. 6 @ USD120/PC 和 Item No. 686 @ USD8. 5/PC 价格偏高。现在要求你给 Manoj 回复一封电邮要求降价 10%，并提出你认为合理的理由。

Task B4 *Lesson 13*

你收到印度公司 JINDAL CRAFTS 的销售经理 Mr. Manoj Aggarwal 的邮件，Mr. Manoj Aggarwal 在邮件中提到价格高但他们的产品质量好，但为了建立长期友好贸易关系，愿意降价 3%，让你尽快决定。

现在你给 Mr. Manoj Aggarwal 写一封电子邮件，认为 3% 的降价幅度太小，价格仍超出了你们的预算，希望对方降价 5%，即：Item No. 382 @ USD9. 3/PC，Item No. 11. 8@ USD114/PC，和 Item No. 686@ USD8. 0/PC，如果接受的话，将立即下单，并可能会续订。

Task B5 *Lesson 25*

印度公司 JINDAL CRAFTS 的销售经理 Mr. Manoj Aggarwal 发来邮件，最终同意了你的还价。现在你给 Mr. Manoj Aggarwal 写一封电子邮件，确认按商定的价格和其他交易条件订购，并随附订单，索要形式发票（Proforma Invoice）。同时，你要求他们尽快生产，严把质量关，按时交货。

Task B6 *Lesson 31*

你刚刚收到 JINDAL CRAFTS 公司销售经理 Mr. Manoj Aggarwal 的电子邮件，内容如下：

Hi，Aaron，

We refer to our P/I No. 022. for 500 pieces of hand-made fashion bracelets and bangles Item No. 382，486 and 686 each for shipment in March.

We wonder whether you have opened the relevant L/C. As the shipment date will soon be over，your prompt answer to this effect will be highly appreciated.

Best regards，
Manoj

现在你立即给 Manoj 回复邮件，说明昨天你方已由中国银行山东分行开出了以 JINDAL CRAFTS 公司为受益人的信用证，请对方今天注意查收。要求对方收到信用证后，立即安排装运。据悉 "President" 轮定于本月 10 日左右开往你地，请对方赶装此轮，装后请电告。

Task B7 *Lesson 35*

最迟交货期马上快要临近，你还未收到 JINDAL CRAFTS 公司发来的有关你方 P/I No. 022 货物装运的相关通知。现在你给 Manoj 写一封邮件，询问一下装运事宜，催促其赶紧装运，以利于你方销售，也避免办理延期信用证的麻烦。

Appendix 1

Letters of Congratulations and Thanks
祝贺升职

1. 正式

Dear Mr. Smith，

I am writing to convey my warm congratulations on your appointment to the Board of Asia Industries Ltd.

My colleagues and I are delighted that the years of service your have given to your company should at last have been rewarded in this way and we join in sending you our very best wishes for the future.

Yours sincerely，

敬爱的史密斯先生：

欣闻你获任命为亚洲实业有限公司董事会成员，我谨向你致以热烈的祝贺。

我和我的同事都感到很高兴，你为贵公司服务多年终以这一方式得到应有的奖赏。我们大家祝你前程远大。

××谨上

2. 非正式

Dear Ruth，

It was a pleasure to hear about your promotion to Vice President of the agency. I know how talented you are and how hard you've worked to attain this goal. It's been a real encouragement to me to see your efforts rewarded.

Sincere congratulations to you. Your expertise and dedication will bring out the best of everyone on your staff. They're learning from a real pro.

Sincerely yours，

亲爱的露丝：

很高兴听说你提升为经销处副经理。我知道你很有才干，而且为获得这个职位付出了巨大努力。看到你如愿以偿，让我深受鼓舞。

衷心地祝贺你。有你这样一位精通业务，工作投入的上司，下属一定能各尽其职。他们是向一位真正的行家学习。

××谨上

祝贺获奖（私人）

Dear Laurie，

The news of your music scholarship to the University made my day. No one could have been more deserving. How exciting it must be for you to realize your dream after all those years of faithful practice and proficient performance.

I wish you all the best in your college years.

Fondly，

亲爱的洛丽：

你获得大学音乐奖学金的消息，真使我高兴。没有人比你更受之无愧的了。经过多年顽强的学习和出色的表现，终于实现了自己的梦想，你一定非常激动。

祝你大学期间一切顺利。

爱你的

祝贺毕业（私人）

Dear Sarah，

Congratulations，Dr. Blake. I love the way that sounds! Now that you're graduating it seems like yesterday that you proclaimed to the world that you were going to be a doctor.

I wish you success and fulfillment in the years ahead.

Lucy，

亲爱的莎拉：

祝贺你，Blake 医生。这样叫你，听起来好极了。你就要毕业了。仿佛就在昨天，你向世界宣告：你将做一名医生。

祝你事业成功，幸福美满，万事如意。

露茜

贺 卡

Dear Mr. Hanks
    Here are special greetings and my best wishes.
    May Christmas bring happiness and health to you and your families. May you have a more prosperous new year for your business.
    Merry Christmas and Happy New Year!
                Yours sincerely
                    Sima
	亲爱的汉克斯：
	    值此表达我真诚问候和美好祝愿！
	    祝福你和家人圣诞快乐健康，祝愿新年生意兴隆！
	    圣诞快乐！新年快乐！
	                司马敬贺

感 谢 信

Dear Mr. Smith，

    I am writing to you just to tell you how very much I appreciate the warm welcome you extended to me during my visit to your country last week.

    The help and advice you gave me and the introductions you arranged for me have resulted in a number of very useful meetings and I should like you to know how very grateful I am for all you have done to make them possible.

    I realized the value of time to a busy person like you and this makes me all the more appreciative of the time you so generously gave to me.

                Yours truly，

敬爱的史密斯先生：

    我写此信是想告诉您我是多么感激您在我上周访问贵国时给予我的热情款待。

    你给予我的协助和宝贵意见，以及为我安排的情况介绍，使我有机会开成几次十分有用的会议，这一切都得助于您才得以办成，我对此真是感激不尽。

    我深知时间对于像您一样忙的人是多么宝贵，而您如此慷慨地拿出时间接待我，我为此更要向您表示衷心的感谢。

                        ×× 谨上

Appendix 2

Invitations

非正式邀请

Dear Miss Smith，
 	
    Our sales representative in New York Mr. Peter Lewis will be staying here for a few days during the Christmas holidays and my wife and I have planned a family dinner for him next Saturday evening at seven o'clock so that he can meet some of our friends. We should be delighted if you could join us. I hope you will let me know that you can come.
                   Mr. & Mrs. Jones
	敬爱的史密斯小姐：
	
	    我公司纽约销售代理彼得·刘易斯先生将在圣诞节假期期间在此地住几天，我和妻子计划在下星期六晚七时在家中为他设便宴，以便他可以和我们一些朋友见面。若您能出席我们会感到很高兴，希望您告诉我您能来。
	                    琼斯夫妇

正式邀请

Mr. Joy Wong
requests the pleasure of your company
at a dinner
in honor of his company's
Fifth Anniversary
on Sunday，the fifth of July
at eight o'clock
New Asia Hotel
100 Deep Water Bay Road
Hong Kong
R. S. V. P.
	谨定于七月五日星期日晚八时在香港深水湾道 100 号新亚洲大酒店为我公司成立五周年纪念举行晚宴
	          敬请光临
	              黄卓敬约
	    敬请回复

非正式接受邀请

Dear Mr. Jones， 　　Thank you for your kind invitation to the dinner you and Mrs. Jones are giving next Saturday for Mr. Lewis. I shall be very happy indeed to come, and look forward with pleasure to meeting him. 　　Yours sincerely 　　Abbi Smith	琼斯先生： 　　感谢您邀请我参加您和夫人下周六为刘易斯先生举行的晚宴。我将很高兴出席，并愉快地期待着见到他。 　　　　　　　　　　艾比·史密斯

正式接受邀请

Mr. and Mrs. John Smith accept with pleasure the kind invitation of Mr. Joy Wong to a dinner at eight o'clock the fifth of July New Asia Hotel 100 Deep Water Bay Road Hong Kong	约翰史密斯夫妇欣然接受黄卓先生的邀请，参加于七月五日晚八时在香港深水湾道 100 号新亚洲大酒店举行的晚宴。

Appendix 3

Most-used Currencies in the World

世界主要货币

中文名称	英文名称	常用符号	国际代码
人民币	Renminbi Yuan	RMB￥	CNY
港元	Hong Kong Dollar	HK $	HKD
英镑	Pound Sterling	STG£	GBP
美元	United States Dollar	US $	USD
欧元	Euro	€	EUR
日元	Japanese Yen	J￥	JPY
加拿大元	Canadian Dollar	CAN $	CAD
澳大利亚元	Australian Dollar	A $	AUD
新加坡元	Singapore Dollar	S $	SGD
马来西亚元	Malaysian Dollar	M $	MYR
瑞士法郎	Swiss Franc	SFR（SF）	CHF
瑞典克郎	Swedish Krone	SKR	SEK
挪威克郎	Norwegian Krone	NKR	NOR
泰铢	Thai Baht	BT.；Tc.	THP
新台币	New Taiwan Dollar	NT $	NTD
韩元	Korean Won	W	KOW
澳门元	Macao Pataca	PAT.	MOP
印度尼西亚盾	Indonesian Rupiah	Rps.	IDR
俄罗斯卢布	Russian Ruble	Rbs. Rbl.	SUR
印度卢比	Indian Rupee	Re	INR
沙特阿拉伯亚尔	Saudi Arabian Riyal	S. R.	SAR
新西兰元	New Zealand Dollar	$ NZ.	NZD
墨西哥比索	Mexican Peso	Mex. $	MXP
埃及镑	Egyptian Pound	£E.；LF.	EGP
特别提款权	Special Drawing Rights	S. D. R.	SDR

Appendix 4

Common Measurement Units

常用度量衡单位表

长度单位

中文名称	英文名称	英文简写	单位换算
千米	kilometer	km	1 千米＝1000 米
米	meter	m	1 米＝100 厘米＝3.28084 英尺
厘米	centimeter	cm	1 厘米＝0.3937 英寸
码	yard	yd	1 码＝3 英尺＝0.9144 米
英尺	foot	ft	1 英尺＝12 英寸＝0.3048 米
英寸	inch	in	1 英寸＝2.5400 厘米

质量单位

中文名称	英文名称	英文简写	单位换算
千克	kilogram	kg	1 千克＝1000 克＝2.2046 磅
克	gram	g	1 克＝0.001 千克
磅	pound	lb	1 磅＝0.4536 千克
盎司	ounce	oz	1 盎司＝1/16 磅＝28.35 克
公吨	metric ton	m/t	1 公吨＝1000 千克
长吨	long ton	l/t	1 长吨＝1016 千克
短吨	short ton	s/t	1 短吨＝907 千克

容积与体积单位

中文名称	英文名称	英文简写	单位换算
立方米	cubic meter	m^3	1 立方米＝1000 升
升	litre	l	1 升＝1000 毫升
毫升	millilitre	ml	1 毫升＝0.001 升
蒲式耳	bushel	Bu	1 蒲式耳＝8 加仑
加仑	gallon	gal	1 美加仑＝3.785 升 1 英加仑＝4.546 升

面积单位

中文名称	英文名称	英文简写	单位换算
平方米	square meter	m^2	1 平方米＝10.764 平方英尺
平方英尺	square foot	ft^2	1 平方英尺＝0.093 平方米
平方码	square yard	yd^2	1 平方码＝0.8361 平方米

Appendix 5

Common Acronyms and Abbreviations in Business Correspondence

商务函电常用缩写

电传（Telex）作为一种交流方式，在国际贸易中虽已被传真和电子邮件等更先进的传递方式所取代，但大量的电传缩写字仍然普遍应用在现代化传递方式上，如信函、传真、电子邮件、手机短信中。不仅如此，缩写字还更广泛地应用在人们的日常生活中，应该说，英语中的缩略语像汉语中的缩略语一样，是使用国语言、文化的一部分。英语中的缩写大致有以下规律：

1. Acronyms：字首缩写

常用在公司、机构名称中，也用在专业术语、习惯说法、常用搭配中，多数严格采用所有单词的第一个字母，有时为方便发音或拼写，也可以有所出入。如：

WTO＝the World Trade Organization

WB＝the World Bank

OECD＝Organization for Economic Cooperation and Development

ISO＝the International Organization for Standardization

L/C＝letter of credit

P/O＝purchase order

S/O＝shipping order

FOB＝free on board

CDMA＝Code Division Multiple Access

ASAP＝as soon as possible

DIY＝do it yourself

2. Abbreviations：单词缩写

英文单词由字母组成，单词有缩写余地，而中文单字无缩写余地，中文缩略均来自词、句。英文单词的缩写并不是任意性的，有一定规律可循。汇总起来，有以下几个规律：

（1）保留辅音字母，去掉元音字母（字首的元音字母除外）：

RCV＝receive

ACPT＝accept

CFM＝confirm

IMPSBL＝impossible

BTWN＝between

（2）保留单词头部，去掉尾部（留头去尾）：

MANU＝manufacture，manufacturer

CONDI＝condition

COMM＝commission

这种方式叫 clipping，由此得到的许多缩略词都被当作了单词，因此 clipping 也成了一种构词方式。如：

memo＝memorandum

info＝information

demo＝demonstration

pro＝professional

bro＝brother

doc＝doctor

sec＝secretary

（3）用谐音缩略

B＝be

R＝are

U＝you

WUD＝would

THRU＝through

BIZ＝business

B4＝before

X'mas＝Christmas

这种缩略方式也是英美人喜欢玩的文字游戏，在谜语、命名中经常使用，如：ESSO 艾索石油公司，原 Standard Oil，简称为 SO。因遭同业反对，改名为 ESSO，仍读为 SO。

OIC 一家眼镜公司的名字，谐音于 Oh，I see!

All-4-One 一个乐队的名字，意思是 All for one。

Boyz II Men 一个乐队的名字，意思是 boys to men。

总之，不管用什么方式缩写，都要记住一个原则，即缩写后的单词不论从结构上还是发音上，都能让人很容易地辨认出它原来是哪一个单词，而不能让人费解。

常用商务函电缩写表

ABT	about	大约
ABV	above	在……之上，超过
AC，A/C，ACCT	account	账，账目
ACDGLY	accordingly	相应地
ADDS，ADS，.ADRS	address	地址
ADV	advice，advise	通知
AFT，AFR，AFTR	after	在……之后
AIRD	airmailed	航空邮寄
ALRDY	already	已经
AMND，AMD	amend	修改
AP（P）ROX，APPR	approximate（ly）	大约
ARVD，ARRVD	arrived	到达
ART	article	商品
ASAP	as soon as possible	尽快
ASRTMT，ASTMT	assortment	搭配
ATN，ATTN，ATT	attention	办理
AVBL，AVLBL	available	可用的
AMNT，AMT	amount	金额
AD	advertisement	广告
AGCY	agency	代理
AGRMT	agreement	协议
AIRFRT	airfreight	航空运费
ATCH	attach（ed/ment）	附件
AVTG	average	平均
B	be	是
BG	bag	袋
BAL，BALCE	balance	余额；平衡
BCOS，BCOZ，BCS，BCAUS	because	因为
BEF，BFR	before	在……之前
BGN	begin	开始
BIZ，BZ，BSNZ，BUS	business	商业，生意
BTWN	between	在……之间
BXS	boxes	盒子

（续表）

BYR	buyer	买主
BK，BNK	bank	银行
CAT，CATLG，CTLG，CA	catalogue	商品目录
CERT	certificate	证书
CFM，CNF，CNFM	confirm	确认
CHQ	cheque	支票
CHRGS	charges	费用
CNT，CANT	can't，cannot	不能
C/OFR，C/OFA	counter offer	还盘
CLR	color	颜色
COMM	commission，commercial	佣金；商业的
COND，CONDL，CNDTN	condition	条件
CONSGNT，CONSGT	consignment	托运的货物
CONSR	consumer	消费者
CONTR，CTNR，CNTR	container	集装箱
CONT，CONTR，CNTRCT	contract	合同
COOP	co-operation	合作
CSTMR	customer	顾客
CR，CRED	credit	信用
C/S	case，cases	木箱
C/SMPL	counter sample	回样
CTN（S）	carton（s）	纸板箱
DD，DTD	dated	日期为……
DIS，DISC，DISCNT	discount	折扣
DLVR，DLV，DELV	deliver	交货
DESTN	destination	目的地
DFRN	different，difference	不同的；差距，不同
DOC，DCMTS	documents	单据
DSGN，DES	design	设计
DZ	dozen	打
EMGNCY	emergency	紧急的
ENQURY，ENQRY	enquiry	询盘
ERLY	early	早的
EXAM	examine	检查
EXCH，EXCHG	exchange	交换
FACTRY	factory	工厂
FLT	flight	航班

(续表)

FLWG，FOLG	following	如下
FM	from	从……开始
FOC	free of charge	免费
FRT	freight	运费
FWD，FORWD	forward	寄送
FYI	for your information	供参考
GDS	goods	货物
GM（S），GRS	grams	克
GV	give	给
GUAR，GURANTE	guarantee	保证
HGT	height	高度
HV	have	有
HVY	heavy	重的
IMM，IMMED，IMED	immediate（ly）	立即
IMP	import	进口
IMPS，IMPSBL	impossible	不可能
IMPT	important	重要的
INCL，INCLD	include	包括
INF，INFM，IFM	inform	通知
INS	insurance	保险
INV，IVO	invoice	发票
INTST	interest	兴趣
I/O	instead of	代替
IVO	in view of	鉴于
KG（S）	kilogram（s）	千克
KM	kilometer	千米
LET，LTR，LTTR	letter	信函
LIT	litre	升
LNTH	length	长度
MANF，MANUF	manufacture	生产
MAX	maximum	最大值的
MIN，MUM	minimum	最小值的
MKT，MRKT	market	市场
MNTH，MTH	month	月
MSG	message	信息
MDL	model	型号
MEAS，MEASMT	measurement	尺寸

（续表）

N，Y	and	和
NEC，NCRY，NSRY，NCSRY	necessary	必要的
NEGO	negotiate	磋商
NO，NBR，NR	number	数
ODR，ORDR，ORD	order	订单
OFR（S），OFA	offer（s）	报盘
OPT，OPTN	option	选择
PCT	percent	百分比
PCS	pieces	件
PLS，PL	please	请
PRC	price	价格
QLTY	quality	质量
QNTY	quantity	数量
QTN，QUTN	quotation	报价
R	are	是
RCPT	receipt	收据
RCV.	receive	收到
RGDS，RGS	regards，best regards	问候
RPY，RPLY	reply	回复，答复
RQST	request	请求
SHP	ship	装运
SHPMT，SHPT	shipment	装运
SMPL	sample	样品
SPEC（S）	specification（s）	规格
SRY	sorry	对不起
SUB，SUBJ	subject	主题
SUPLY	supply	供货
SZ	size	尺寸
THRU	through	通过
TKS	thanks	感谢
TTL	total	总共
U	you	你
UR，YR	your	你的
V，W	we	我们
VLDY，VLDTY	validity	有效期
WK	week	星期
WL	will	将
WUD	would	将

REFERENCES

[1] 董晓波. 国际贸易英语函电. 北京：清华大学出版社，北京交通大学出版社，2010.

[2] 黄水乞等. 外贸英文信函范例. 广州：广东经济出版社，2011.

[3] 刘志伟. 国际商务函电. 北京：对外经济贸易大学出版社，2011.

[4] 李宏亮. 国际商务函电. 北京：对外经济贸易大学出版社，2008.

[5] 李艳丽等. 外贸英语函电. 济南：山东人民出版社，2009.

[6] 檀文茹. 商务英语函电. 北京：对外经济贸易大学出版社，2010.

[7] 滕美荣. 外贸英语函电. 北京：首都经济贸易大学出版社，2011.

[8] 袁秋红等. 外贸跟单业务英语. 北京：对外经济贸易大学出版社，2014.

[9] 王乃彦等. 对外经贸英语函电. 北京：对外经济贸易大学出版社，2005.

[10] 诸葛霖等. 对外经济贸易大学出版社. 北京：对外经济贸易大学出版社，2005.

[11] 福步论坛：http：//bbs. fobshanghai. com/.

[12] http：//www. nidera. com.